IMAGES
of Rail

SOUTHEASTERN PENNSYLVANIA TROLLEYS

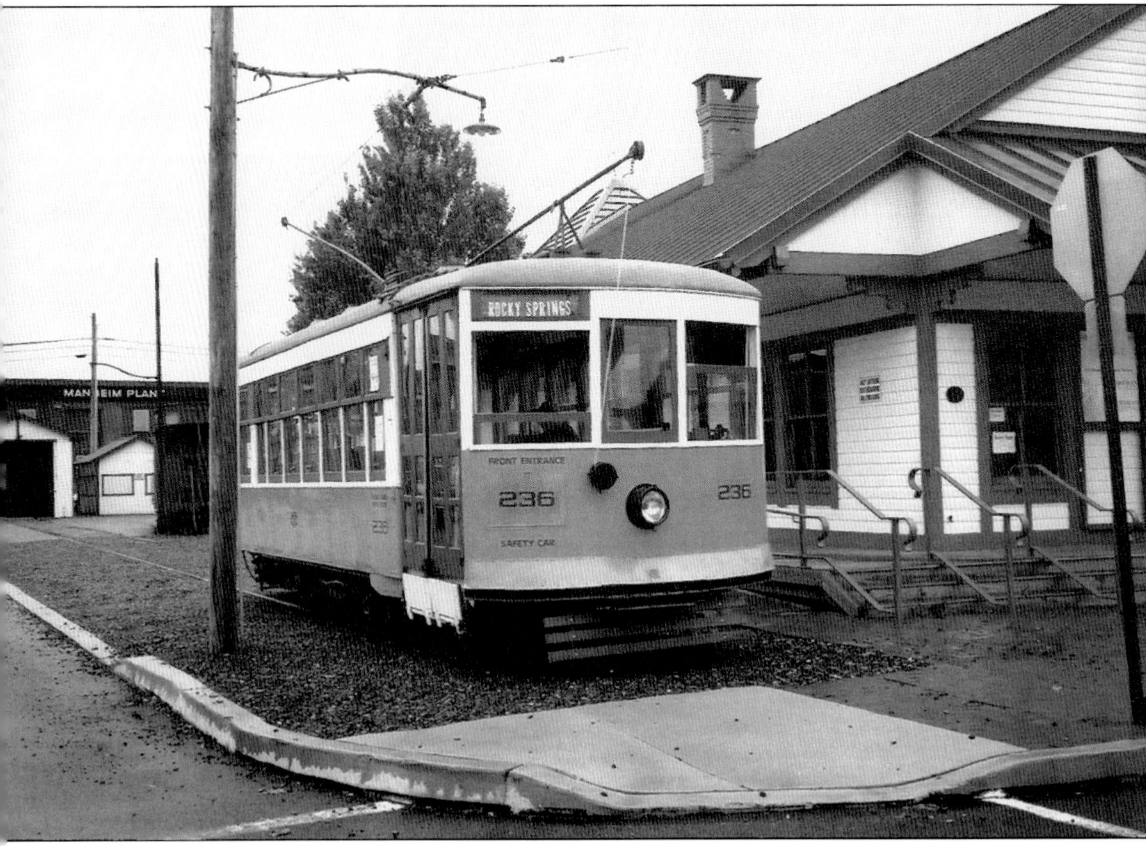

Conestoga Traction Company–restored, double-end trolley car No. 236, built by J. G. Brill Car Company during 1926, is at the ex–Reading Railroad train station in the borough of Manheim during October 2004. Buses replaced trolleys on the Lancaster-to-Manheim line on April 10, 1932. Lancaster trolley service ended on September 21, 1947. (Photograph by James A. Gillin.)

On the cover: Southeastern Pennsylvania Transportation Authority trolley car No. 2168 and former Philadelphia Transportation Company car No. 8534 are at the Sixty-third Street and Malvern Avenue loop of route 10 in Philadelphia on July 6, 1997. Car No. 2168 was powered by four General Electric model 1220A motors. Car No. 8534 was powered by two General Electric model 275A motors. (Photograph by Kenneth C. Springirth.)

IMAGES
of Rail

SOUTHEASTERN PENNSYLVANIA TROLLEYS

Kenneth C. Springirth

ARCADIA
PUBLISHING

ISBN 978-0-7385-5692-5

Published by Arcadia Publishing
Charleston, South Carolina

Printed in the United States of America

Library of Congress Catalog Card Number: 2008922386

For all general information contact Arcadia Publishing at:
Telephone 843-853-2070
Fax 843-853-0044
E-mail sales@arcadiapublishing.com
For customer service and orders:
Toll-Free 1-888-313-2665

Visit us on the Internet at www.arcadiapublishing.com

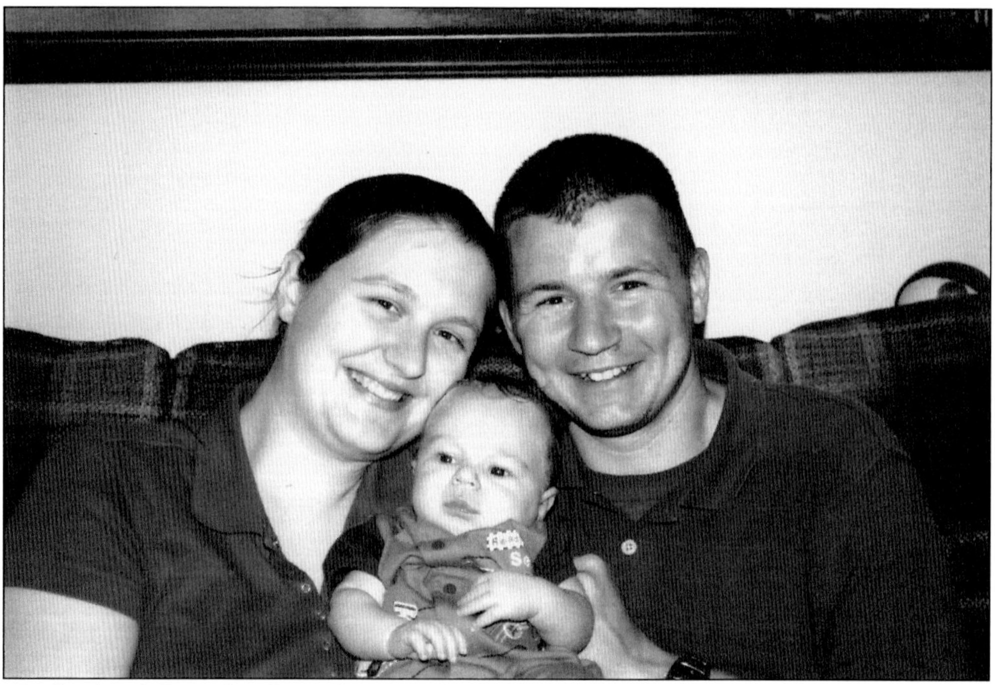

This book is dedicated to the author's grandson Nathan Caleb Springirth, who is shown with his parents Peter and Rachel Springirth. His inquisitive look inspires me to want to keep learning. Writing this book required a lot of research to help preserve the history of trolley cars in this region. (Photograph by Kenneth C. Springirth.)

Contents

ACKNOWLEDGMENTS

A special thanks to my parents, Clarence and Sallie Springirth, and brother Clarence Springirth Jr. for the time they spent with me and the knowledge that they shared along the way. My father was a trolley car motorman in Philadelphia. He went to work with an immaculate uniform. My mother was skilled in making sure dinner was always ready in a household that had a complicated schedule. My brother was an expert in just about everything. Craig Knox provided photographs and schedules; Henry J. Adamcik provided Philadelphia map information; James A. Gillin and Robert G. Lewis provided photographs; Oliver J. Ogden of the Museum of Bus Transportation provided historical photographs and information; John and Jan Haigis, co-coordinators of the OC Trolley Fest, worked to organize interest in surface rail transportation; and William Neil, Yeadon Borough emergency management coordinator, created outstanding transportation displays. Matthew W. Nawn, president of Railways to Yesterday, Inc., provided Philadelphia route history information. Raymond E. Grabowski Jr., president of the Lake Shore Railway Museum, provided information from their excellent North East, Pennsylvania museum files. Edward A. Springer provided trackless trolley information. Dennis M. Linsky, Rev. Edward J. Casey, Edward B. Havens, Charles Greene, and the other list members of the Philly_Traction@yahoogroups.com Web site over the years have provided information on Philadelphia public transportation. McGraw Electric Railway List August 1918, *Street Railway Journal, Electric Railway Journal, Electric Railroaders' Association Headlights, Philadelphia Evening Bulletin, Philadelphia Inquirer,* and *Pennsylvania's Street Railways* by Benson W. Rohrbeck were sources of information. Our thanks to the trolley car operators and employees behind the scenes who have provided accessibility to the riding public.

INTRODUCTION

In southeastern Pennsylvania, it was possible to travel from Philadelphia 140 miles westward to the borough of Newville in central Pennsylvania by electric railway transportation, by taking the Market Street subway elevated line from Center City Philadelphia to the Sixty-ninth Street terminal and transferring to another trolley at Sixty-ninth Street terminal, West Chester, Coatesville, Lancaster, Elizabethtown, Hummelstown, Harrisburg, and Carlisle. The Reading Transit and Light Company and its leased Schuylkill Valley Traction Company linked Reading with Philadelphia. Allentown had a direct connection to Philadelphia via the Lehigh Valley Transit Company's Liberty Bell Limited route. Stroudsburg and the Delaware Water Gap were linked to Philadelphia by transferring to another trolley at Doylestown, Easton, Bangor, and Portland. The Philadelphia and West Chester Traction Company operated trolley service from the Sixty-ninth Street terminal to Ardmore, Media, Sharon Hill, and West Chester. High-speed rail service was available on the Philadelphia and Western Railway line from the Sixty-ninth Street terminal to Norristown and Strafford.

On December 10, 1892, the first electric trolley car operated in Chester, and on July 1, 1910, the Southern Pennsylvania Traction Company was chartered, which leased a number of Pennsylvania trolley routes between Darby and Chester. Abandonment of its trolleys began in 1930 with the last line, Linwood–Wilmington, closing on February 29, 1936. In Northeast Philadelphia during 1896, the Holmesburg, Frankford and Tacony Electric Railway Company opened a trolley line along Frankford Avenue to the city line and another line using Tacony State Road and Rhawn Street. Following receivership, under new owners, the line became the Frankford, Tacony and Holmesburg Street Railway Company and was sold to the Philadelphia Rapid Transit Company on January 2, 1926.

The Philadelphia and Bristol Passenger Railway Company, chartered on January 3, 1896, began operation on April 24, 1897, and eventually linked Philadelphia with Trenton, New Jersey. Following its second reorganization on September 22, 1909, as the Trenton, Bristol and Philadelphia Street Railway Company during September 1929, it became the Delaware River Coach Company with buses replacing trolleys on November 22, 1931, except for a franchise run, which operated until 1932. Trolley service between Langhorn and Newtown began on December 21, 1897, by the Newtown Electric Street Railway Company. Service from Newtown to Bristol began on October 21, 1899, followed by Newtown to Doylestown on February 25, 1900. The company became the Pennsylvania-New Jersey Railway Company on May 15, 1917. The Bristol–Doylestown line was abandoned on November 1, 1923. On September 21, 1924, the Yardley–Lambertville and Yardley–Newtown lines were abandoned. The final run was made from Trenton to Yardley and Morrisville on September 2, 1934.

The Philadelphia and Easton Railway Company began service from Doylestown to Easton on September 14, 1904. With its connections at Doylestown with the Philadelphia Rapid Transit Company to Philadelphia and at Easton with Lehigh Valley Transit Company, it was now possible to travel from Philadelphia to the Delaware Water Gap by trolley car. It reorganized as the Philadelphia and Easton Transit Company on August 1, 1921, with trolley service ending on November 25, 1926. Trolley service from Easton to Nazareth began on May 18, 1902, by the Easton and Nazareth Street Railway Company. After consolidating into the Northampton Traction Company on October 13, 1902, service was extended to Bangor on May 28, 1903. It reorganized into the Northampton Transit Company in January 1922, and trolley service ended on February 28, 1933.

The Bangor, East Bangor and Portland Transit Company began service from Bangor to East Bangor in 1901 and became the Bangor and Portland Traction Company on May 26, 1904. Following receivership, it emerged as the Bangor and Portland Transit Company during 1923, with all trolley service ending in September 1927. Trolley car service in Stroudsburg began on March 11, 1902, and reached the Delaware Water Gap on July 3, 1907, with two companies forming the Stroudsburg, Water Gap and Portland Railway Company on April 1, 1911 (which became the Stroudsburg Traction Company in July 1917), and trolley service ended on September 4, 1928. Bangor-to-Nazareth trolley car service began during 1900 by the Slate Belt Electric Street Railway. A 1918 fire at the Pen Argyl carbarn plus financial problems forced the company to reorganize as the Slate Belt Transit Company during 1921. Employees purchased the company during 1925, and it became the Bangor and Nazareth Transit Company with trolley service ending during 1929.

Connecting Nazareth and Bath, the Allen Street Railway Company emerged as a consolidation of several trolley companies on June 26, 1906. Because the line was not allowed to cross the Lehigh and New England Railroad, it operated in two sections: Penn Allen to Nazareth and Penn Allen to Bath, with trolley service ending on January 24, 1927. Beginning on July 24, 1903, and ending on January 31, 1931, the Whitehall Street Railway Company operated between Lehigh Valley Transit's Egypt line and Slatington line. The Blue Ridge Traction Company began trolley service on February 9, 1903, from Walnutport to Danielsville and ended service on May 30, 1924. The South Bethlehem and Saucon Street Railway Company began service from South Bethlehem to the village of Center Valley on May 2, 1909, and service ended on January 29, 1929.

Electric trolley car service began in Allentown on Hamilton Street on July 1, 1891, by the Allentown and Bethlehem Rapid Transit Company. During two separate reorganizations, ownership came under the Lehigh Valley Transit Company on June 20, 1905. The Chestnut Hill section of Philadelphia was linked via Lansdale to Allentown by trolley car with hourly service effective on May 16, 1903. A faster route to Philadelphia was established by connecting with the Philadelphia and Western Railway at Norristown, which opened on December 12, 1912. The Chestnut Hill-to-Lansdale section was converted to bus operation on July 31, 1926. Norristown-to-Allentown service ended on September 7, 1951, followed by the last official trolley from Bethlehem to Allentown on June 8, 1953.

Allentown-to-Kutztown trolley service began on February 6, 1902. Under a July 10, 1902, reorganization into the Allentown and Reading Traction Company, a wide-gauge line was opened from Kutztown to Reading on October 16, 1902. Passengers from Allentown to Reading had to transfer between standard-gauge and wide-gauge cars at Kutztown. Service was abandoned in sections, with the final end on March 27, 1936. The Reading Traction Company, chartered on March 14, 1893, electrified all the horsecar lines in Reading. By 1913, the Reading Transit and Light Company operated all Reading's trolley lines. On January 7, 1952, route 16 Mohnton made its last run, ending trolley car service in Berks County. The Neversink Mountain Railway Company began operation from Ninth and Penn Streets in Reading to Neversink Mountain on July 23, 1890, and closed during September 1917.

At Reading, the Mount Penn Gravity Railroad Company, originally a steam railroad, reopened as an electric line on April 16, 1898, and was closed during 1924. During June 1902, the Souderton, Skippack and Fairview Electric Railway Company was formed to construct and operate a line from Trooper, which by 1912 was completed to Harleysville. Following several reorganizations, it became the Montgomery Transit Company during November 1911, with service ending on June 7, 1925. The Pottstown Passenger Railway Company began regular service in Pottstown on June 15, 1893, followed by service from Pottstown to Boyertown on May 28, 1908. The name was changed to Pottstown and Phoenixville Railway Company on July 15, 1913. The last trolley car operated in Pottstown on September 30, 1936. The Montgomery and Chester Electric Railway Company began service from Phoenixville to Spring City on July 5, 1899. Following the overturn of a trolley on a curve onto Main Street in Spring City on July 8, 1924, all trolley service ended. The Phoenixville, Valley Forge and Strafford Electric Railway Company began trolley service in Phoenixville on July 15, 1911, reaching Valley Forge in 1912 and ending service on December 24, 1923. Regular trolley car service began in West Chester on September 23, 1891, by the West Chester Street Railway Company. During October 1923, the West Chester Street Railway Company took over the West Chester, Kennett and Wilmington Electric Railway Company from Kennett Square to West Grove. West Chester Street Railway Company trolley service ended on November 30, 1929.

Trolley car service began in Lancaster during May 1890. Lancaster area trolley lines were taken over by the Conestoga Traction Company, and service from Lancaster reached Strasburg on December 18, 1901; Adamstown on May 9, 1903; Blue Ball on July 21, 1904; Leaman Place on July 7, 1906; and Elizabethtown on September 5, 1908. Following reorganization into the Conestoga Transportation Company on December 4, 1931, trolley car routes were converted to bus operation, with the last run on September 21, 1947. The Lancaster and York Furnace Street Railway Company operated a trolley line from Millersville to Pequea from December 1903 until closure on October 15, 1930. The Lebanon and Annville Street Railway Company began operation on August 17, 1891, followed by the Lebanon and Myerstown Street Railway Company on August 25, 1893, with both companies combined into the Lebanon Valley Railway Company on May 19, 1899, and trolley service ending on July 20, 1930. The Ephrata and Lebanon Traction Company began service during June 1914 but only lasted until May 1931.

Trolley service in Hummelstown began in October 1904 and became part of Hershey Transit Company on December 13, 1913, which operated trolley car service until December 21, 1946. Harrisburg Traction Company took over trolley car operation in Harrisburg on July 1, 1895, and became Harrisburg Railways Company on November 29, 1912. The first Harrisburg trolley car route to be abandoned was the Capital Street line during May 1930. Trolley car lines were converted to bus operation with all Harrisburg trolley car service ending on July 16, 1939. Valley Traction Company was formed on November 17, 1903, and became Valley Railways Company during July 1912, connecting Harrisburg with Carlisle, Mechanicsburg, and New Cumberland, with trolley service ending on April 9, 1938. The Carlisle and Mount Holly Street Railway Company began service on May 14, 1901, and was sold to the Cumberland Railway Company on August 7, 1909, which completed a line from Carlisle to Newville on September 21, 1910, with trolley car service ending on December 1, 1930.

Trolley car service in York opened on August 18, 1892. On May 21, 1904, service began from York to Wrightsville, where passengers could walk across the bridge over the Susquehanna River to Columbia, where connections could be made for trolley service to Lancaster and beyond. This line closed on February 1, 1933, and the last trolley operated in York on February 4, 1939.

The Hanover and McSherrystown Street Railway Company began service on September 8, 1893, with the main line connecting McSherrystown with the village of Littlestown by 1908. Buses replaced trolleys beginning on January 20, 1932. On October 20, 1894, trolley service began from the Barren Hill section of Philadelphia to the Chestnut Hill section of Philadelphia and reached Norristown by May 19, 1895, under what became the Roxborough, Chestnut Hill and Norristown Railway Company, with service ending in December 1931. Fairmount Park Transportation Company, which later became Fairmount Park Transit Company, opened a line in Philadelphia's Fairmount Park on November 10, 1896, which was replaced by Philadelphia Transportation Company bus route 85 on September 10, 1946.

By May 28, 1898, Chestnut Hill was linked to Eighth and Dauphin Streets in North Philadelphia by trolley. This line became route 23 and reached Eleventh and Pattison Streets in South Philadelphia on June 1, 1926. The line was converted to bus operation on February 21, 1992. The Philadelphia Rapid Transit Company was reorganized as the Philadelphia Transportation Company on January 1, 1940.

In 1954, Philadelphia had 1,513 trolley cars operating on 45 routes. By 1959, there were 555 trolley cars serving 14 routes. North Philadelphia trolley routes 6 (Ogontz–Willow Grove), 53 (Wayne Avenue), 56 (Erie Avenue), 60 (Allegheny Avenue), plus north-south routes 47 (Godfrey–Eighth–Ninth Streets) and 50 (Lawndale–Fourth–Fifth Streets) survived these cuts, with the exception of route 50, which was cut back from Fox Chase to the Lawndale section of Philadelphia on January 28, 1956, and the portion of route 6 from City Line to Willow Grove, which was replaced by buses on June 8, 1958. The southern portion of route 47 from Spring Garden Street to Wolf Street became a bus line on July 9, 1967. Buses operated the northern section of route 47 from Spring Garden Street to Godfrey Avenue beginning on June 15, 1969. Route 60 was converted to bus operation on September 4, 1977, followed by route 50 on October 12, 1980, route 6 from Ogontz and City Line Avenues to Broad Street and Olney Avenue on January 12, 1986, route 53 on May 16, 1985, and route 56 on June 14, 1992.

Philadelphia's subway surface routes 10 (Lancaster Avenue), 11 (Darby), 13 (Chester Avenue), 34 (Baltimore Avenue), and 36 (Elmwood Avenue) connected West Philadelphia with downtown Philadelphia. Horsecar service to Darby began on December 24, 1858. Routes 10, 11, and 34 began using the new subway on December 15, 1906. On November 6, 1955, route 36 was rerouted into the subway followed by route 13 on September 9, 1956. The five subway surface trolley lines received new trolley cars beginning in 1980.

The Girard Avenue line later known as route 15 was established on May 30, 1895. Workers once used route 15 to reach William Cramp and Sons Ship and Engine Building Company along the Delaware River. On September 11, 1955, the eastern end of the line was cut back to Richmond Street and Allegheny Avenue. Richmond and Westmoreland Streets became the eastern terminus on February 24, 1956. A temporary bus replacement for route 15 began on September 13, 1992. Brookville Equipment Company rebuilt 18 Presidents' Conference Committee cars for route 15. Tracks and overhead wire were repaired. Trolley service was restored on route 15 on September 4, 2005.

Philadelphia's first trackless trolley line was route 80 (Oregon Avenue) on October 14, 1923. The second trackless trolley line was route 61 (Ridge Avenue) on October 5, 1941. Route 29 (Morris and Tasker Streets) became a trackless trolley line on December 14, 1947, followed by route 75 (Wyoming Avenue) on April 19, 1948, route 59 (Castor Avenue) on June 25, 1950, and route 66 (Frankford Avenue) to City Line loop on October 2, 1955. During 1980, the Southeastern Pennsylvania Transportation Authority purchased 110 new trackless trolleys from AM General Company. Routes 59, 66, and 75 were temporarily converted to bus operation on June 16, 2002, followed by route 29 on February 23, 2003, and route 79 on July 1, 2003. New trackless trolleys will begin serving routes 59, 66, and 75 during 2008.

One

Trolley Links to the Country

In southeastern Pennsylvania, there were 38 trolley companies operating over 4,700 trolley cars on over 2,000 miles of track in 1917. Eight trolley systems made it possible to travel about 140 miles by trolley car from Philadelphia through the state capital at Harrisburg west to Newville, which is close to the center of the state of Pennsylvania. The trip would begin using the Philadelphia Rapid Transit Company from Philadelphia to the Sixty-ninth Street terminal, connecting with the Philadelphia and West Chester Traction Company to West Chester, transferring to the West Chester Street Railway Company to Coatesville, transferring to the Conestoga Traction Company for Lancaster and at Lancaster changing to the Elizabethtown line, transferring to the Hershey Transit Company for Hershey and changing at Hershey for Hummelstown, transferring to the Harrisburg Railways Company for Harrisburg, transferring to the Valley Railways Company for Carlisle, and transferring to Cumberland Railway Company for Newville. That trip would have required at least 10 hours, plus whatever time was involved between connections. Stroudsburg, about a 100-mile trip by trolley car from Philadelphia, was a popular tourist destination point to the scenic Delaware Water Gap. Densely populated Philadelphia was linked by trolley car to the rich farmland and picturesque towns and small cities of the Pennsylvania Dutch region. The Philadelphia Traction Company opened the first electric trolley car line in Philadelphia on December 15, 1892, on Catharine and Bainbridge Streets, which later became trolley route 63. The many trolley lines in Philadelphia linked residential areas with commercial and industrial districts of the city. On March 1, 1955, National City Lines took over the Philadelphia Transportation Company. Between 1954 and 1959, 31 trolley lines had been abandoned. The Southeastern Pennsylvania Transportation Authority took over the Philadelphia Transportation Company on September 30, 1968, and the Philadelphia Suburban Transportation Company on January 29, 1970. In 2008, the trolley car has survived in Philadelphia, with subway surface trolley routes 10, 11, 13, 34, and 36 serving West Philadelphia, trolley route 15 connecting West Philadelphia with North Philadelphia, the Media and Sharon Hill trolley lines in Delaware County, and the Norristown High Speed Line linking the Sixty-ninth Street terminal with Norristown.

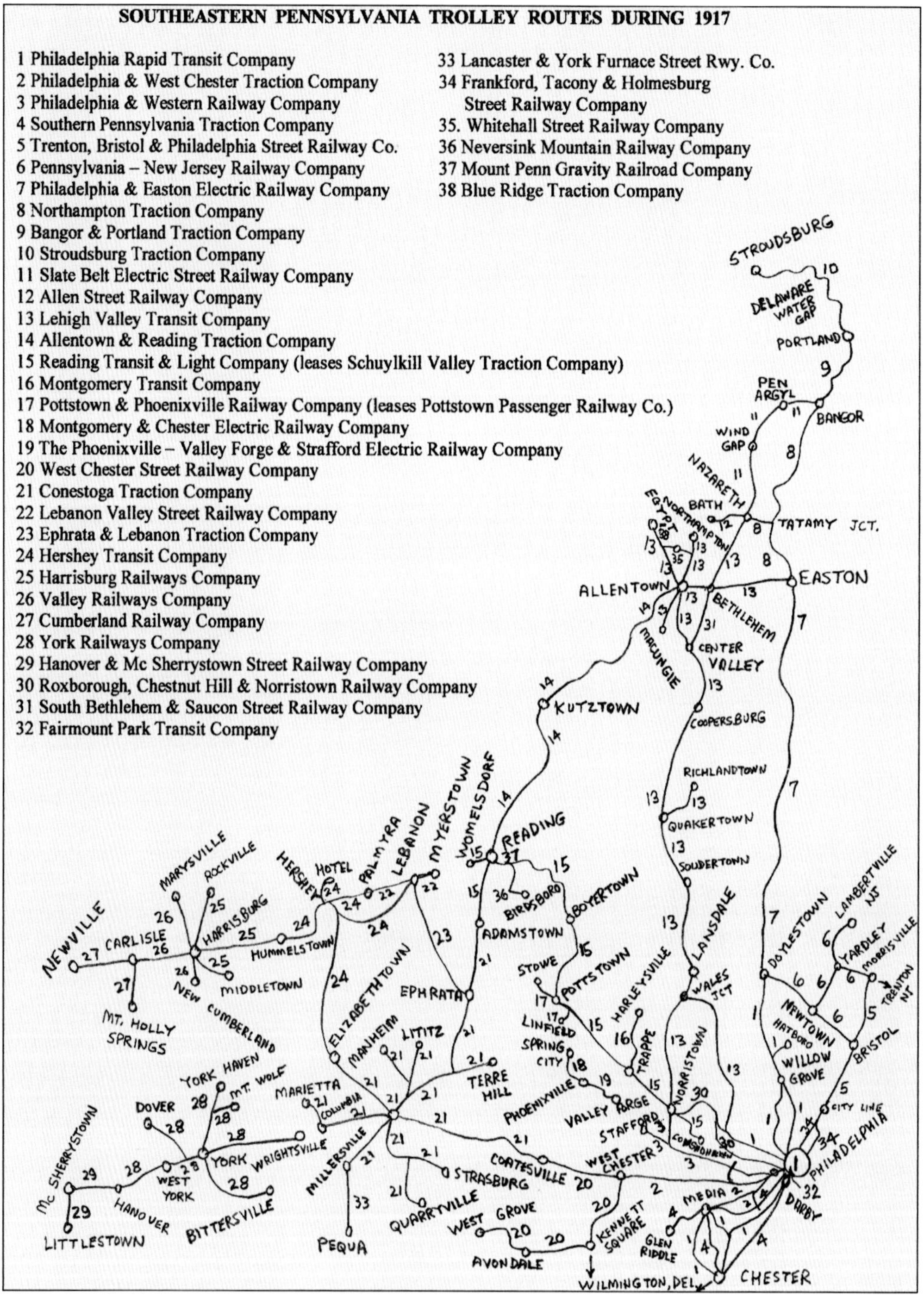

This map of southeastern Pennsylvania trolley car routes during 1917 shows 38 different trolley companies. A trolley line served virtually every community of any significant size. Farmers used the trolley to get milk and produce to market. The factory and office worker could live in outlying areas and commute to work. People used trolley cars to get to work, school, social events, and religious services, and just for the fun of it.

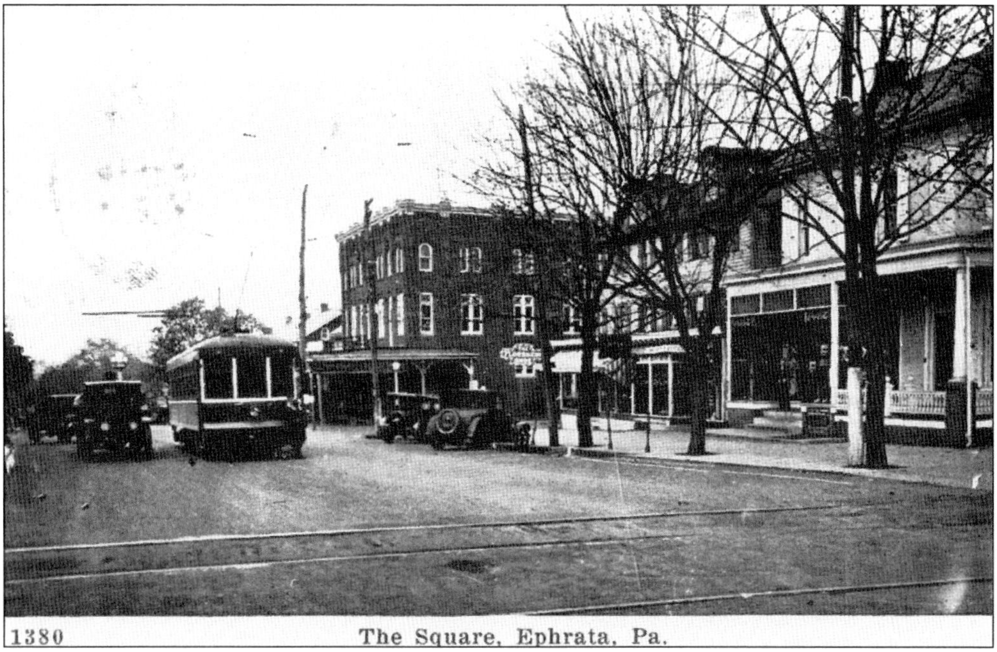

An Ephrata and Lebanon Traction Company double-truck, double-end trolley car is at the Square in the borough of Ephrata in this postcard postmarked July 19, 1928. The Cincinnati Car Company built this car in 1914. Following the closure of this line in May 1931, the car was sold to the Hershey Transit Company and was retired during the 1940s.

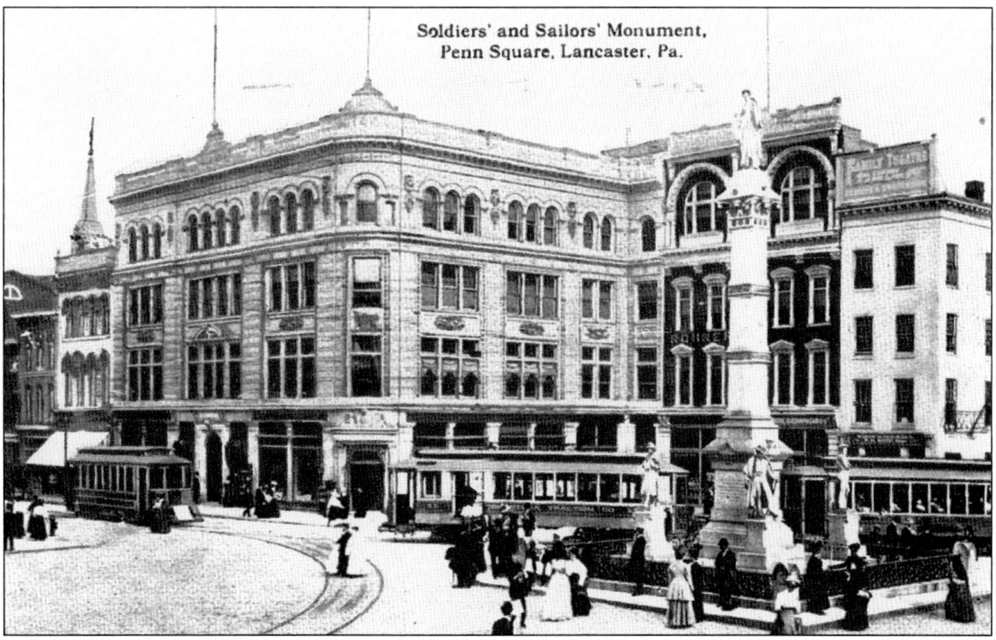

Three Conestoga Traction Company trolleys are at the Soldiers' and Sailors Monument at Penn Square in the city of Lancaster in this postcard postmarked July 1, 1912. This was a prosperous time for the trolley company, which during 1913 carried almost 12 million passengers on routes that served the major communities of Lancaster County.

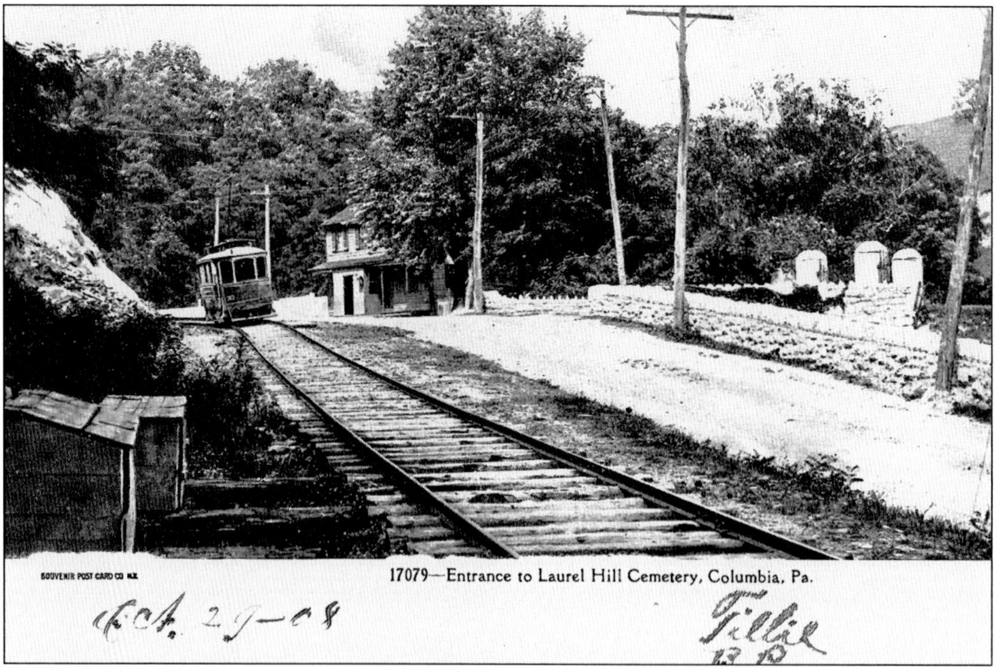

Car No. 30 is at the entrance to Laurel Hill Cemetery in the borough of Columbia around the year 1900 on the Columbia–Marietta line. The Columbia and Donegal Railway Company opened this line on December 31, 1893. This line became part of the Conestoga Traction Company, and trolley service on this line ended on April 25, 1932.

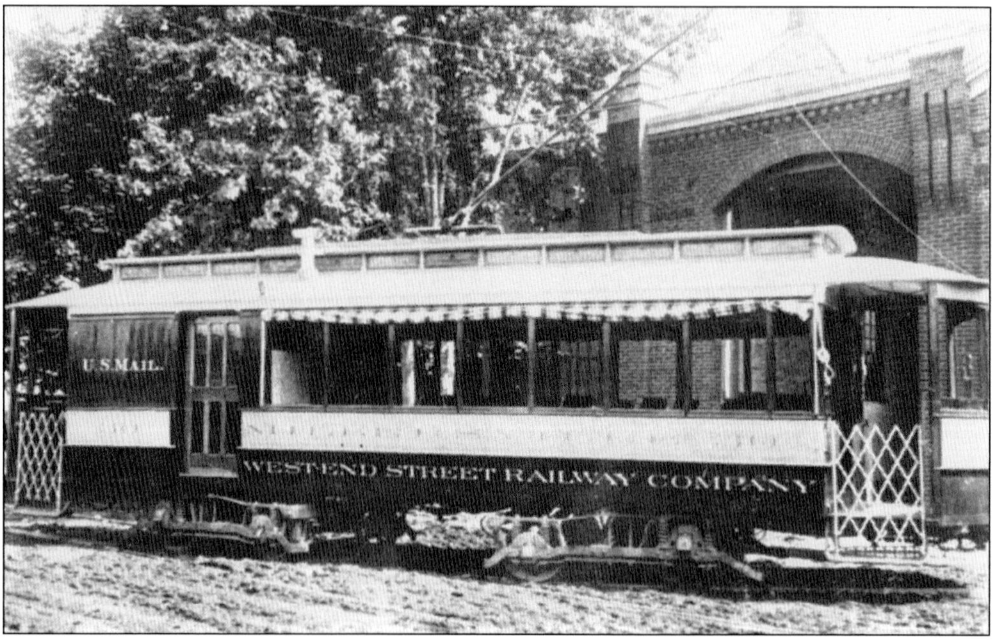

Combination passenger and mail trolley car No. 30 of the West End Street Railway Company is shown in front of the North Prince Street carbarn in the city of Lancaster around the year 1900. On February 1, 1900, the Conestoga Traction Company acquired all the Lancaster and Columbia area electric trolley car lines.

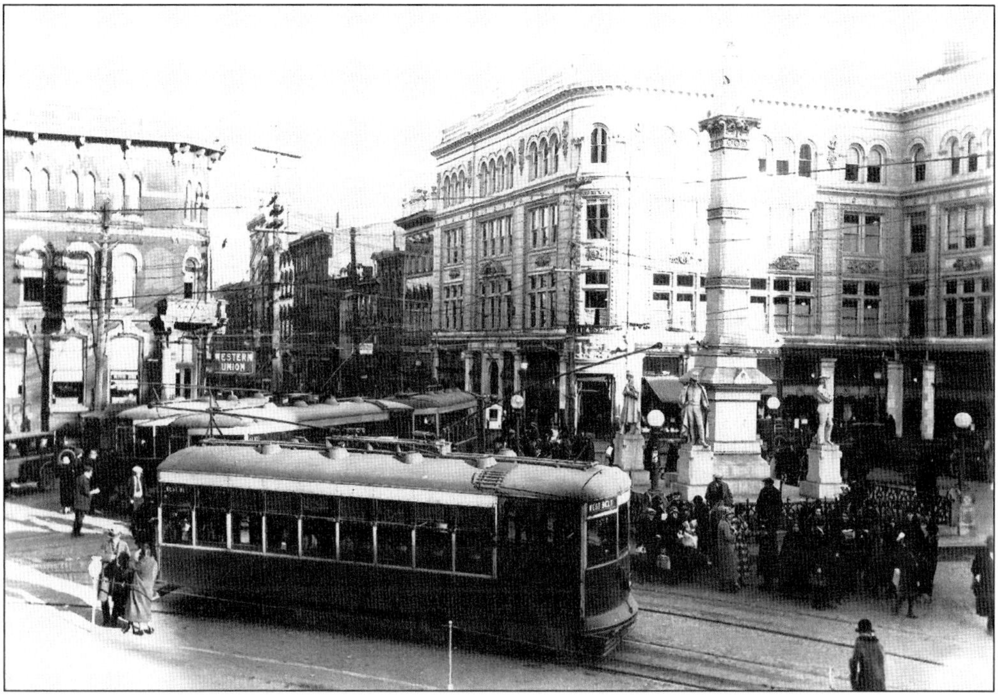

Conestoga Traction Company trolley cars are at Penn Square in downtown Lancaster on February 18, 1925. The trolley at the bottom of the picture with West Belt on the destination sign was one of 40 Birney-type safety cars purchased under seven different orders during 1920 to 1926 from J. G. Brill Car Company.

Conestoga Traction Company Official Time Table and Fares

Safe and Convenient Traneportation

10-18-28

CITY LINES

Single fare 7c. Four tickets for 25c
"For a Dollar and a Dime Ride All the time"

College Ave. Every 6 minutes 5:41 a. m. to 12:07 a. m., last car.

Duke St. First car 5:52 a. m., then at .05, .12, .18, .25, .32, .38, .45; .52, .58, to 11:18 p. m., then 11:24, 11:33, 11:42, 11:51 12:00 p. m.. last car.

Rossmere Belt. 5: 56 a. m. to 8:41 a. m. car at :11, :26, :41, :56, then 8:41, 9:11, 9:41, 10:11, 10:41, 11:11, 11:41, 11:56 a. m. then at :11, :26, :41, :56 until 9:11 p. m. then every 30 minutes at :11 and :41 to 11:41 p. m. last car.

East Belt. Every 6 minutes 5:56 a. m. to 11:26 p. m. then 11:34, 11:43, 11:52 p. m., then Night car leaving Penn Square a. m. 12:08, 12:23, 12:38, 12:53, 1:08, 1:23, (1:38 Sunday only) 1:53, 2:15, 3:20, 4:00, 4:20, 4:40, 5:00, 5:20, 5:38, 5:56.

Ann St. Belt. Every 12 minutes. Sunday 9:10 a m to 1;58 p m. 4;22 p m. to 9:22 p m. Monday, Wedneaday and Thuraday 6:22 a. m. to 8:22 a. m , 11:34 a. m. to 1;58 p. m , 4:22 p. m. to 8:22 p. m. Tuesday and Friday 6:22 a m. to 8;22 a. m., 11;34 a. m. to 8,22 p. m Saturday 6;22 a. m. to 8;22 a. m., 11:34 a m. to 9:22 p. m.

7th Ward Belt. Every 6 minutes 5:39 a. m. to 11:15 p. m., then 11:24, 11:33, 11:42, 11:51, 12:00 p. m., last car.

South Queen St. Every 30 minutes 5:45 a. m. to 7:15 p. m., then 7:50 p. m. and every 20 minutes to 11:50 p. m., last car.

Laurel St. Every 10 minutes 5:40 a. m. to 11:00 p. m., then 11:07, 11:15, 11:22, 11:30, 11:37, 11:45, 12:00 p. m. last car.

West Belt. Every 5 minutes 5:47 a. m. to 12:02 a. m.. last car.

Marietta Ave... Every 12 minutes 5:46 a. m. to 11:22 p. m., then 11:46 p. m. last car.

6th Ward Belt. Every 7 minutes 5:52 a. m. to 11:29 p. m., then 11:35, 11:45, 11:55 p. m., 12:05 a. m., last car.

Conestoga Park. A. M., 5:45, 6:15, 6:45, 7:15, 7:45, 8:45, 9:45, 10:45, 11:15, 11:45, p.m., 12:15 12:45, 1:15, 1:45, 2:15, 2:45. 3:15, 3:45, 4:15, 4:45, 5:15, 5:45, 6:15, 6:45, 7:15, 7:45, 8:15, 9:15, 9:45, 9:59, 10:29, 10:59, 11.15 last car.

SUBURBAN

Leaving Lancaster

Columbia and Marietta. First car 4:30 a. m., then every half hour to 8:00 p. m., then 9:00, 10:00, 11:00 p. m. Sunday, first car 6:00 a. m. Single fare, Columbia, 35c. Round trip 49c. Single fare Marietta, 49c. Round trip 70c.

Mt. Joy and Elizabethtown. First car 4:15 a m. then every hour until 7:15 p m, then 9:15, 11:15 p. m. Sunday, first car 6:15 a. m. Single fare Mt. Joy, 35c. Round trip 56c. Single fare Elizabethtown. 56c. Round trip 91c.

Manheim. First car 4:45 a. m., next car at 5:30 a. m., then every hour until 7:30 p. m., then 9:00 and 11:00 p. m. Sunday, first car 6:45 a m. Single fare 35c. Round trip 49c.

Lititz. First car 5:00 a. m., then every hour until 8:00 p. m., then 9:30 and 11:00 p. m. Saturday, every hour 5:00 to 11:00 a. m., then every half hour to 7:00 p. m., then every hour to 11:00 p. m. Sunday, first car 7:00 a. m. Single fare 28c. Round trip 42c.

Ephrata and Adamstown. First car 4:00 a. m.. then every hour until 8:00 p. m., then 10:00 and 11:00 p. m. (11:00 p. m. car to Ephrata only.) Sunday, first car 6:00 a. m. Single fare Ephrata 42c. Round trip 63c. Single fare Adamstown 63c. Round trip 98c

New Holland and Terre Hill. First car 4:00 a. m., 5:00 a m., 5:30 a m , then every hour until 7:30 p. m., then 9:30 and 11:00 p.m. (11:00 p m. car to New Holland only except Saturday and Sunday to Terre Hill) Sunday, first car 6:00 a. m., next car 6:30 a. m. Single fare New Holland 35c. Round trip 56c. Single fare Terre Hill 56c. Round trip 91c.

Coatesville. First car 3:45 a. m., then every hour until 7:45 p. m., then 9:45 and 11:15 p. m. Saturday, half hour service 8:45 a. m. to 8:45 p.m. Sunday, first car 5:45 a.m. Single fare 77c. Round trip $1.33.

Strasburg. First car 4:45 a. m., next car 6:00, 7:00, 8:00, 9:30, 10:30. 11:30, 12:30, p.m., 1:30, 2:30, 3:30, 4:00, 4:30, 5:00, 5:30, 6:00.6:30, 7:30, 9:00, 11:00, Saturday 4:45 a. m., 6:00, then every hour until 11:00 p. m. Sunday, first car 7:00 a. m. then every hour to 9:00 p. m , then 11:00 p. m. Single fare 35c, Round trip 49c

Quarryville. First car 4:30 a m., then every hour until 7:30 p. m., then 9:00 and 11:00 p.m Sunday, first car 6:30 a.m. Single fare 42c. Round trip 63c.

Millersville. First car 5:30 a. m., then every half hour until 7:00 p. m., then 8:00, 9:00, 10:00 and 11:00 p. m. Saturday, half hour service, 5:30 a. m. to 11:00 p. m. Sunday, first car 7:00 a. m Single fare, 14c. Round trip 21c.

JOSEPH S. BRIENTNALL, Publisher

The Conestoga Traction Company timetable of October 18, 1928, shows service on the West Belt line every five minutes, Sixth Ward Belt line every seven minutes, and every six minutes on College Avenue, East Belt, and Seventh Ward Belt lines. Suburban service was hourly with 30-minute daytime service on the Columbia–Marietta and Millersville lines.

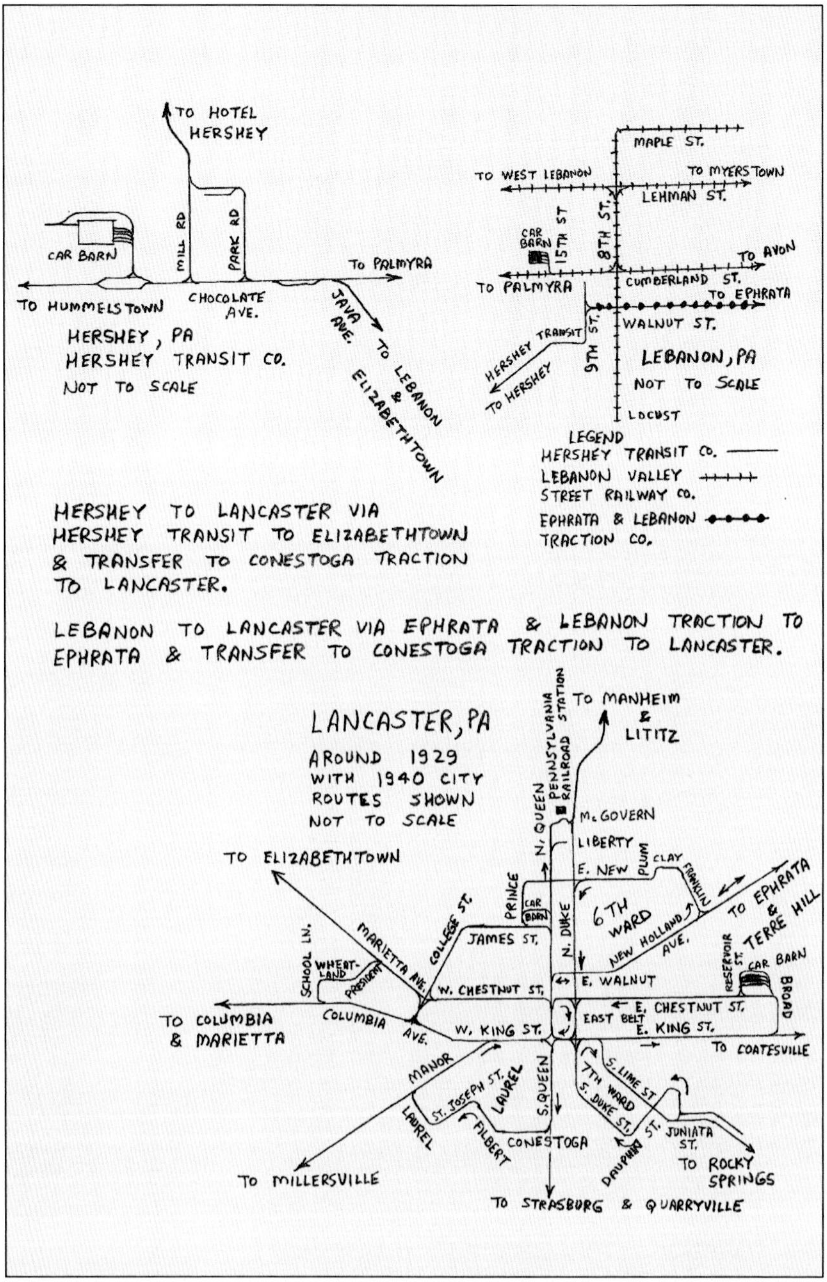

In 1917, the Conestoga Traction Company operated daytime service every 30 minutes from Lancaster to Millersville and from Lancaster to Columbia and Marietta, with hourly evening service on these lines. Service was hourly from Lancaster to Strasburg, Terre Hill, Elizabethtown, Coatesville, and Quarryville. The Hershey Transit Company operated hourly service from Lebanon via Campbelltown and Hershey to Hummelstown. Service from Hershey to the Hotel Hershey and Hershey to Elizabethtown was hourly, while service from Hershey to Palmyra was every 30 minutes. The Lebanon Valley Street Railway Company operated service hourly from Lebanon to Palmyra, Avon, and Myerstown. The Ephrata and Lebanon Traction Company operated every 90 minutes from Lebanon to Ephrata.

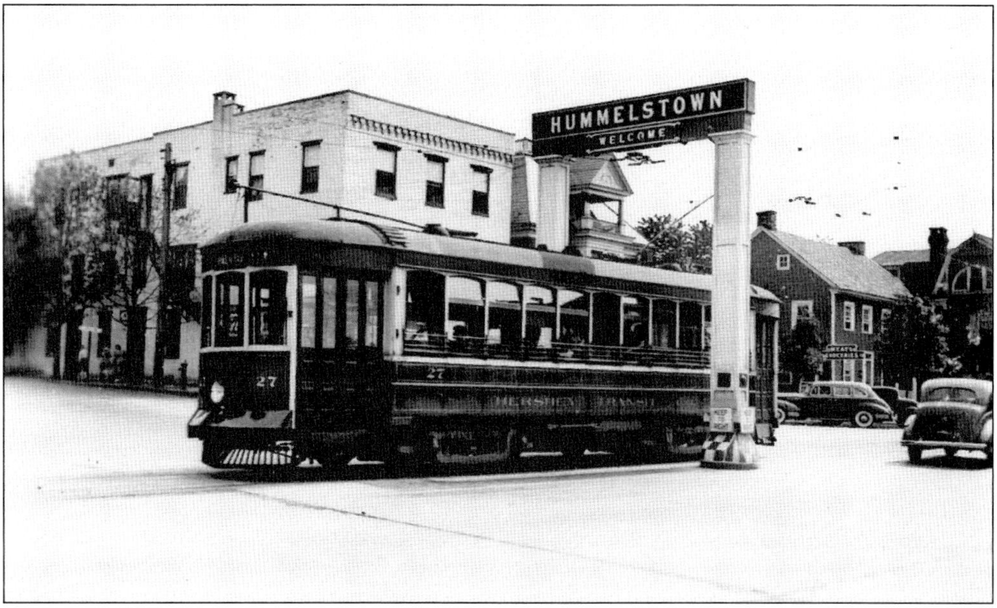

Hershey Transit Company car No. 27 is on Main Street in downtown Hummelstown around 1940. This double-truck trolley car was built by J. G. Brill Car Company during 1920 and was retired in 1946. A connection could be made at this point with Harrisburg Railways Company route 7, which provided trolley car service via Middletown to downtown Harrisburg until through service was abandoned on January 10, 1937.

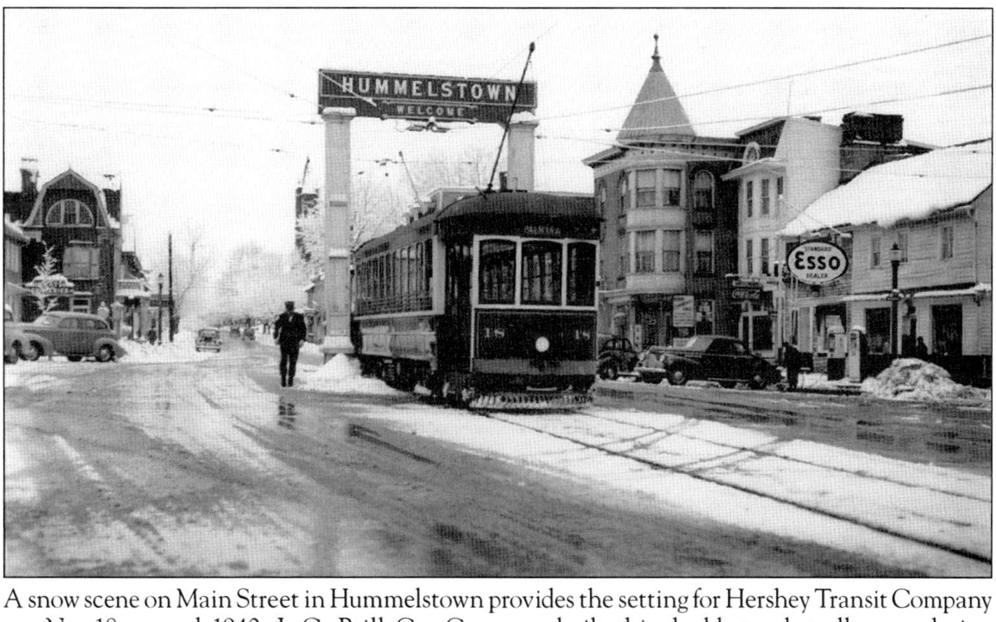

A snow scene on Main Street in Hummelstown provides the setting for Hershey Transit Company car No. 18 around 1940. J. G. Brill Car Company built this double-truck trolley car during 1915, and it was retired in 1946. On June 23, 1940, the Elizabethtown line was abandoned. The Lebanon line was cut back to Campbelltown on January 9, 1942.

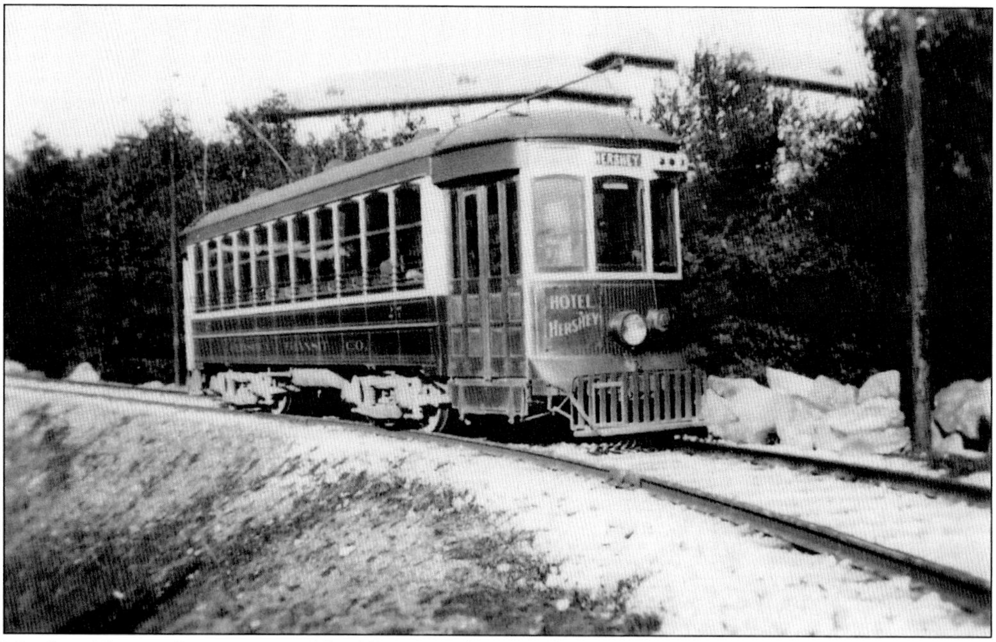

Hershey Transit Company car No. 27 is near the Hotel Hershey on December 30, 1934. Milton S. Hershey established the chocolate factory, the town of Hershey, and the trolley system. The Hotel Hershey, which opened on May 23, 1933, had trolley service until the system closed on December 21, 1946. (Photograph by Robert G. Lewis.)

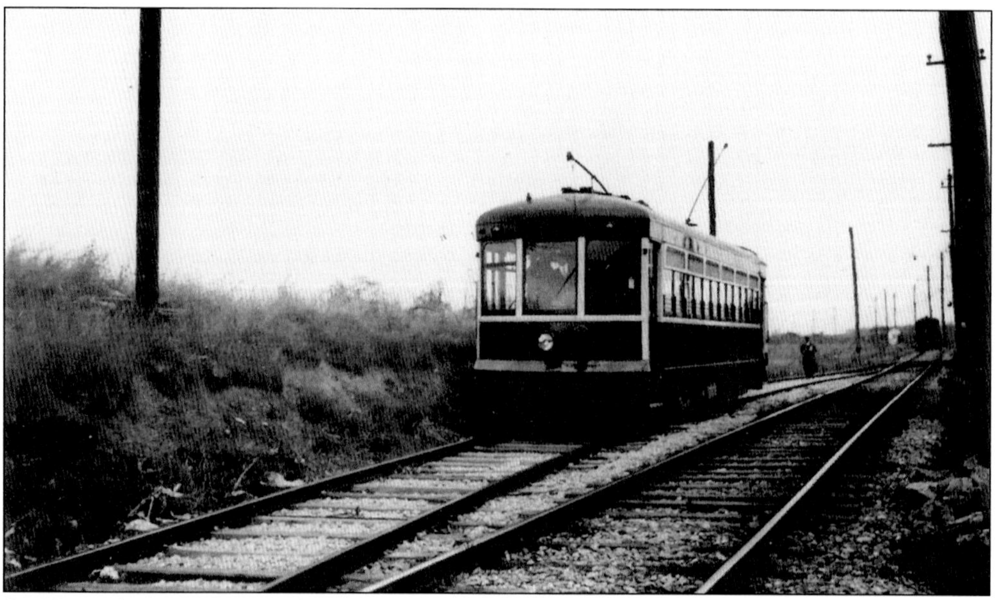

On November 22, 1936, Hershey Transit Company car No. 7 is on the Lebanon line. Built by the Cincinnati Car Company in 1914 for the Ephrata and Lebanon Street Railway Company as car No. 21, it was purchased in 1934 and became car No. 7. It was retired in the 1940s. On January 9, 1942, the line from Campbelltown to Lebanon was closed. (Photograph by Robert G. Lewis.)

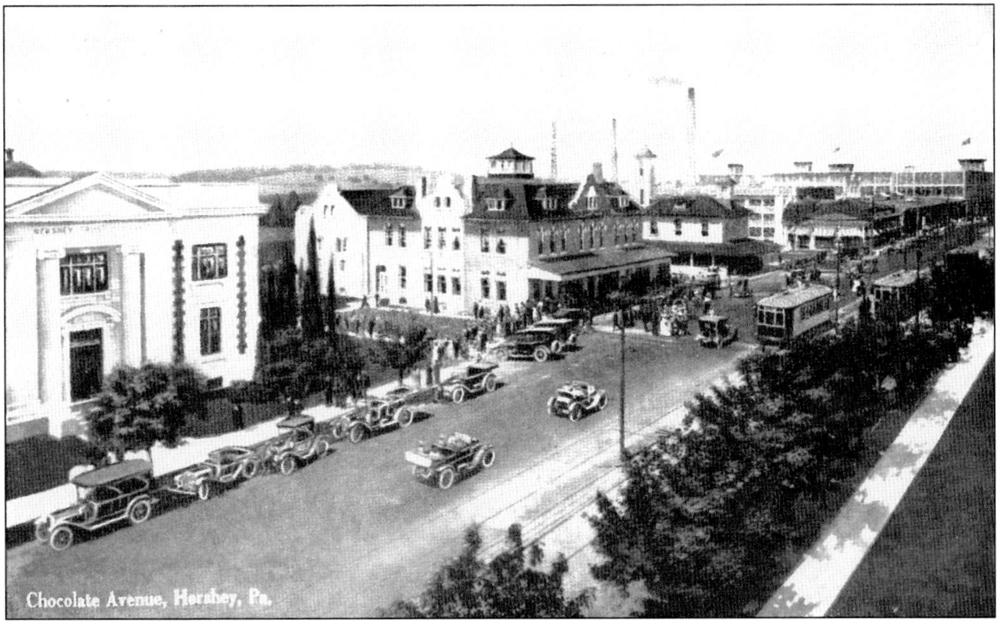

Two Hershey Transit Company trolley cars are on Chocolate Avenue in Hershey around 1920. From this point, trolley service operated to Hummelstown, Palmyra, Lebanon, Elizabethtown, and Hotel Hershey. The Philadelphia and Reading Railroad delivered cocoa beans and sugar, and the trolleys delivered milk and workers to the Hershey chocolate factory.

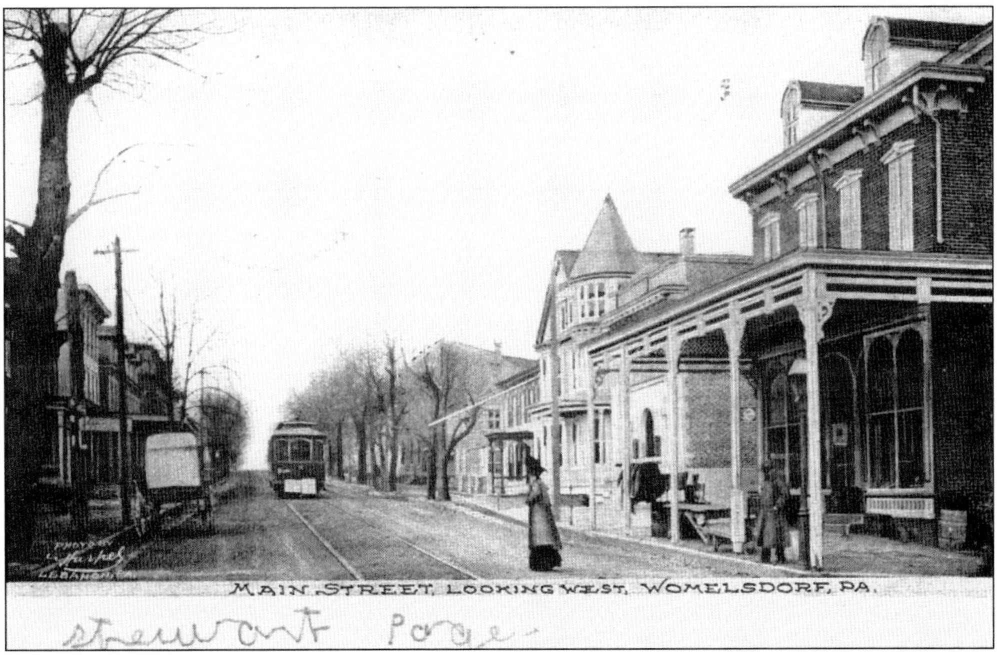

Main Street looking west in the borough of Womelsdorf finds a Reading and Womelsdorf Electric Railway Company trolley car in this postcard postmarked July 8, 1908. This line was leased by the Reading Traction Company on January 1, 1896, and later became part of the Reading Transit and Light Company.

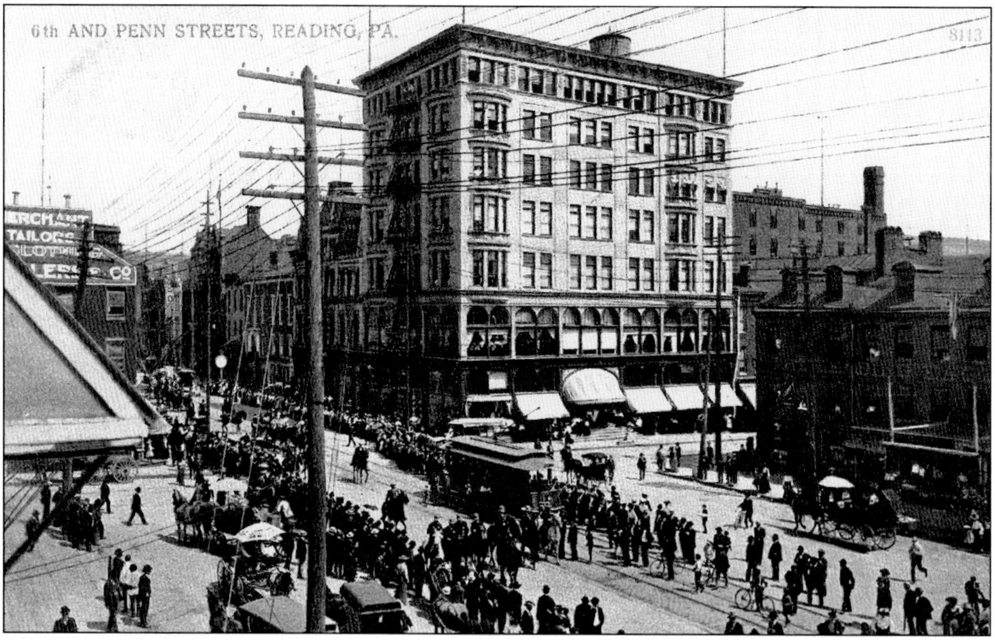

An open trolley car in the city of Reading makes its way along Penn and Sixth Streets during a parade in the early 1900s. The McGraw Electric Railway List of August 1918 noted that the Reading Transit and Light Company operated 218 miles of track with 254 trolley cars serving Reading, Pottstown, Norristown, Conshohocken, and Lebanon.

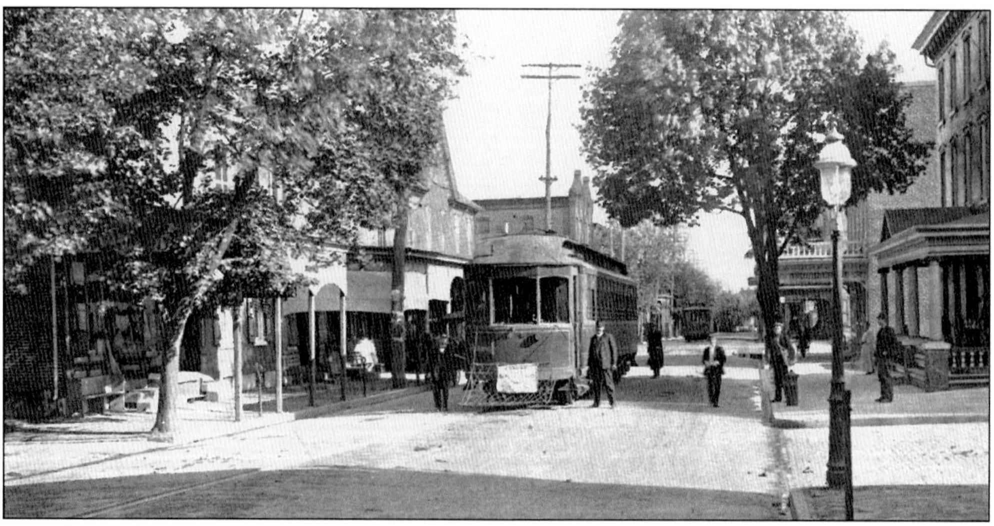

An Oley Valley Railway Company trolley car is in the borough of Boyertown on Philadelphia Avenue around 1910. Chartered on September 21, 1899, the line from Reading reached the Boyertown borough line on May 23, 1902, and by 1906 served downtown Boyertown. The Reading Transit and Light Company controlled this line.

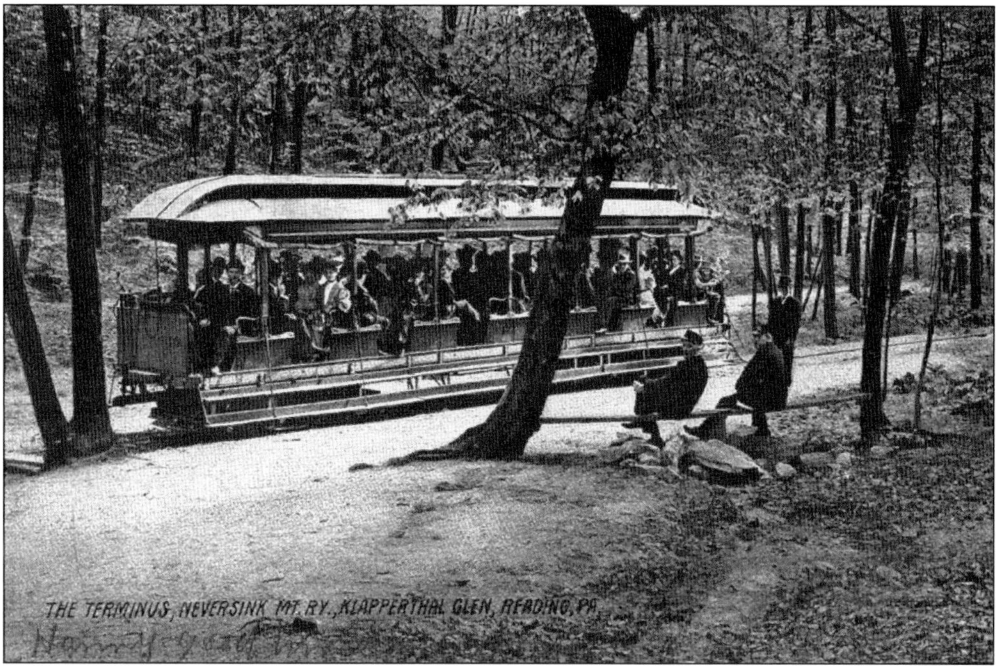

Open car No. 10 is at the Klapperthal Glen terminus of the Neversink Mountain Railway Company in this postcard postmarked June 8, 1907. The eight-mile line using eight cars operated from Ninth and Penn Streets in the city of Reading to Neversink Mountain. The Reading Transit and Light Company controlled the company through stock ownership.

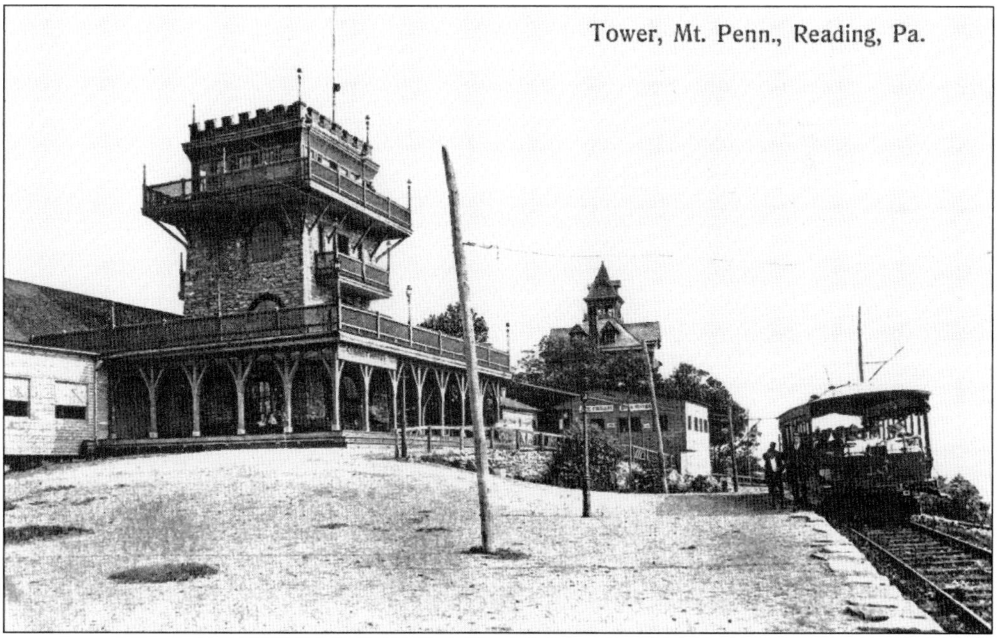

A Mount Penn Gravity Railroad Company trolley car is at the top of Mount Penn in this postcard view around 1900. Originally a steam railroad, the line was electrified and reopened on April 16, 1898. The observation tower shown in the postcard was destroyed by fire on April 13, 1923. Under new owners the line was scrapped during 1924.

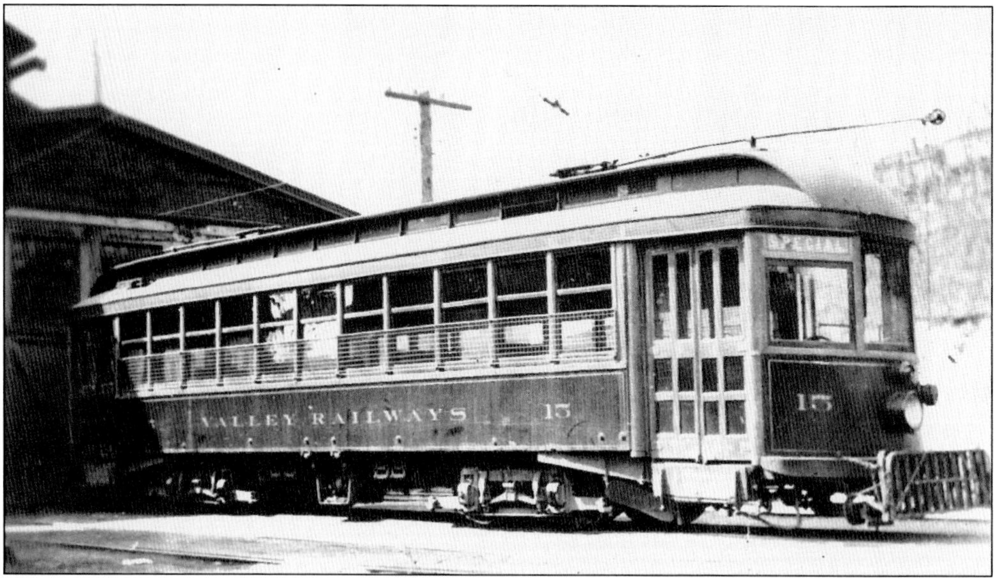

Valley Railways Company car No. 15 is a 1907 product of J. G. Brill Car Company. It had Brill model 27G1 trucks and four Westinghouse motors model 101B and was retired around 1936. The first cutback occurred with the establishment of bus service from Mechanicsburg to Carlisle by the subsidiary Valley Transportation Company on June 23, 1930. Valley Railways Company ended trolley service on April 9, 1938.

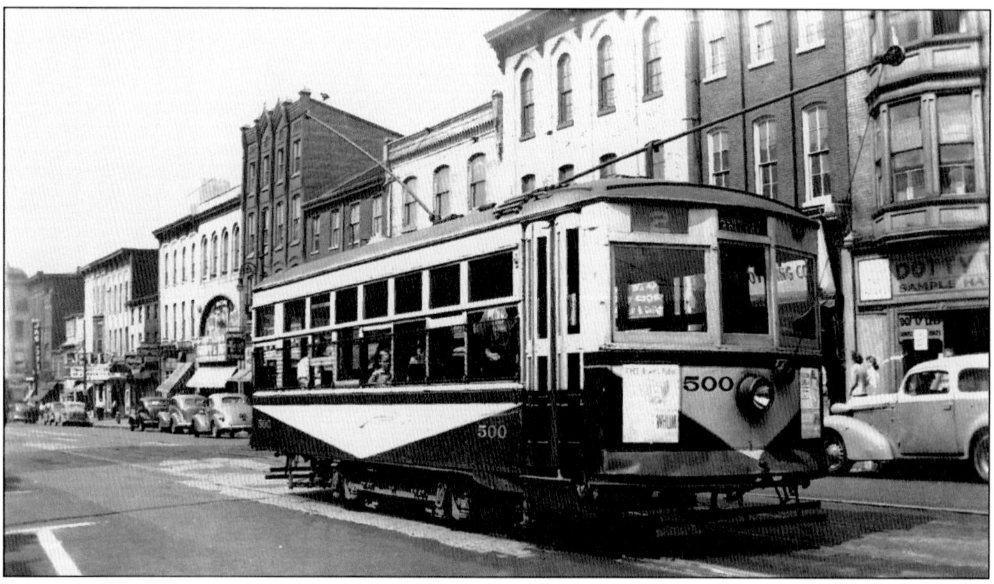

Penn Street in downtown Reading provides the setting for Reading Transit Company car No. 500 operating on route 2 with Albright College on the destination sign around 1940. Route 2 was established on November 2, 1924, and provided service every 10 minutes with six cars. The four-wheel, Birney-type trolley was built by the Wason Car Company in 1920 and was retired around 1947.

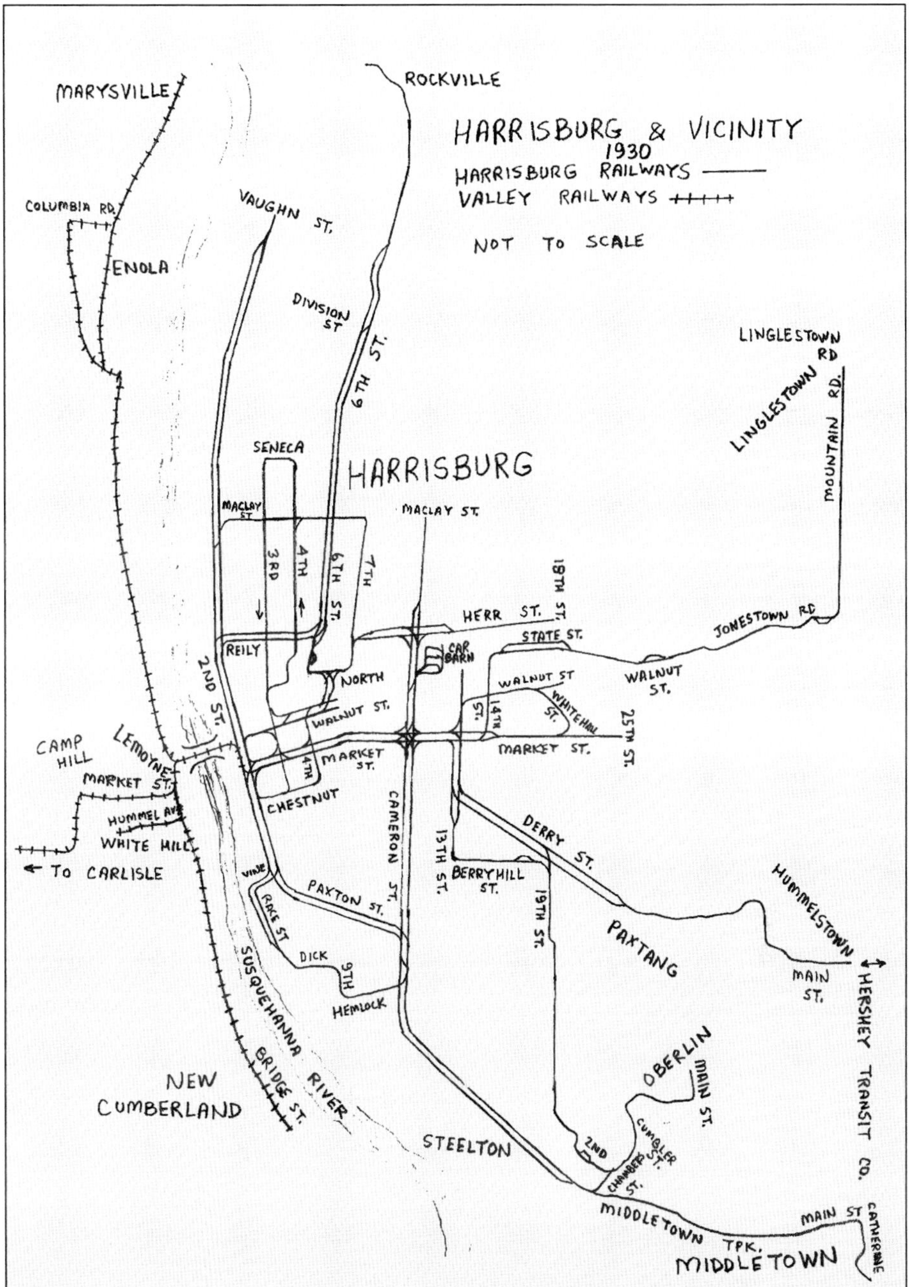

The Harrisburg Railways Company operated 136 trolley cars on 73.51 miles of track, providing trolley car service within the city of Harrisburg and suburban trolley car service to Oberlin, Middletown, Linglestown, Rockville, and Hummelstown (where connections were made with the Hershey Transit Company for Lebanon, Hershey, and Elizabethtown). The Valley Railways Company served the towns of the west shore of the Susquehanna River with 39 trolley cars and 44 miles of track connecting Harrisburg with Marysville, White Hill, New Cumberland, and Carlisle where connections were made via the Cumberland Railway Company to Newville and Mount Holly Springs. This data is according to the McGraw Electric Railway List of August 1918.

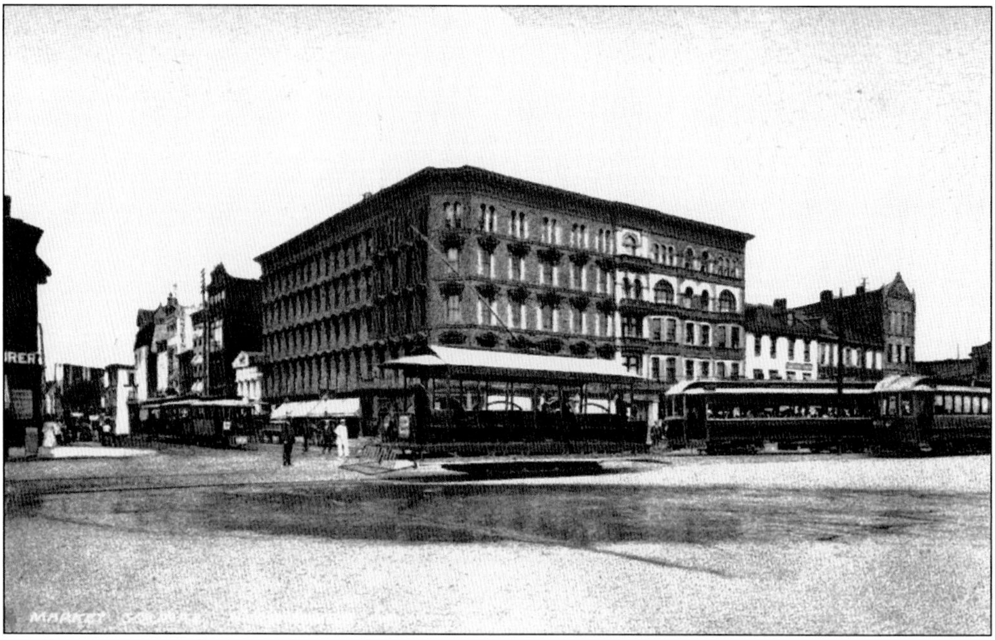

Market Square in the city of Harrisburg, around 1910, has open trolley car No. 150 built by J. G. Brill Car Company in the center of the picture, and car No. 63 built by Jackson and Sharp is to the right of the open car. The Harrisburg Railways Company served industrial areas, which contributed to heavy ridership until the business decline after 1923.

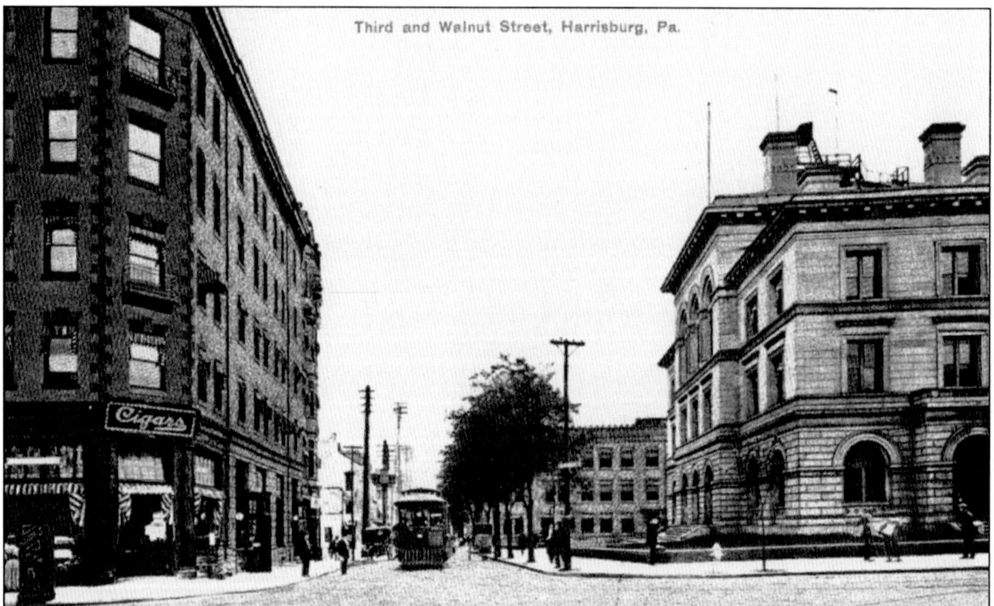

A Harrisburg Railways Company trolley car is on Third and Walnut Streets in traffic-free downtown Harrisburg during 1913. By November 1931, transit routes were designated as follows: 2 (Second Street–Reservoir), 3 (Third Street), 5 (Rockville–Oberlin), 6 (Sixth Street), 7 (Hummelstown–Middletown), 8 (Paxtang–Steelton), 9 (Twenty-third Street–Race and Vine), 10 (Cameron Street), 11 (Fairgrounds), 18 (Herr Street), and Penbrook (Linglestown).

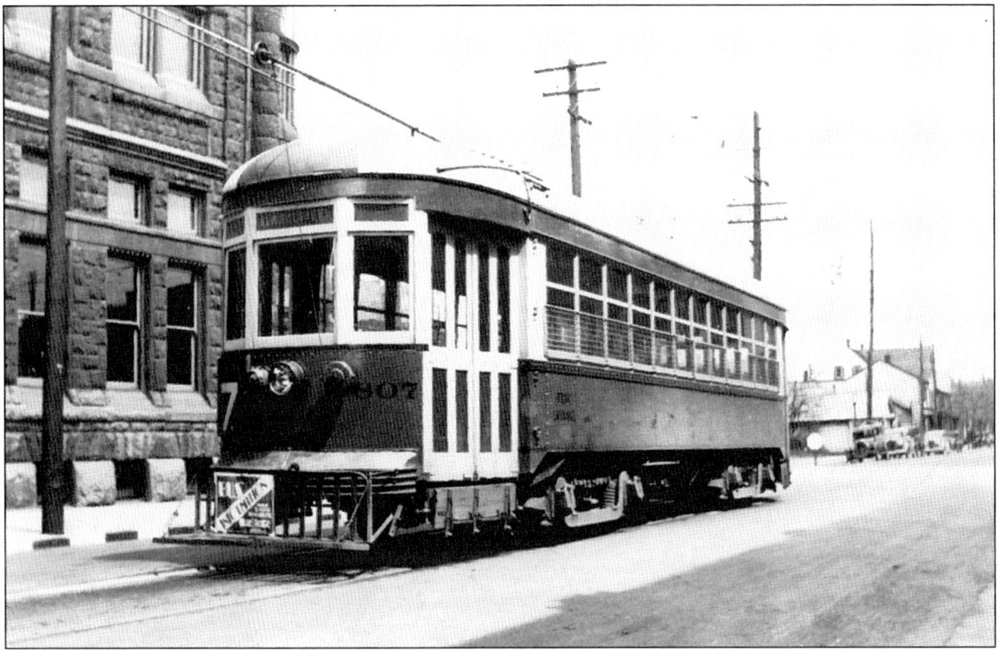

Harrisburg Railways Company car No. 807 is at the end of the route 7 Middletown line with Hummelstown on the destination sign during 1936. This was one of five cars in the series 807 to 811 ordered from J. G. Brill Car Company in September 1917. The last trolley cars purchased by the Harrisburg Railways Company were numbered 812 to 816, ordered from J. G. Brill Car Company in July 1919.

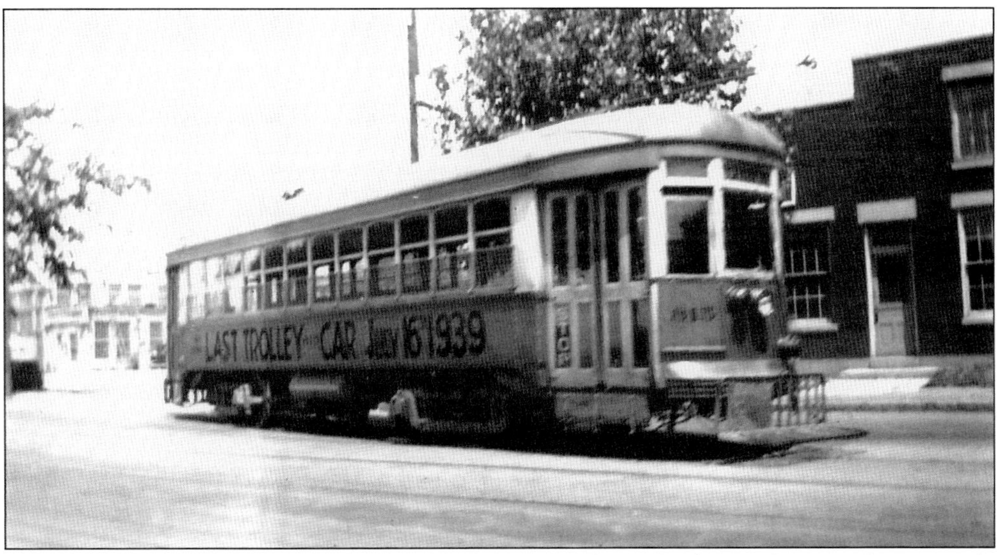

Trolley car No. 815 made the last run on Harrisburg Railways Company's nine-mile Middletown–Steelton line on July 16, 1939. The last trip started at 2:00 p.m. in downtown Harrisburg and arrived back at Market Square in Harrisburg at 3:30 p.m., ending trolley car service in Harrisburg. Regular trolley car service from Harrisburg to Middletown began on December 18, 1892.

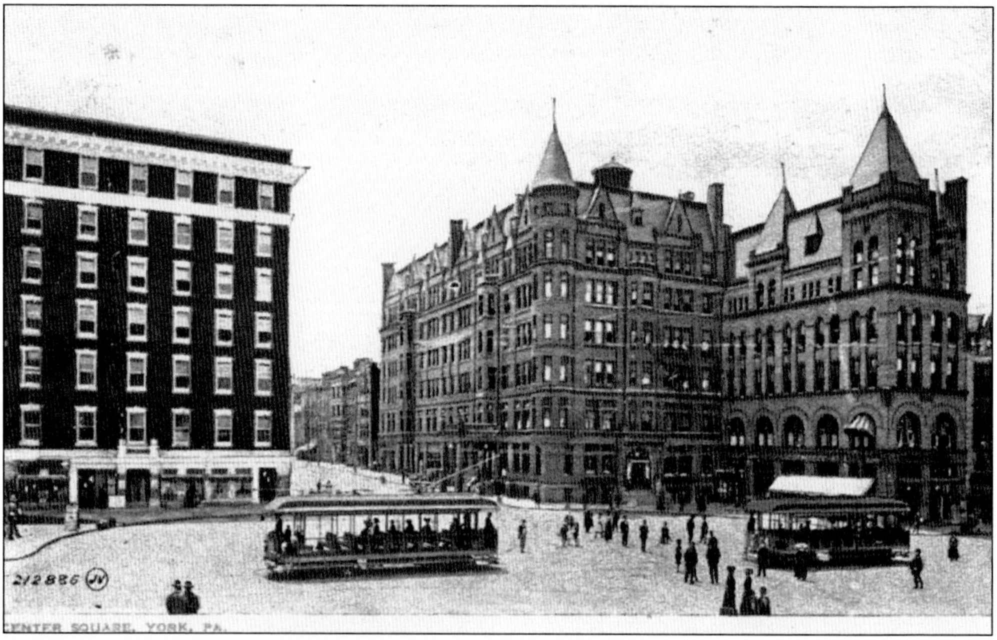

Center Square in downtown York shows two open summer trolleys around 1900. The York Street Railway Company began electric trolley car service in York on August 18, 1892, and by 1896 had about 11 miles of track in operation. The last major line built was from York to Hanover, which opened on February 28, 1908.

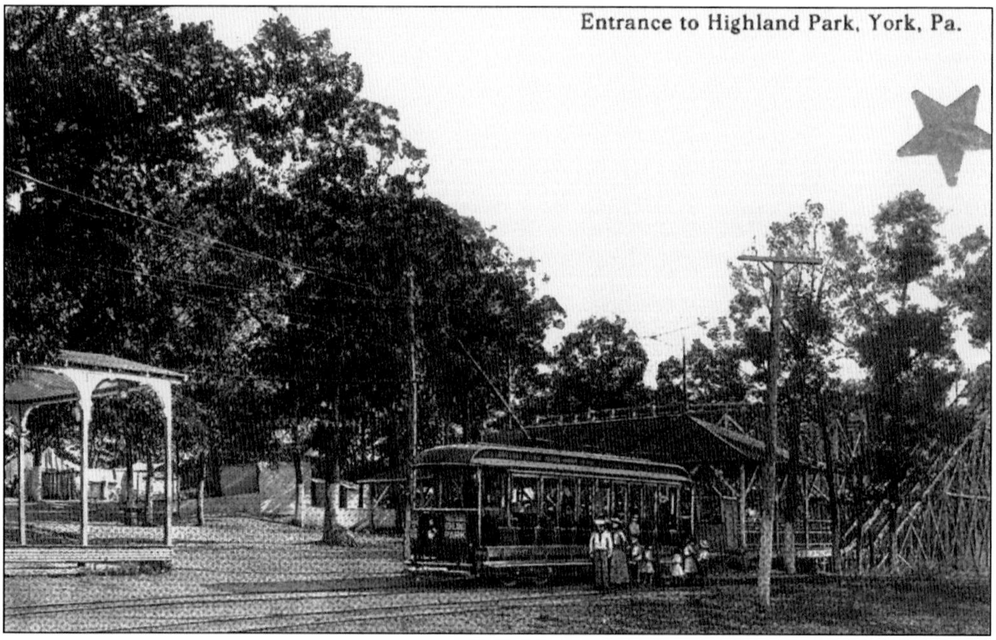

During 1919, an open summer car is at the entrance to Highland Park (located two miles from downtown York), which featured a theater, dancing pavilion, circle swing, merry-go-round, roller coaster, penny arcade, and picnic grove. On November 15, 1907, the York Railways Company was formed as a reorganization of the York County Traction Company, and by 1918, the system operated 70 trolley cars on 84 miles of track.

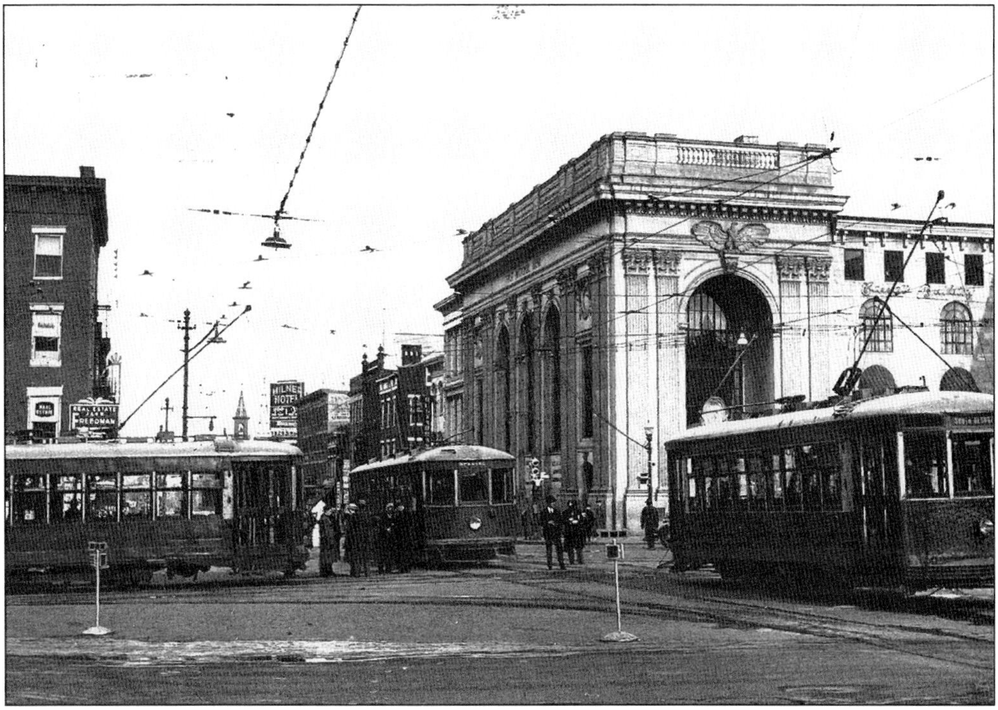

York Railways Company cars are at York's City Square in December 1935. Much of the system had been abandoned, with the Broad Street line making its last run on December 1, 1931, followed by Dover on May 1, 1932; York Haven was cutback to North York on June 1, 1932; Wrightsville was abandoned on February 1, 1933; and North York was abandoned on April 22, 1934. (Photograph by Robert G. Lewis.)

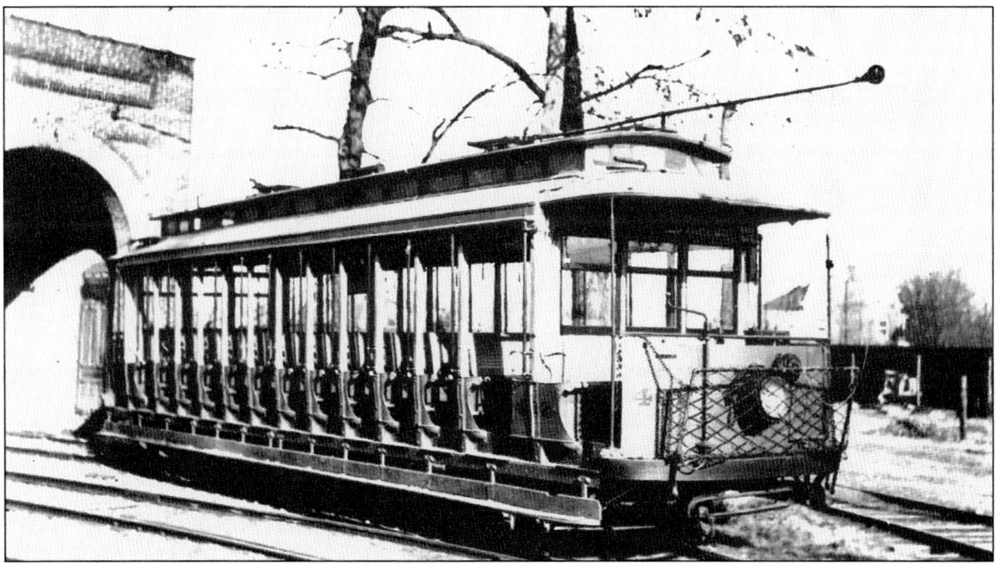

York Railways Company car No. 402 is at the Maryland Avenue carbarn around 1910. This was a group of 10 open cars in the series 400 to 408 and 411, which were all retired by 1939. When the company sold its electric utility operation to satisfy creditors, plans were made to convert to bus operation with trolley car service ending on February 4, 1939.

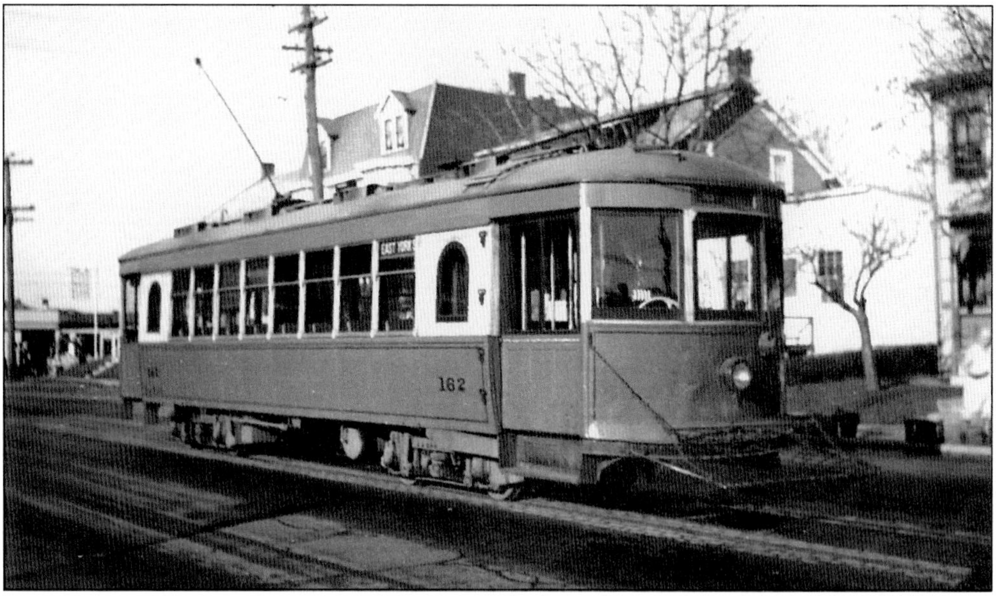

Double-truck, double-end, curved-side, lightweight York Railways Company car No. 162 is on West Market Street around 1930. J. G. Brill Car Company built this car along with No. 163 during 1924 powered by four General Electric model 264A motors. Car No. 162 was retired in 1939, and car No. 163 has been restored to operating condition at the Rockhill Trolley Museum located in the borough of Rockhill Furnace.

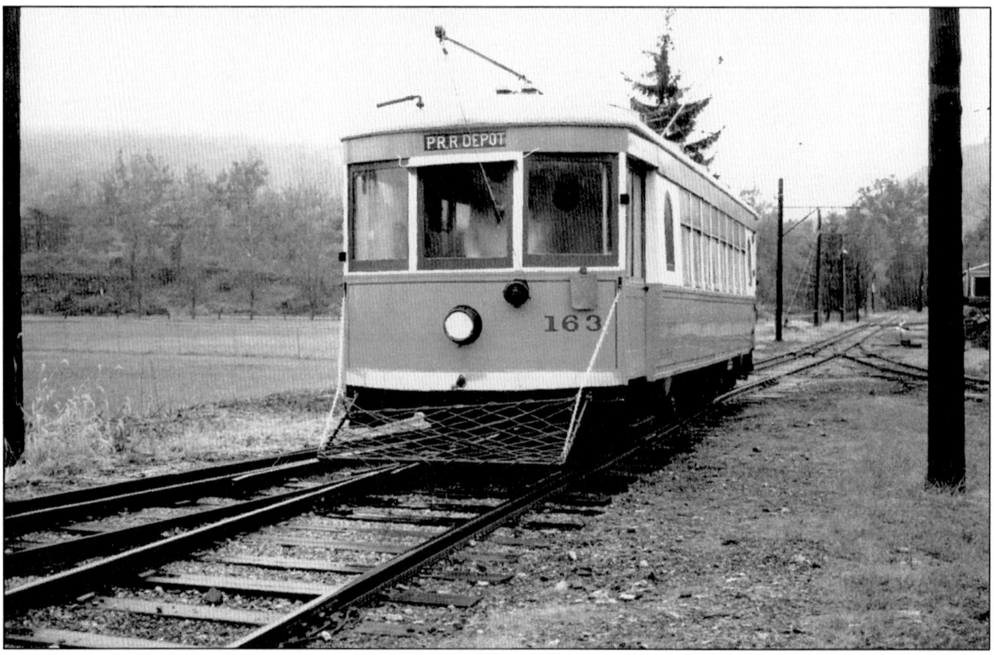

Former York Railways Company trolley car No. 163 is at Rockhill Trolley Museum on October 8, 2005. This car, built by J. G. Brill Car Company in 1924, was used until trolley service in York ended on February 4, 1939, and became a summer home. Following the 1972 Hurricane Agnes, it was donated to the Rockhill Trolley Museum, where volunteers restored the car. (Photograph by Kenneth C. Springirth.)

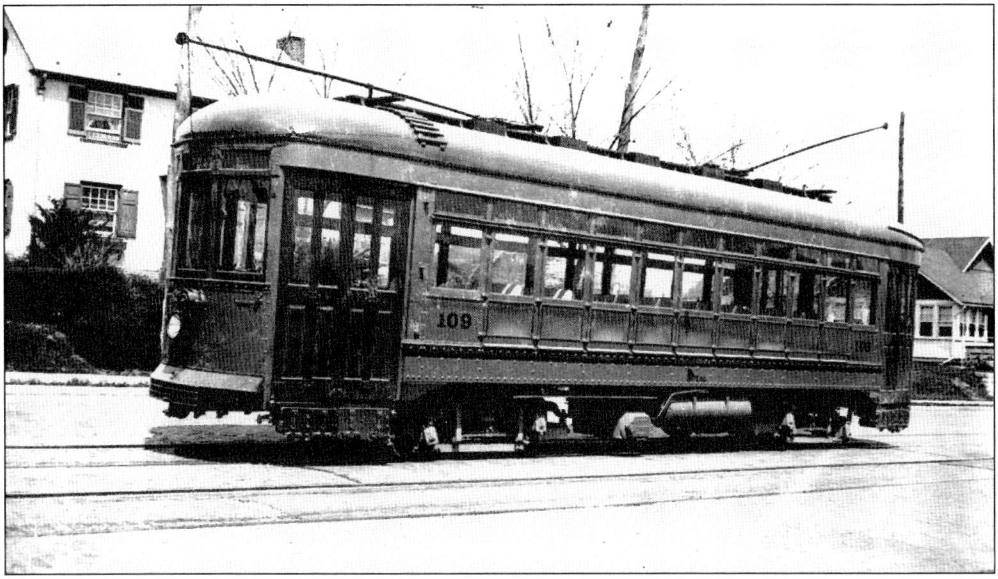

Pottstown Transit Company car No. 109 is on High Street in Pottstown around 1935. This was one of six new trolley cars ordered from J. G. Brill Car Company and placed in service during January 1917. It was known as a "convertible" car because the side panels and windows could be removed and replaced with screens, making it like an open summer car. This trolley system closed on September 30, 1936.

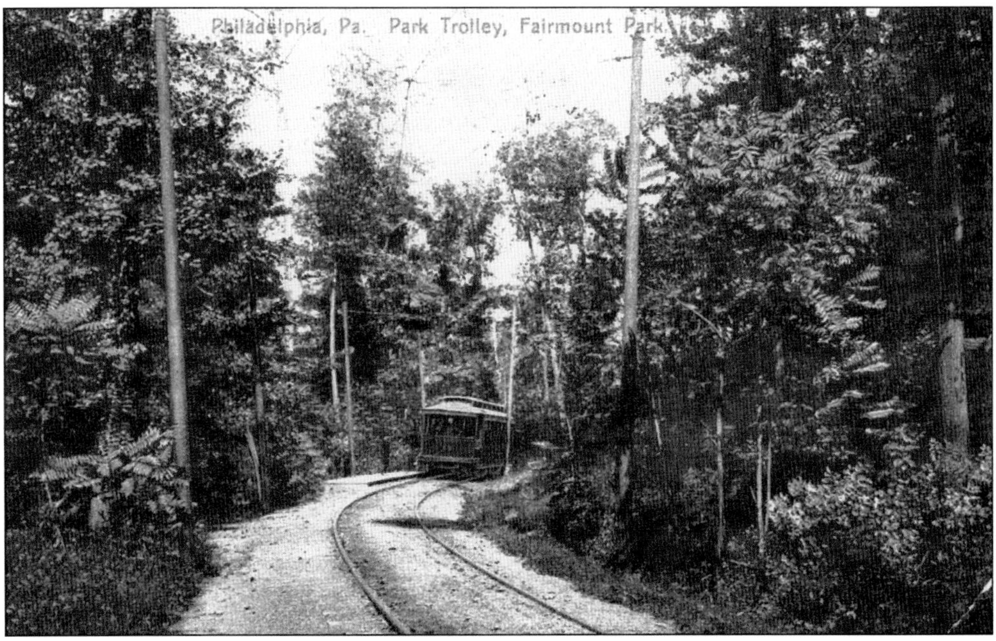

A Fairmount Park Transportation Company open trolley is operating through Philadelphia's Fairmount Park during 1908. The line opened on November 10, 1896 with 20 closed and 50 open cars, of which 30 were open trailer cars. It became Fairmount Park Transit Company in 1917, making its last regular service run on September 9, 1946.

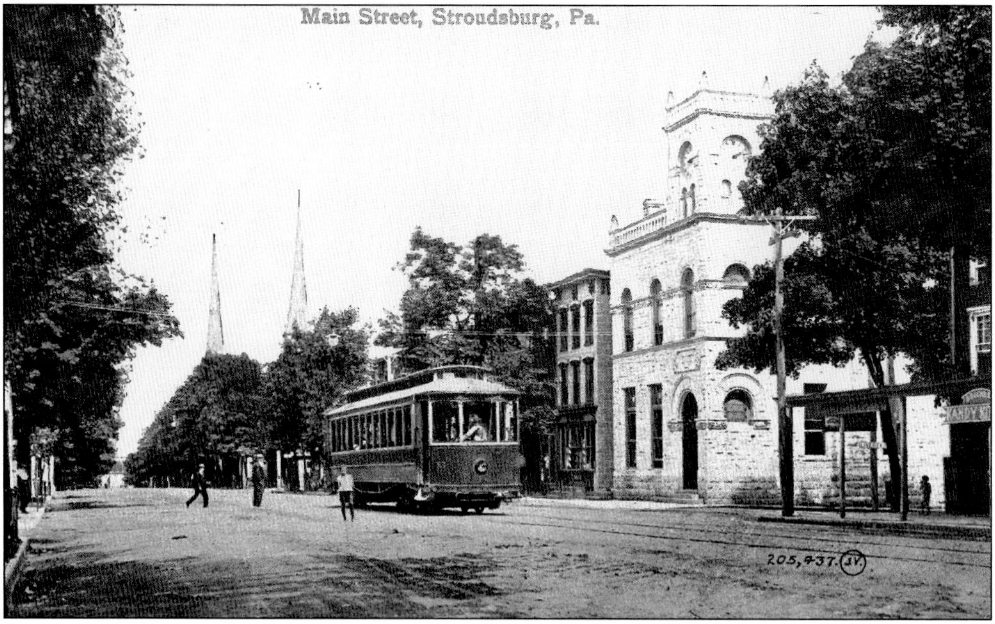

A Stroudsburg and Water Gap Street Railway Company trolley car is on Main Street in the borough of Stroudsburg around 1910. Trolley service reached the borough of Portland during October 1911, and service from Stroudsburg to Portland continued until November 30, 1926, when it was cut back to the borough of Delaware Water Gap.

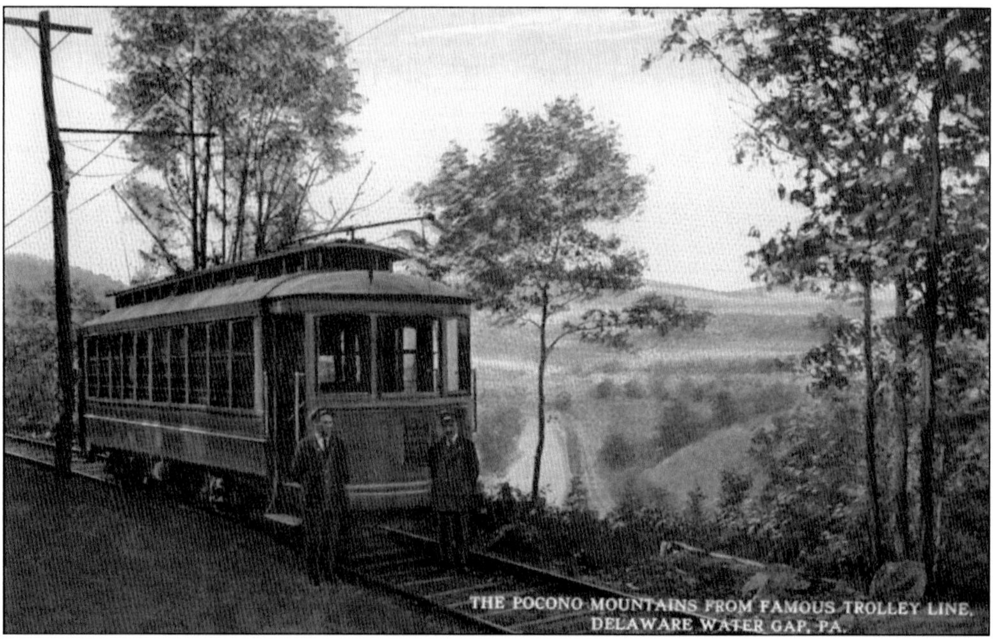

The motorman and conductor are posing with a Stroudsburg Traction Company trolley car at the Delaware Water Gap around 1917. On July 3, 1907, trolley service began from Stroudsburg to the Delaware Water Gap by the Stroudsburg and Water Gap Street Railway Company. With a July 1917 consolidation into the Stroudsburg Traction Company, the system had 12.5 miles of track and 12 trolley cars.

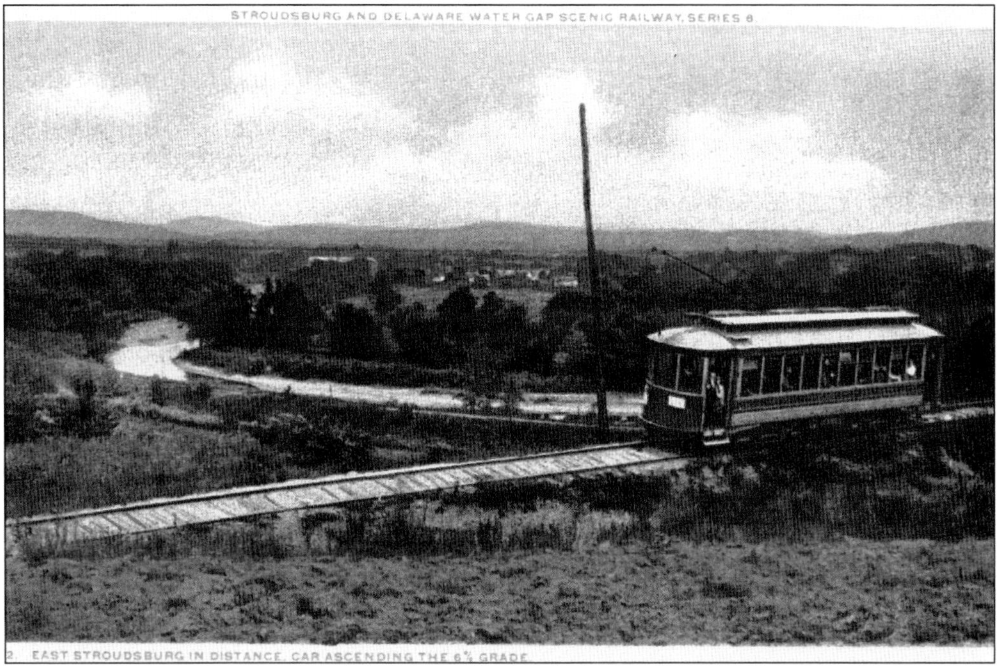

With East Stroudsburg in the distance, a Stroudsburg and Water Gap Street Railway Company trolley car is ascending a 6 percent grade. The nine-mile Stroudsburg-to-Portland line had a scheduled time of 50 minutes, and two trolleys provided hourly service. This was an attractive area for visitors who could reach this area by trolley.

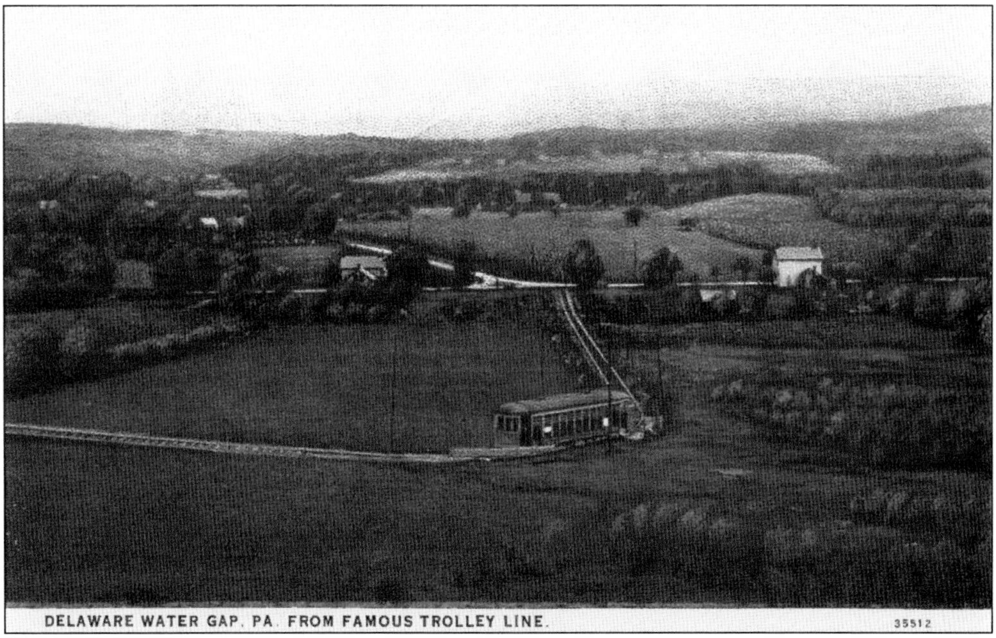

Viewing the beautiful Delaware Water Gap from the Stroudsburg Traction Company trolley initially was popular, but on January 1, 1927, buses temporarily replaced trolley service between Stroudsburg and the Delaware Water Gap. Trolley service was restored for the summer season on June 1, 1927, and permanently ended on September 4, 1928.

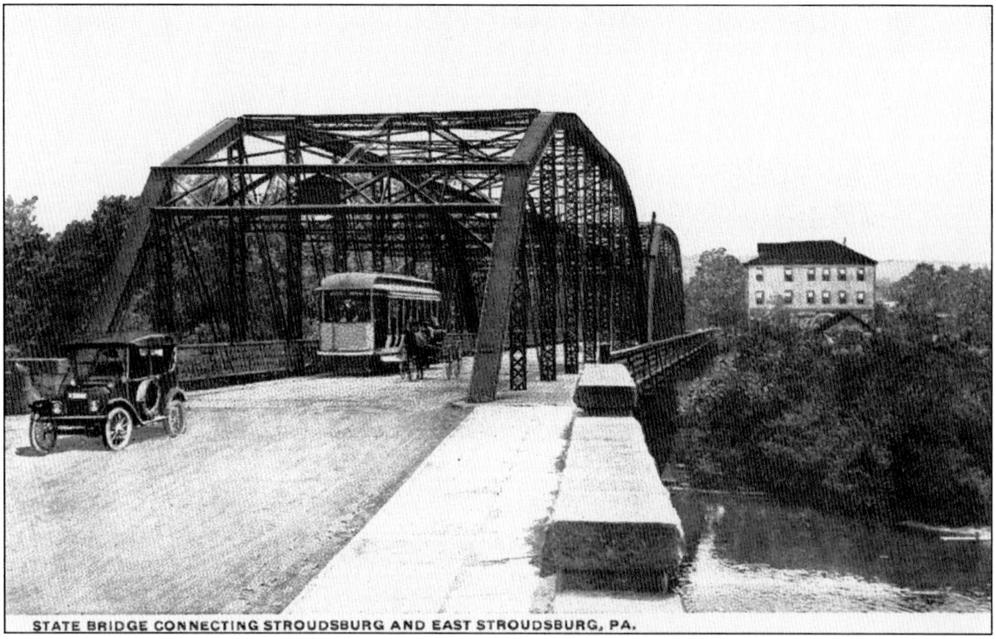

A Stroudsburg, Water Gap and Portland Railway Company trolley car is crossing the bridge connecting Stroudsburg and East Stroudsburg during 1912. Trolley car service began on March 11, 1902, and the first electric trolley car from Stroudsburg reached the Delaware Water Gap on July 3, 1907. Trolley car service ended on September 4, 1928.

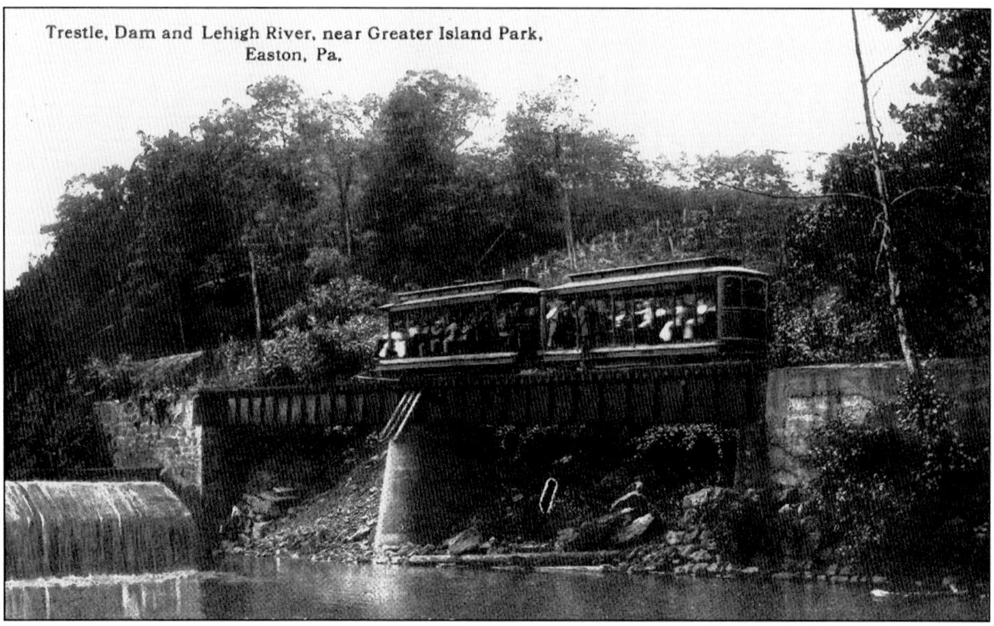

Easton Transit Company open summer cars are crossing the Lehigh River to Greater Island Park in this 1911 scene. The bridge was completed on April 21, 1905, to reach the amusement center at Greater Island Park. On October 31, 1931, the last trolley car operated over the Delaware River into Phillipsburg, New Jersey.

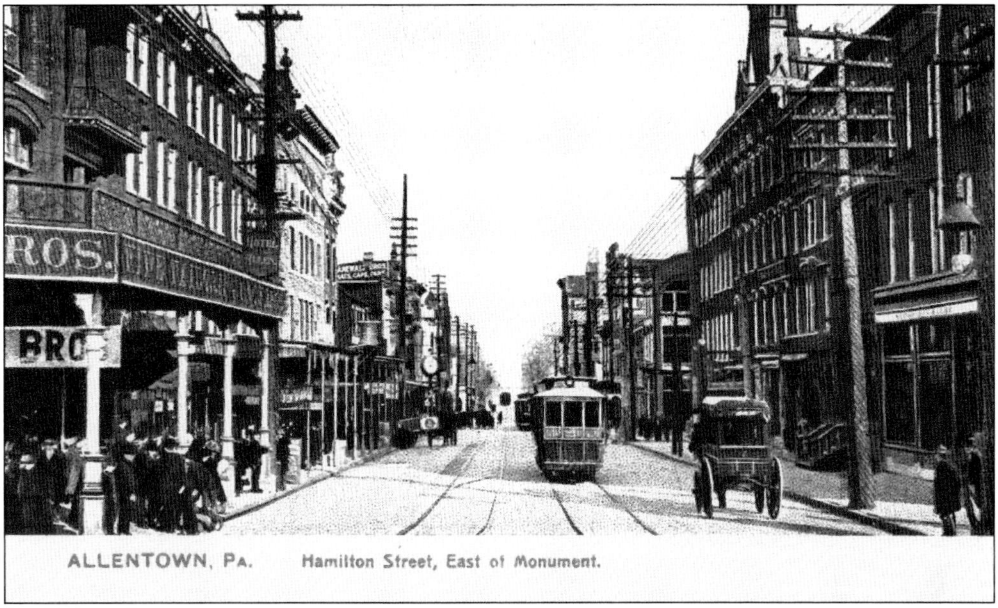

Several Allentown and Bethlehem Rapid Transit Company trolley cars are in this scene on Hamilton Street around 1900. Electric trolley car service in Allentown began on Hamilton Street on July 1, 1891. On November 17, 1899, a number of trolley lines were brought under control of the Lehigh Valley Traction Company. Another merger on July 20, 1905, resulted in the formation of the Lehigh Valley Transit Company.

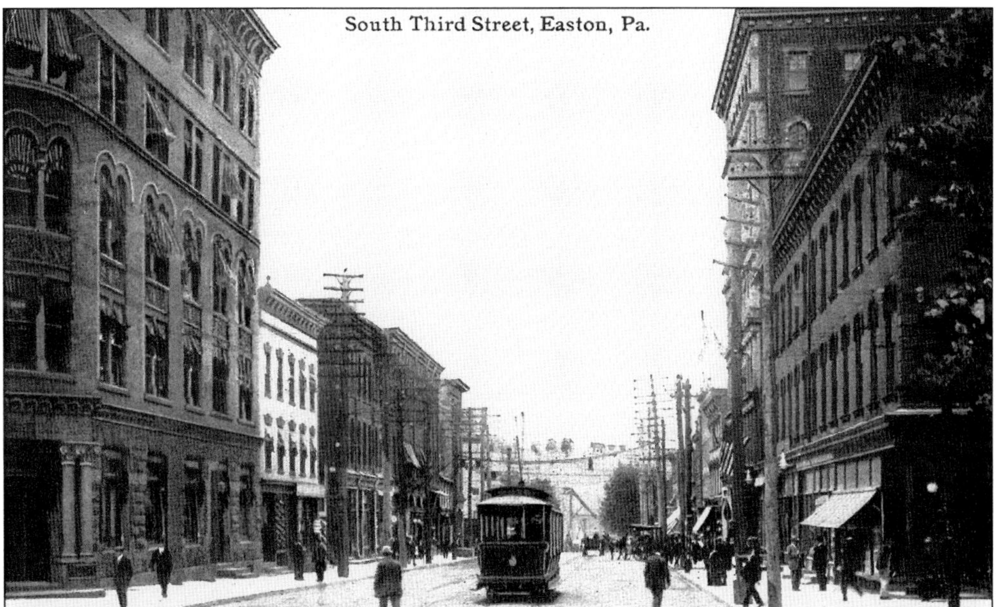

South Third Street in Easton around 1910 is the scene for this Easton Transit Company trolley car. Electric trolley car service in Easton began on January 7, 1888, by the Lafayette Traction Company. The Easton Transit Company was leased by the Lehigh Valley Transit Company on March 1, 1922. Easton–Bethlehem–Allentown limited trolley car service was converted to bus operation on August 15, 1949.

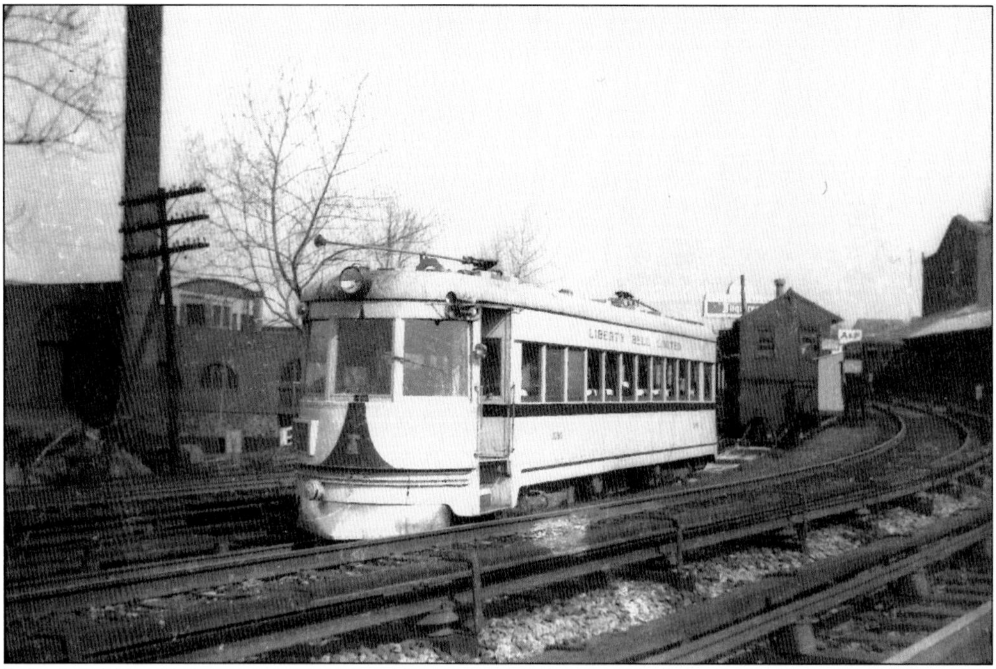

Lehigh Valley Transit Company car No. 1030 is at Sixty-ninth Street terminal during 1942. This was originally Indiana Railroad Company car No. 55 built by American Car and Foundry Company during 1931. The Lehigh Valley Transit Company discontinued service between Norristown and Sixty-ninth Street terminal on September 24, 1949, and ended Allentown-to-Norristown service on September 7, 1951. This car is preserved at the Seashore Trolley Museum at Kennebunkport, Maine.

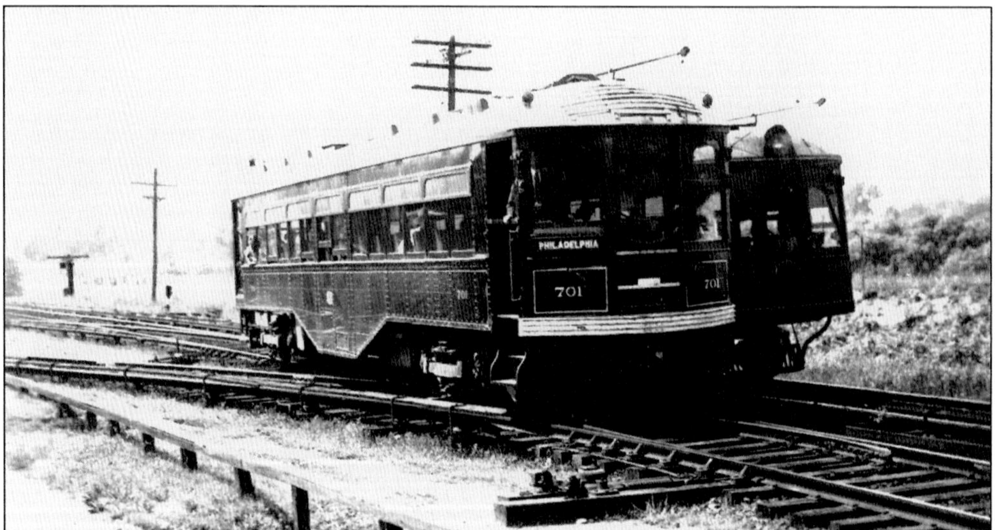

Lehigh Valley Transit Company car No. 701 is shown on Philadelphia and Western Railway Company trackage around 1936. This was one of 12 center-entrance, all-steel-body cars purchased from the Southern Car Company of High Point, North Carolina, in 1916. It had Brill model MCB2X trucks and four Westinghouse model 547A motors. This car was converted to one-man operation in 1932 and scrapped on January 8, 1952.

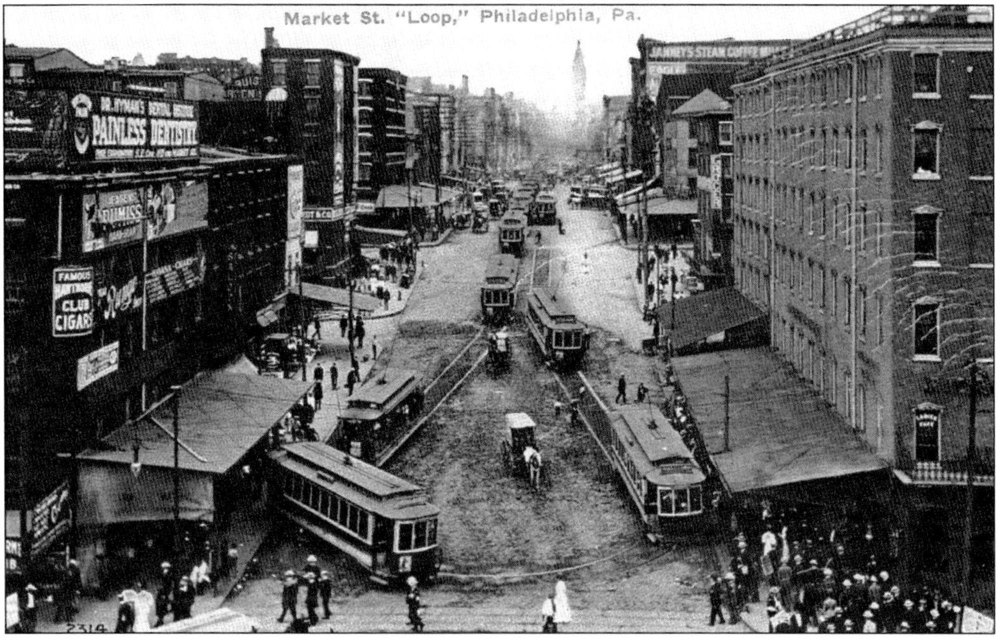

Market Street Loop at the intersection of Market Street and Delaware Avenue in Philadelphia shows a constant flow of Philadelphia Rapid Transit Company trolley cars handling passengers to and from the seashore during 1913. Philadelphia's fleet of trolleys was 3,399 in 1911. By 1913, there were 1,500 new trolley cars placed in service.

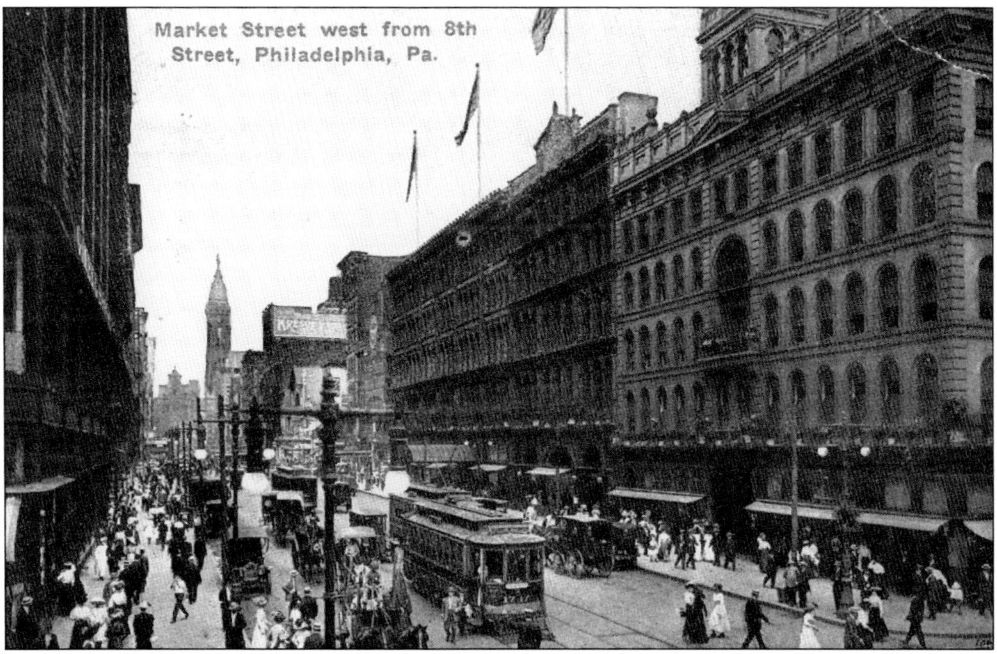

Philadelphia Rapid Transit car No. 1747 is on Market Street, looking west from Eighth Street in Philadelphia during 1916. There were 772 cars of this series built by J. G. Brill Car Company between 1899 and 1906. This was known as a pay-within car with the conductor located on the car body instead of the front platform. All the cars in this series were scrapped by 1941.

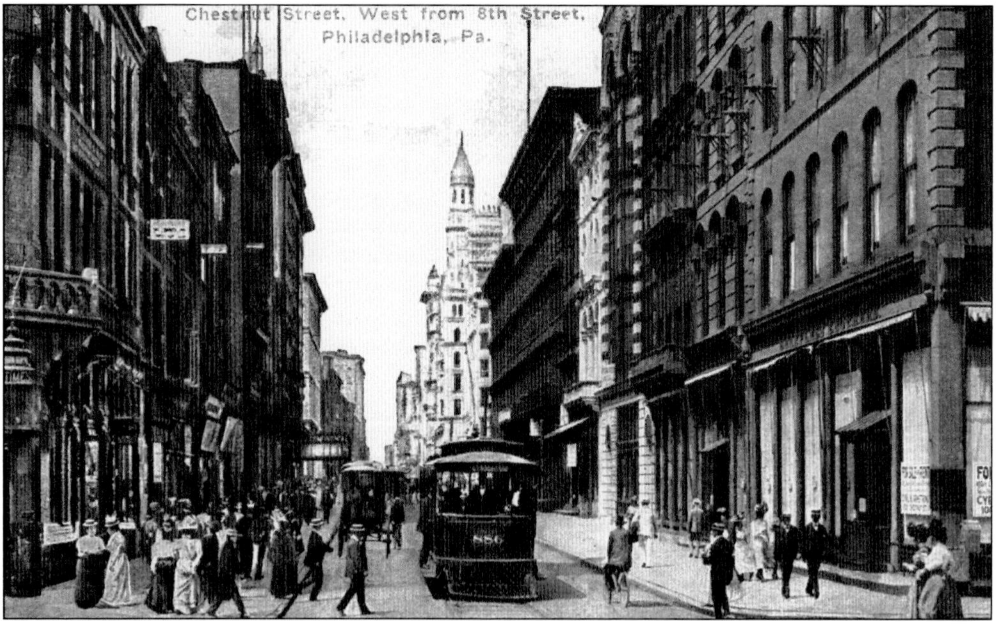

The first-class stores of Chestnut Street west from Eighth Street in Philadelphia provide the setting for Philadelphia Rapid Transit Company double-truck open platform car No. 886 during 1910. This was a large group of cars, numbered from 501 to 1517. The last trolley cars operated on Chestnut Street on September 9, 1956.

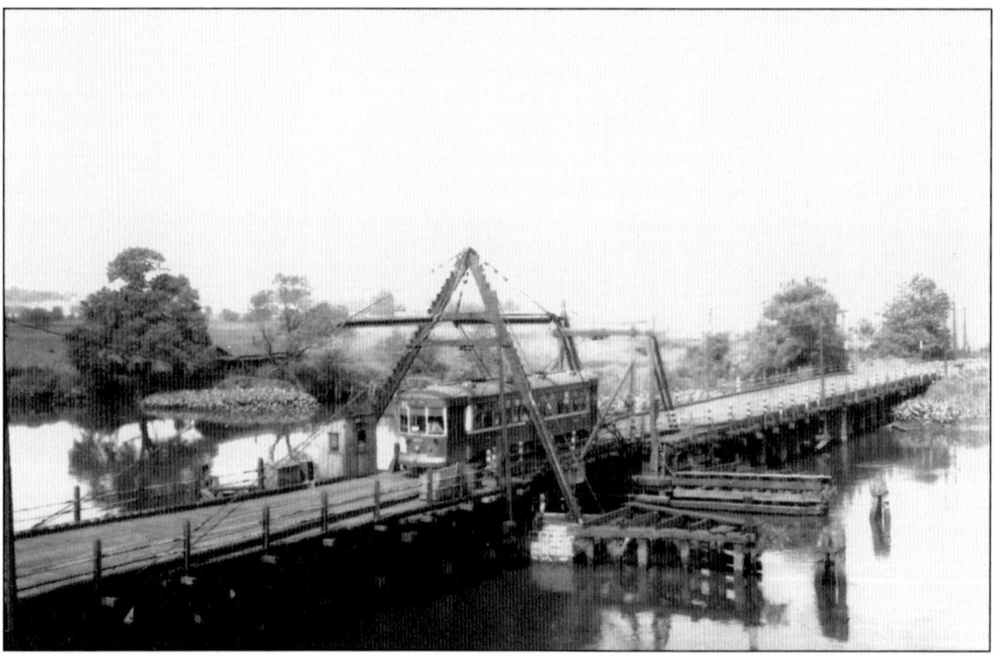

A Philadelphia Rapid Transit Company trolley car on route 37 is crossing the drawbridge heading for Chester in 1934. On February 15, 1911, route 37, Chester, was established operating from Third and Market Streets in Chester to Philadelphia using Elmwood and Woodland Avenues, to the subway. On November 24, 1946, buses replaced trolleys between Westinghouse Loop and Chester. (Photograph by Robert G. Lewis.)

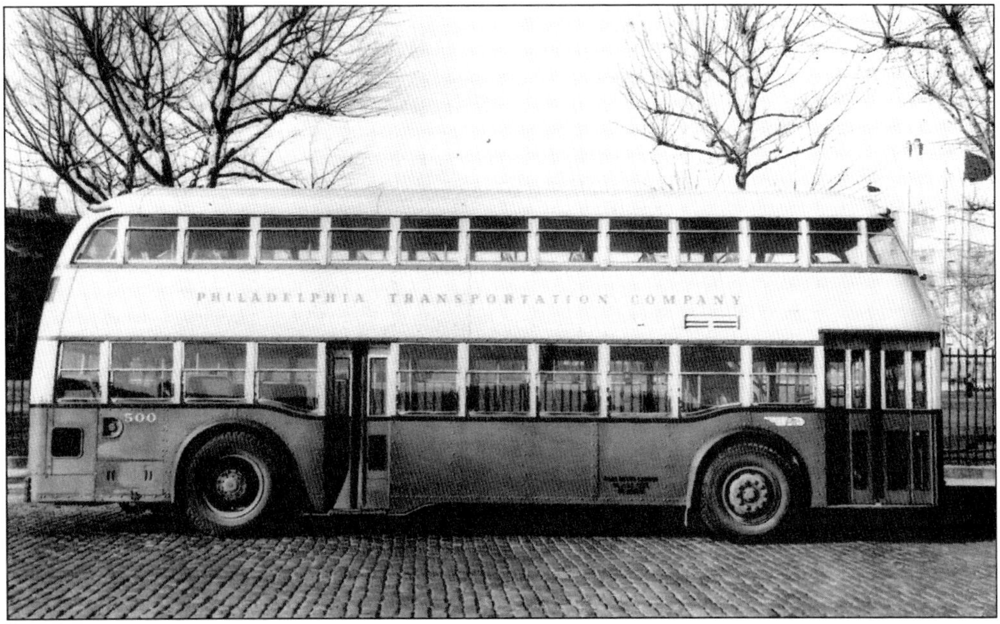

Philadelphia Transportation Company bus No. 500 is in North Philadelphia on December 23, 1940. This 1936 Yellow Coach model 735 was former Fifth Avenue Coach No. 2025 that was purchased in 1940 and operated on route C in Philadelphia during World War II. It was serial number 1 and is the first Fifth Avenue Coach of that model. (Oliver J. Ogden, Museum of Bus Transportation photograph.)

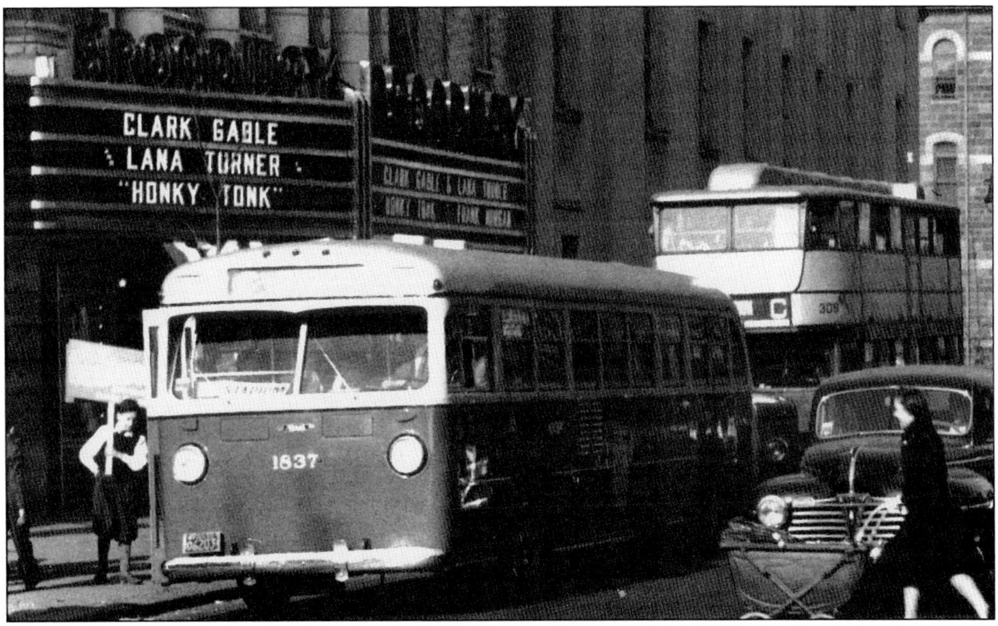

Broad Street at Snyder Avenue in Philadelphia is the scene for Philadelphia Transportation Company route C bus No. 1837 around 1946. The Mack Truck Company of Allentown built this model CM bus during 1941. The CM model produced from 1939 through 1942 was second only to the model AB as Mack's most popular pre–World War II model with 1,877 built. (Oliver J. Ogden, Museum of Bus Transportation photograph.)

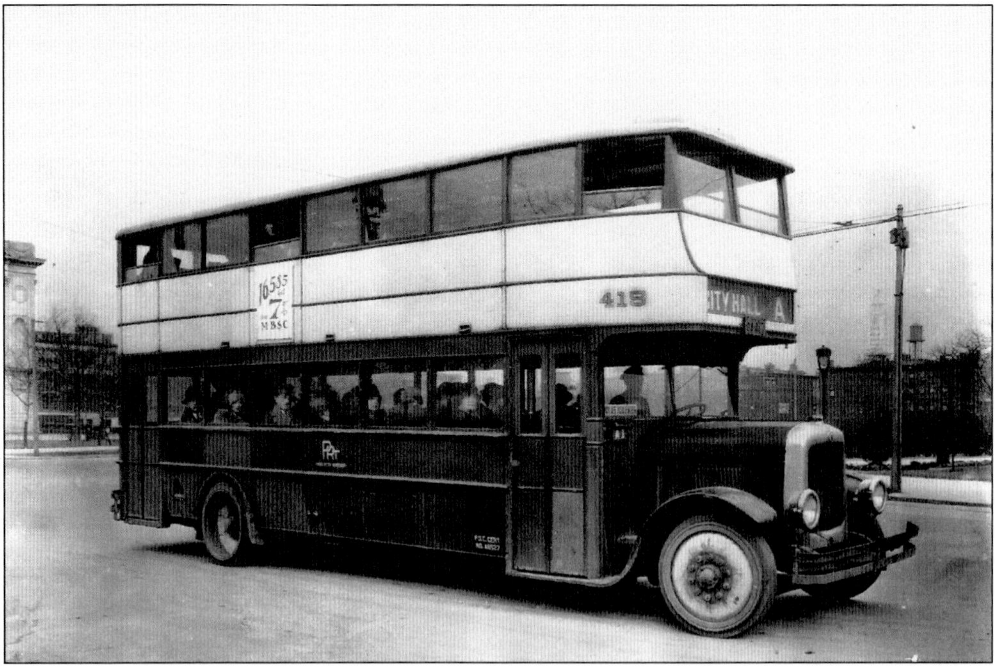

On February 15, 1928, Philadelphia Rapid Transit Company double-decker bus No. 415 is at Logan Circle on route A in Philadelphia. Yellow Coach built this bus in the Z model class in 1926. In 1923, the first bus line and first trackless trolley line in Philadelphia was started. (Oliver J. Ogden, Museum of Bus Transportation photograph.)

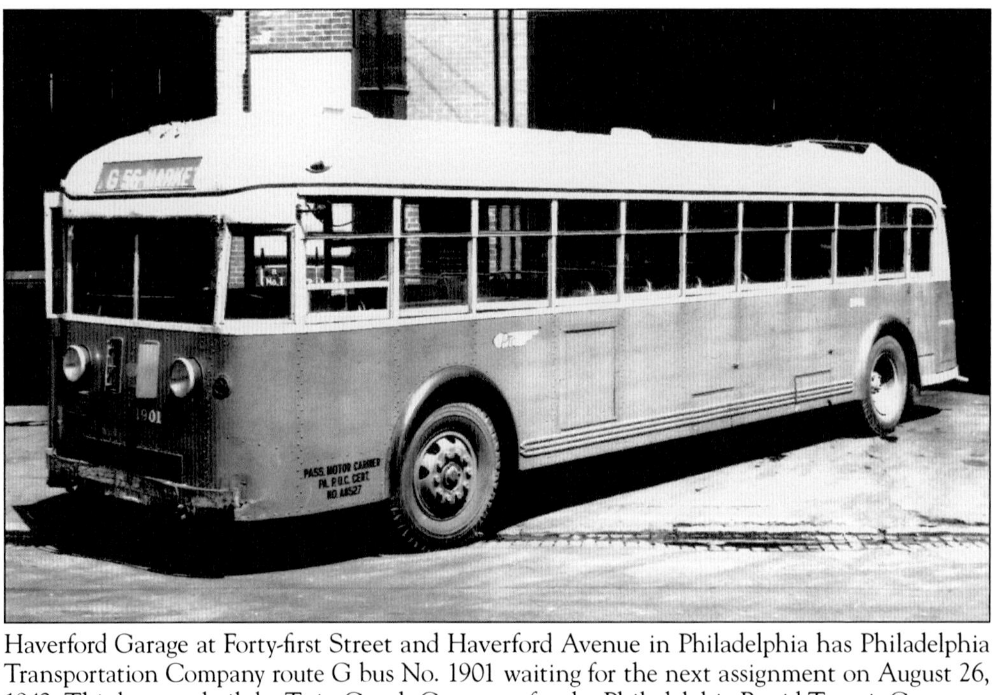

Haverford Garage at Forty-first Street and Haverford Avenue in Philadelphia has Philadelphia Transportation Company route G bus No. 1901 waiting for the next assignment on August 26, 1942. This bus was built by Twin Coach Company for the Philadelphia Rapid Transit Company in 1938. (Oliver J. Ogden, Museum of Bus Transportation photograph.)

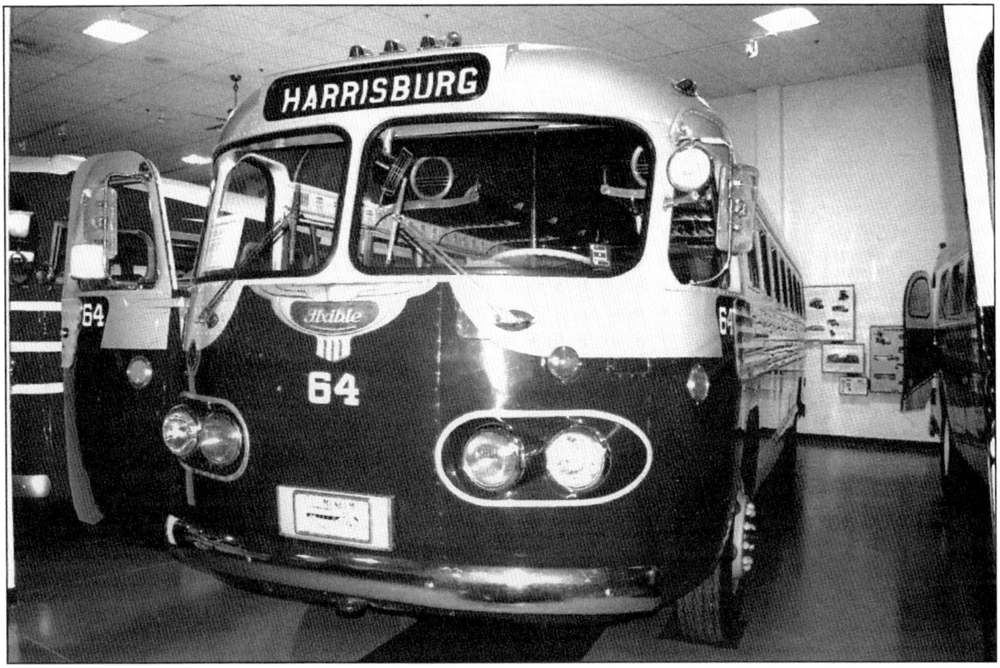

Capitol Bus Company bus No. 64 is a 29-passenger bus built by the Flxible Company in 1947 for Meridian Transit Company of Belleville, Kansas. It was purchased by Richard Maguire for his historical fleet and donated by his estate to the Museum of Bus Transportation located at 161 Museum Drive in Hershey. These Flxible Clipper buses were used in Pennsylvania intercity bus service. (Photograph by Kenneth C. Springirth.)

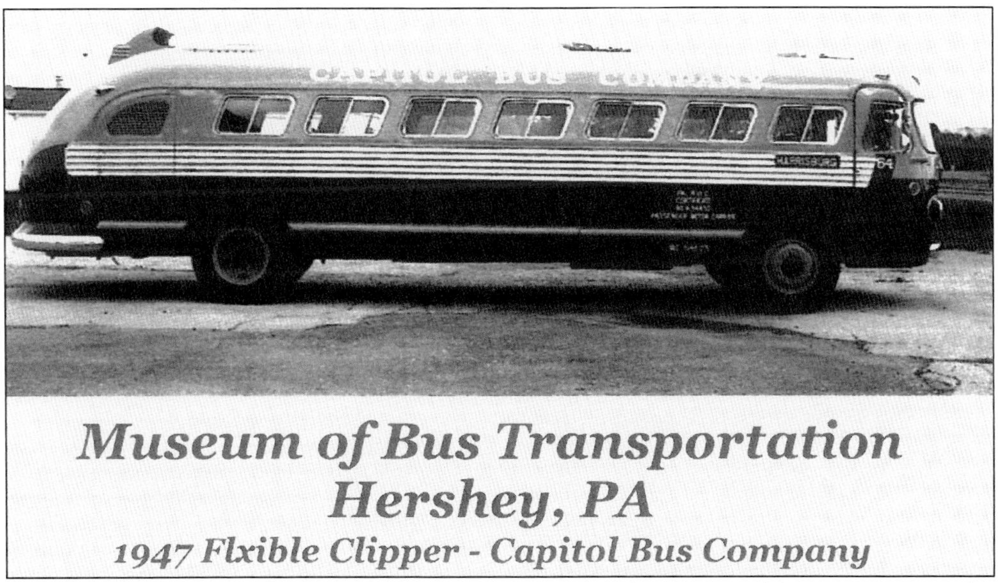

The 1947 Flxible Clipper bus No. 64 model 29B1-47 with Buick engine model FB320 was a popular intercity coach produced in Loudonville, Ohio, and is at the Museum of Bus Transportation in Hershey. Capitol Bus Company, founded in 1936, has a Harrisburg–Reading bus route serving Hummelstown, Hershey, and Palmyra that was once a Hershey Transit Company trolley route. (Oliver J. Ogden, Museum of Bus Transportation photograph.)

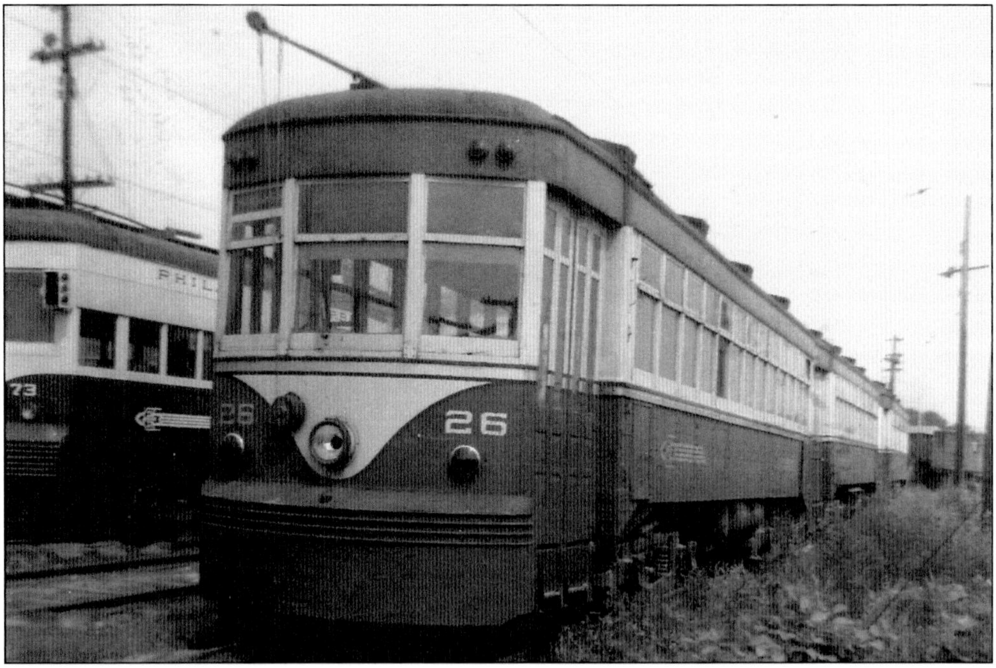

Philadelphia Suburban Transportation Company car No. 26 is at the Llanerch carbarn around 1959. This was one of three cars, 4024, 4045, and 4106 (built by J. G. Brill Car Company in 1917–1918), purchased from the Philadelphia Transportation Company in 1942 to handle the increased ridership during World War II. They became cars Nos. 20–22 and were renumbered in 1949 to cars Nos. 25–27. (Photograph by Craig Knox.)

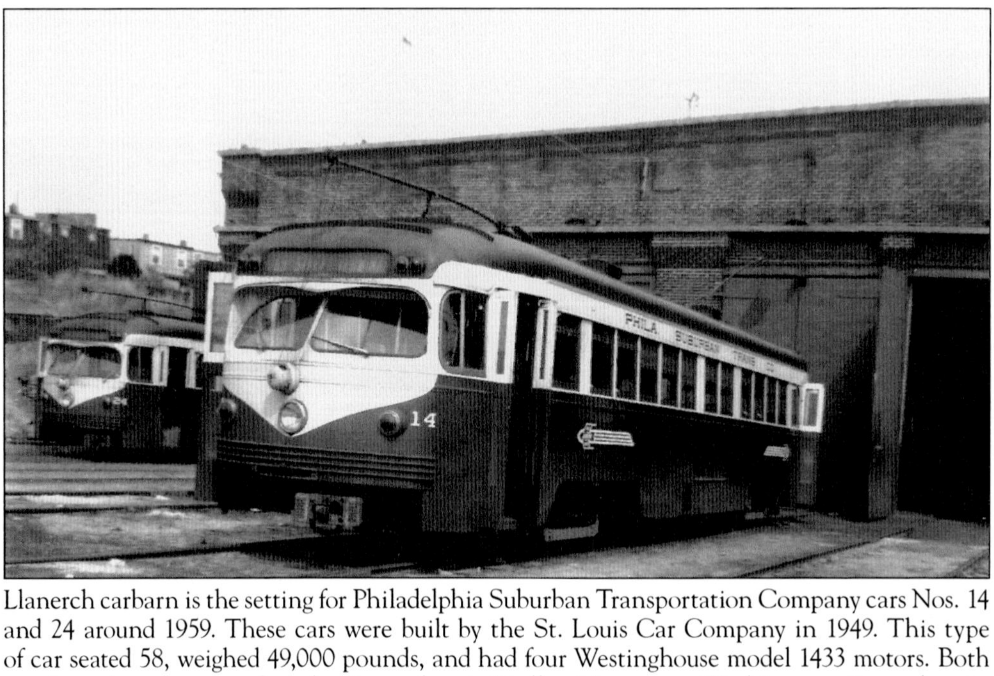

Llanerch carbarn is the setting for Philadelphia Suburban Transportation Company cars Nos. 14 and 24 around 1959. These cars were built by the St. Louis Car Company in 1949. This type of car seated 58, weighed 49,000 pounds, and had four Westinghouse model 1433 motors. Both cars have been preserved at the Pennsylvania Trolley Museum at Washington, Pennsylvania. (Photograph by Craig Knox.)

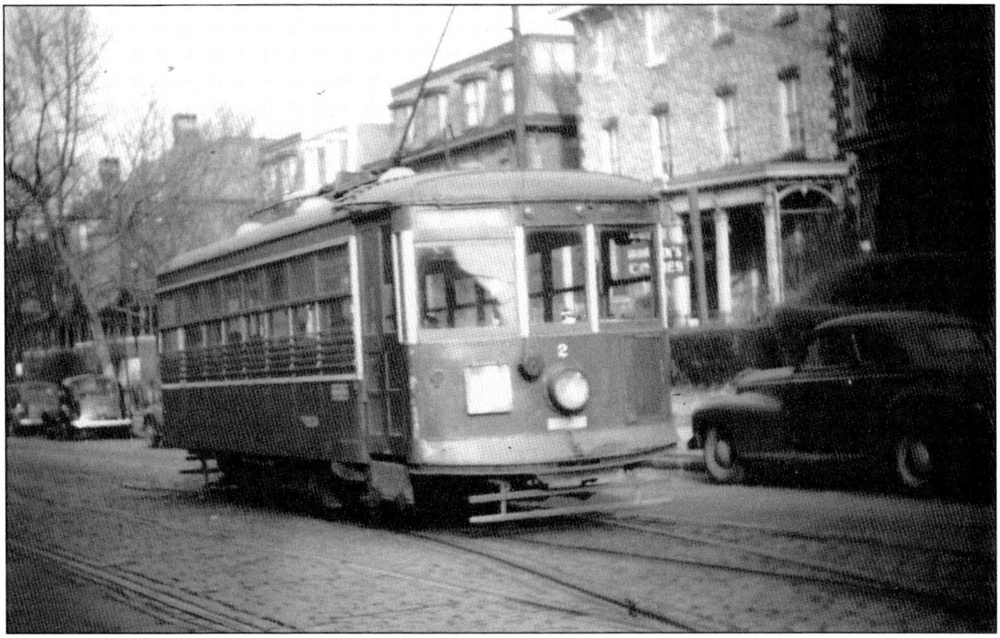

Around 1930, Birney-type trolley car No. 2 is on route 14 at Forty-second Street and Chester Avenue in Philadelphia. This was one of five cars, numbered 1 to 5, purchased in 1922 by the City of Philadelphia for the Bustleton line and transferred to the Philadelphia Rapid Transit Company for lines like route 14 until conversion to bus on June 22, 1947. The five trolleys were scrapped during 1948. (Craig Knox collection.)

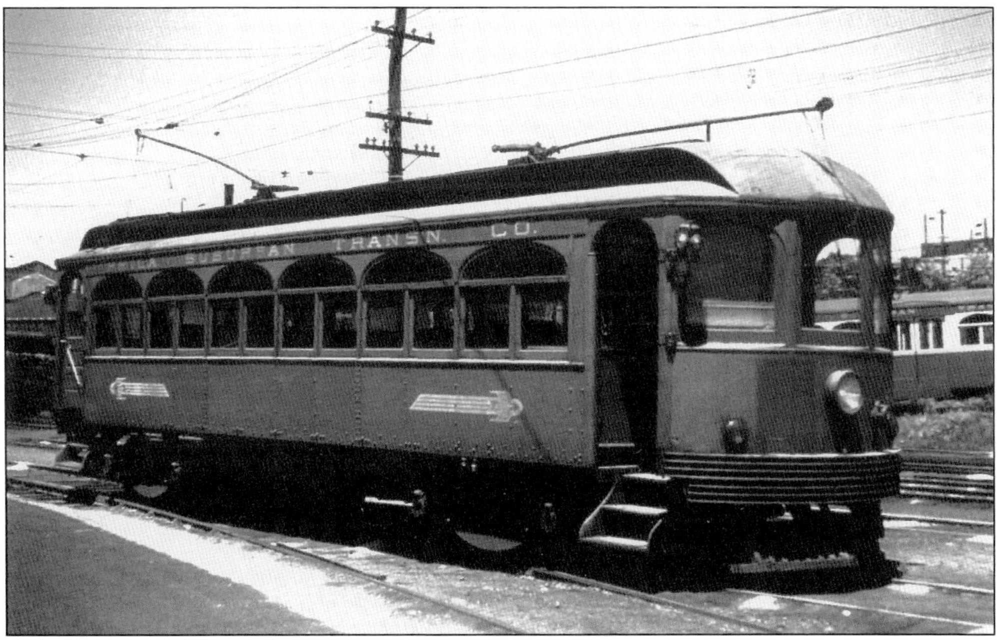

A 40-series trolley car is waiting for the next assignment at Llanerch carbarn around 1945. This was one of five cars, Nos. 40–44, built by the Jewett Car Company in 1914. Seating 48 passengers, the car weighed 50,000 pounds and had four General Electric model 203L motors. (Craig Knox collection.)

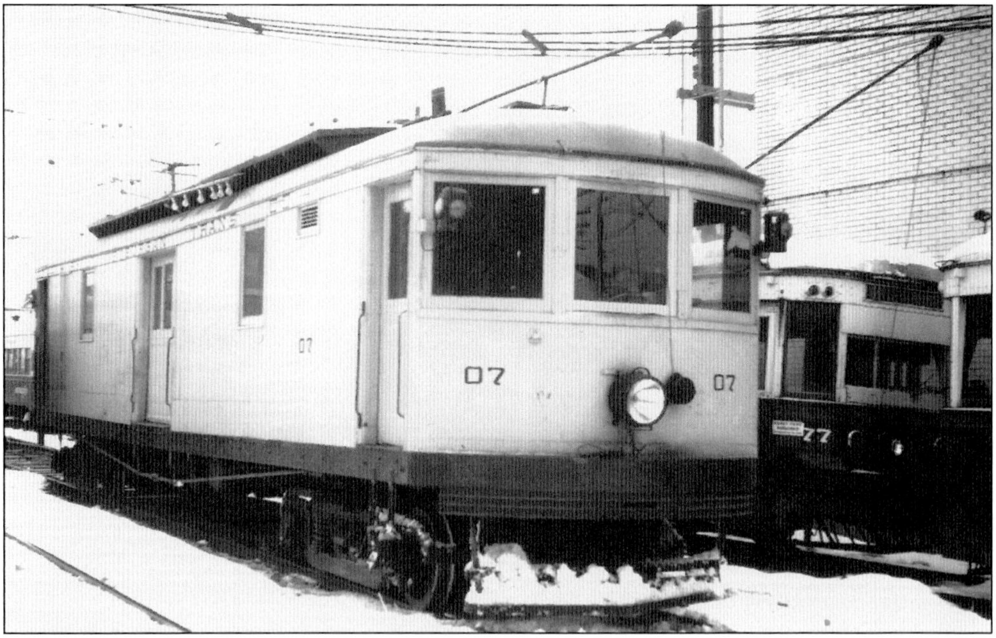

Philadelphia Suburban Transportation Company work car No. 07 is on the West Chester Pike siding, just west of Sixty-ninth Street terminal on December 26, 1969. This was a former freight car built by the Jewett Car Company during 1911 and was later revamped to handle a variety of maintenance assignments. (Photograph by Kenneth C. Springirth.)

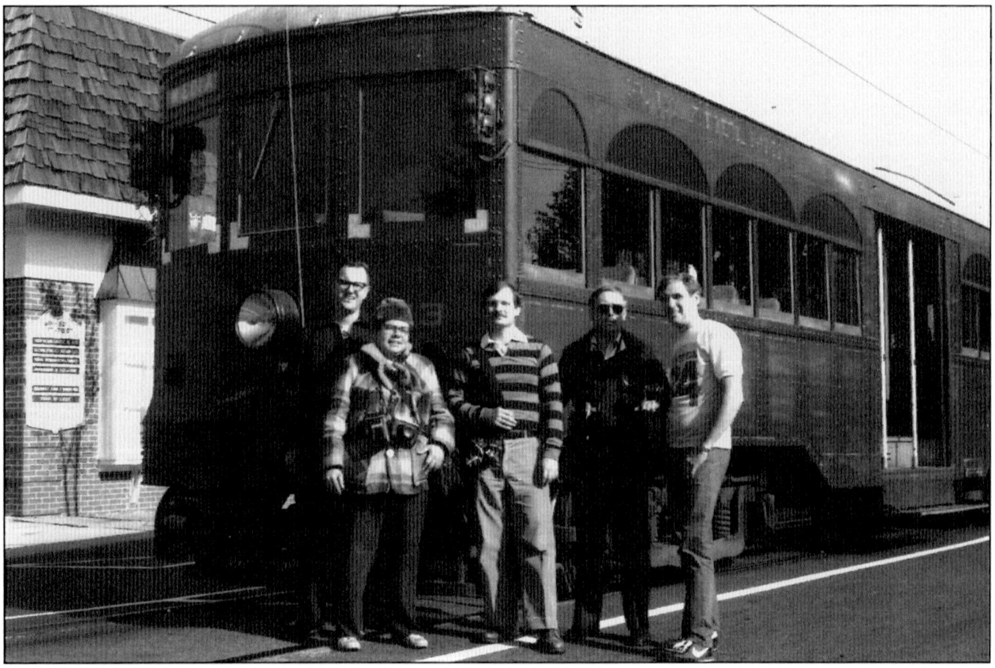
On November 7, 1982, from left to right, Carl Schmidt, Kenneth C. Springirth, John Gbur, Jim Gillin, and Craig Knox chartered center-door car No. 73 and posed on State Street near Orange Street in Media. Built by J. G. Brill Car Company in 1926, this car was restored during June 1972 by the Southeastern Pennsylvania Transportation Authority. (Kenneth C. Springirth collection.)

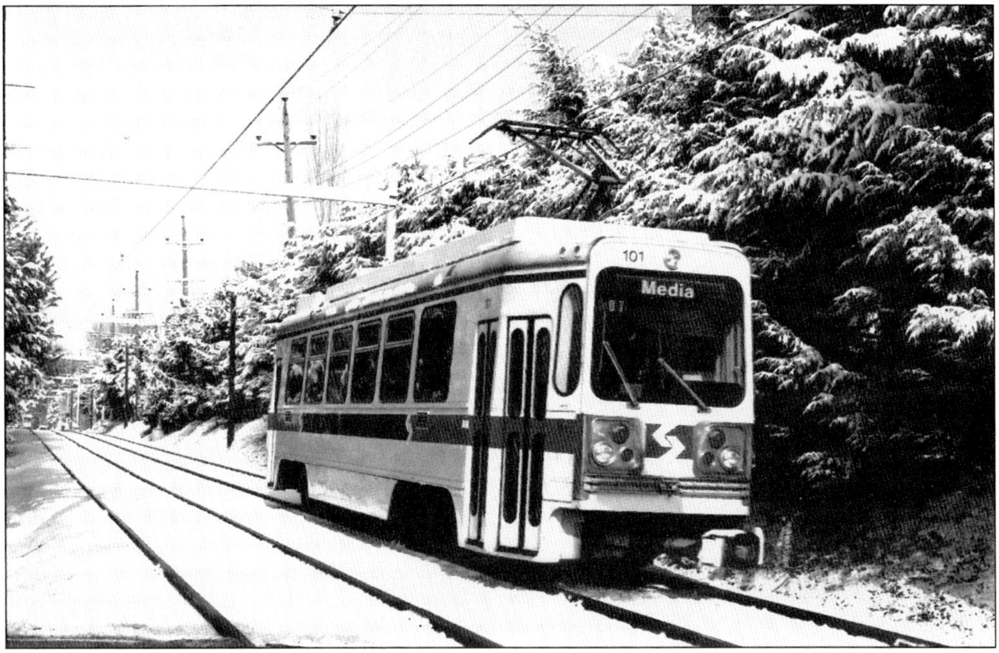

Westbound on route 101 (Media) with the sun shining on the beautiful morning snow, Southeastern Pennsylvania Transportation Authority car No. 101 has just crossed Beatty Road on March 23, 1992. Built by Kawasaki Heavy Industries, this car was placed in revenue service on September 29, 1982. (Photograph by Kenneth C. Springirth.)

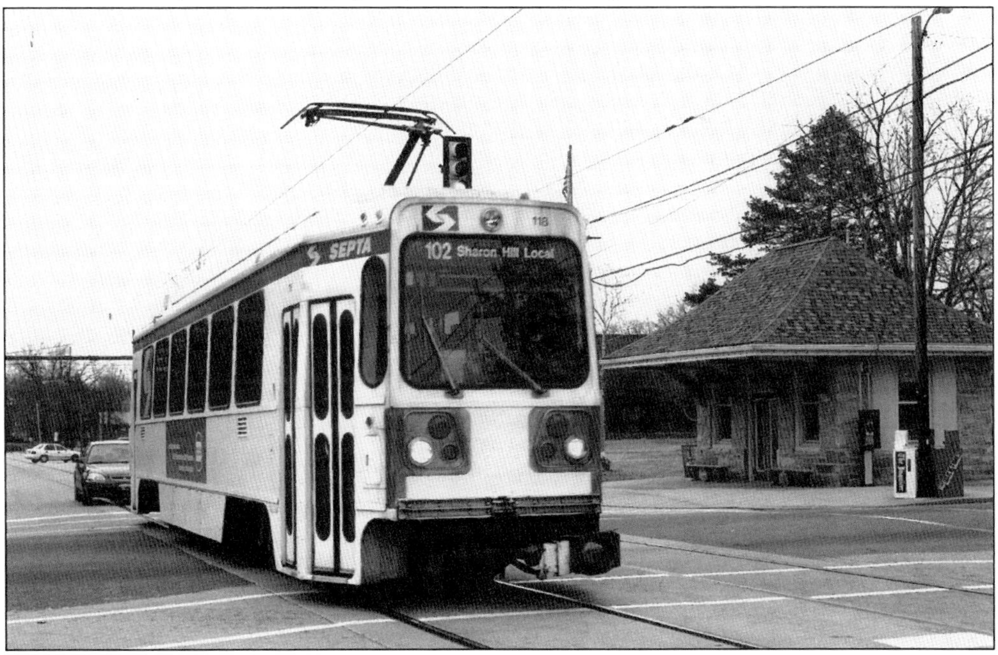

Southeastern Pennsylvania Transportation Authority route 102 (Sharon Hill) car No. 118 built by Kawasaki Heavy Industries is on Woodland Avenue at Providence Road on February 26, 2004. The station on the right of the picture is now the Aldan Borough Historical Museum and Memorial Park. (Photograph by Kenneth C. Springirth.)

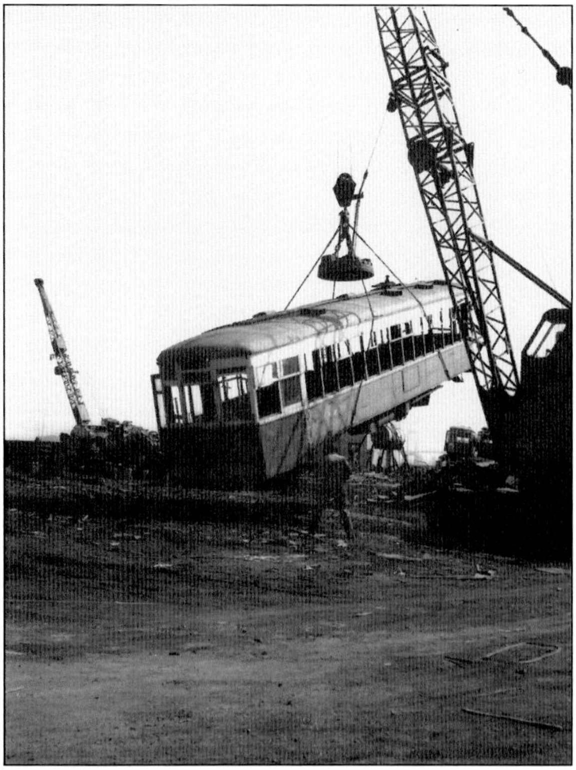

An 8000-series trolley car, minus trucks, is being lifted at the R. and S. Ballis scrap yard in South Philadelphia during 1958. Following the last full day of trolley car service on routes 17 and 32 on December 28, 1957, all 8000-series cars were taken out of regular public transit service and most of them were scrapped. (Photograph by Craig Knox.)

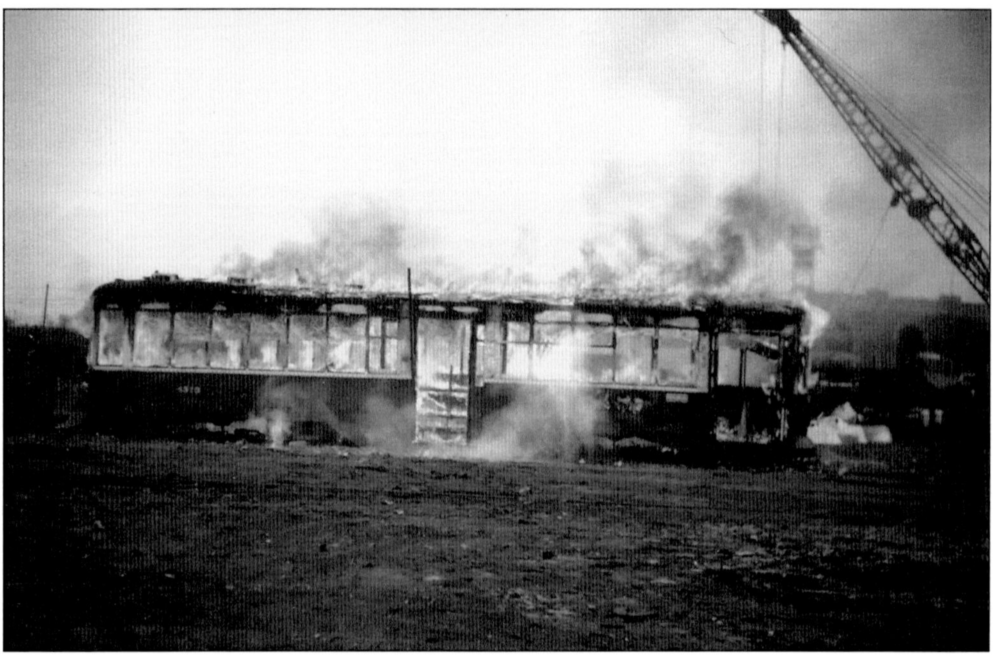

Philadelphia Transportation Company trolley car No. 8373 is being burned at the R. and S. Ballis scrap yard during August 1957. J. G. Brill Car Company built cars numbered 8000 to 8384 in 1923, cars numbered 8385 to 8484 in 1925, and cars numbered 8485 to 8534 in 1926. (Photograph by Craig Knox.)

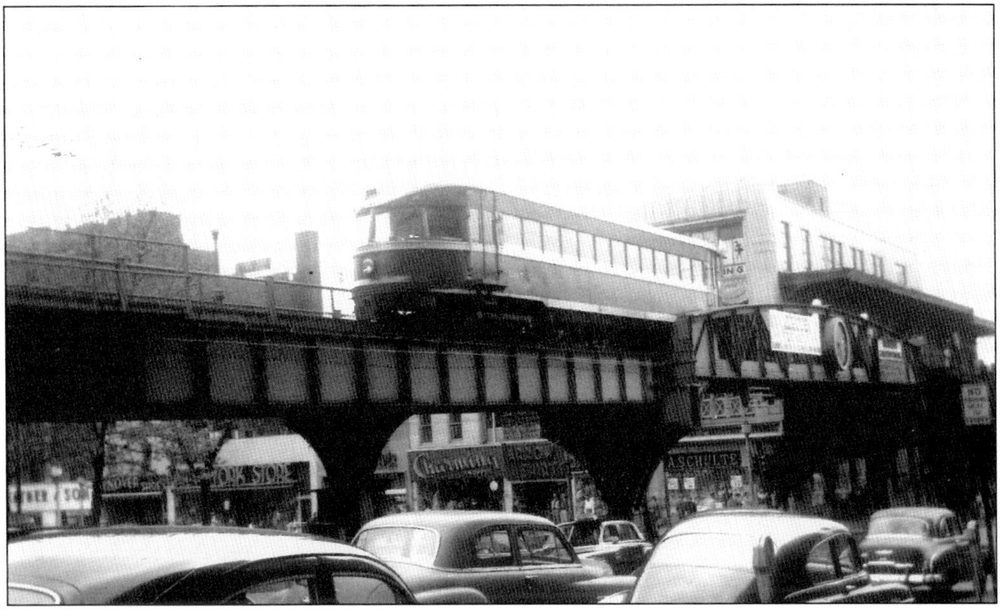

Philadelphia and Western Railway Company car No. 207 is at Norristown on April 24, 1954. J. G. Brill Car Company built the 10 cars of this series 200 to 209 during 1931. These aluminum cars weighed 52,290 pounds and were powered by four General Electric model 706B-2 motors. This car, retired on January 26, 1987, was sold to the Seashore Trolley Museum for parts. (Craig Knox collection.)

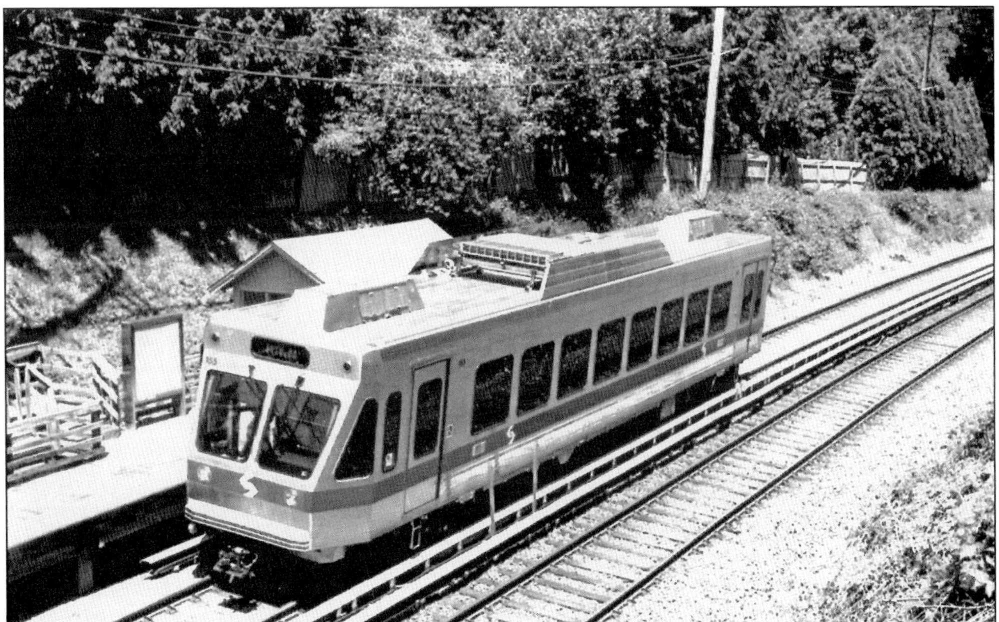

County Line Station on May 20, 2007, is the scene for this Rockhill Trolley Museum excursion on the Southeastern Pennsylvania Transportation Authority route 100 Norristown High Speed Line using type N5 car No. 155. This was one of 26 cars built by Asea Brown Boveri during 1990 to 1994 for the Norristown-to-Sixty-ninth Street terminal line. (Photograph by Kenneth C. Springirth.)

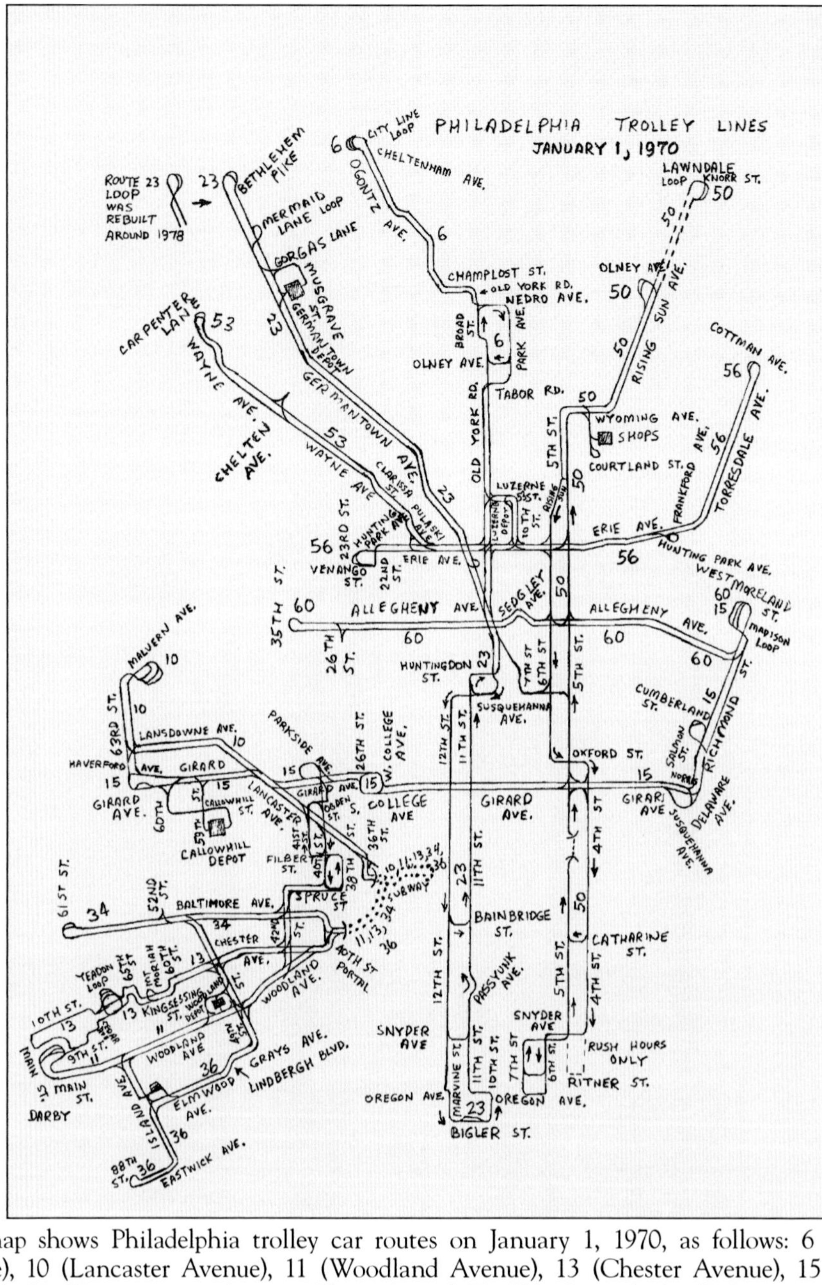

This map shows Philadelphia trolley car routes on January 1, 1970, as follows: 6 (Ogontz Avenue), 10 (Lancaster Avenue), 11 (Woodland Avenue), 13 (Chester Avenue), 15 (Girard Avenue), 23 (Germantown Avenue–Eleventh and Twelfth Streets), 34 (Baltimore Avenue), 36 (Elmwood Avenue), 50 (Rising Sun Avenue–Fourth and Fifth Streets), 53 (Wayne Avenue), 56 (Erie Avenue–Torresdale Avenue), and 60 (Allegheny Avenue). Route 15 was cut back from Sixty-third Street to Twenty-sixth Street and Girard Avenue on October 26, 1969, to permit reconstruction of the Girard Avenue Bridge over the Schuylkill River, and the remainder was temporarily converted to bus operation on June 21, 1970. Route 15 trolley service was restored on January 30, 1972. Route 50 on Rising Sun Avenue from Olney Avenue to Knorr Street was out of service because of reconstruction of Rising Sun Avenue Bridge over Tacony Creek from October 7, 1968, until restoration of service on October 16, 1972.

Two

Chestnut Hill to South Philadelphia Trolleys

Trolley route 23, prior to 1887, began operation as the Germantown line from Germantown Depot to Eighth and Dauphin Streets. By 1890, it was consolidated with the Fourth and Fifth Streets line and renamed the Pelham line. On August 31, 1913, the Pelham, Mermaid, and Chestnut Hill lines were combined into the Germantown Tenth and Eleventh Streets line and operated from City Line and from Erdenheim Road via Germantown Avenue southbound on Tenth Street to Ritner Street and northbound via Eleventh Street and Germantown Avenue to City Line and Erdenheim Road. On October 31, 1920, Bethlehem Pike loop became the northern terminus of route 23. Service north of Bethlehem Pike loop was by route 23A, which operated via Germantown Avenue, Hillcrest Avenue, and Bethlehem Pike to Erdenheim Road and by route 23B, which operated via Germantown Avenue to City Line. Bus route X replaced route 23B on June 7, 1928, and 23A on July 16, 1928. Route 23 was extended southward, reaching Oregon Avenue on September 9, 1923, and Pattison Avenue on June 1, 1926. On December 29, 1957, routes 20 and 23 were combined into route 23 and designated Germantown Avenue–Eleventh and Twelfth Streets line. Starting in South Philadelphia, route 23 went through a neighborhood of narrow streets and row homes whose residents were proud working-class Americans. These were the people who have built America. The line passed through crowded Center City and north of Market Street on Twelfth Street traversed challenging neighborhoods. At Huntingdon Street, the route turned east for one block and swung north onto Germantown Avenue. A transfer could be made with the Broad Street Subway at Broad Street. Heading northwest on Germantown Avenue, the line was on a continuous climb and entered the picturesque affluent Chestnut Hill section of Philadelphia. Depending on the time of day, a one-way trip could take from 60 to 90 minutes. From skid row to classy neighborhoods with stops at everything in between, this 12-mile trolley line was the longest and busiest trolley line in Philadelphia. Following conversion to bus operation on February 21, 1992, limited trolley car service operated from Chestnut Hill to the Germantown carbarn until June 1996.

CHANGES TO BE MADE

Four major changes will be made. They are:

1. Combination of Route 23 (10th and 11th sts.—Germantown ave. line) and Route 20 (12th and 13th sts.—Old York Road line) into one streamlined streetcar route on 11th and 12th sts. and Germantown av.
2. Combination of Route 2 (15th and 16th sts. line) with Route 21 (North 17th and 18th sts. line) and Route 32 (South 17th and 18th sts. line) into one bus route on 16th and 17th sts.
3. Rerouting of Route 33 buses (Arch st.—North 19th and 20th sts. line) to run on Market st. instead of Arch st. between 20th st. and Front st.
4. Conversion of Route 17 (Market st.—South 19th and 20th sts. line) from old streetcars to modern buses, and extension south to Moyamensing av.

In addition, free transfer privileges will be made available between Route C buses on Broad st. and intersecting lines between Olney and Snyder avs. (Transfer privileges already exist to and from Route C north of Olney av. and south of Snyder av.)

NEW ROUTE 23

New Route 23, resulting from the combination of Routes 23 and 20, will follow the present Route 23 between Chestnut Hill and Susquehanna av., then run south on 12th st. and north on 11th st. between Susquehanna av. and Bigler st. in South Philadelphia. More cars will be operated on the combined route than on either of the present routes, giving riders more frequent service.

A shuttle bus service, Route 23-s, will run between 10th & Bigler sts. and the Philadelphia Naval Base during hours of Naval Base shift changes.

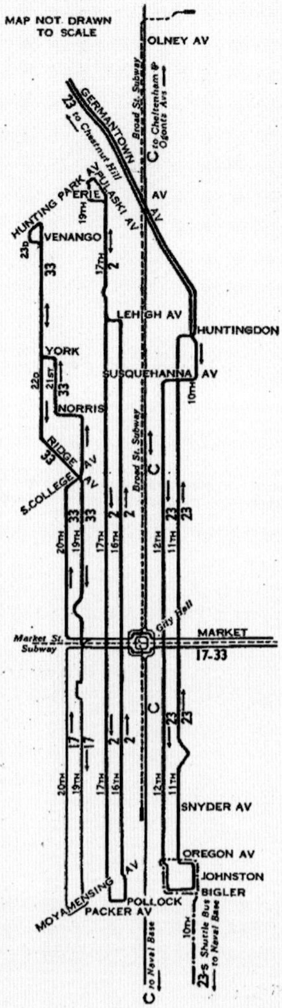

Special school bus service, principally serving Little Flower High School and Cooke Jr. High School, will be operated on Old York Rd. and Germantown av. between the Broad & Olney subway station and Lehigh av. on school days during hours when students are riding to and from schools.

NEW ROUTE 2

New Route 2, resulting from the combination of Routes 2, 21 and 32, will run between Pollock st. in South Philadelphia and Hunting Park & Pulaski avs. in Nicetown. Route 2 will operate south on 16th st. and north on 17th st. between Pollock st. and Lehigh av., and on 17th st. and the present Route 21 routing between Lehigh av. and Hunting Park av.

This concentration of transit service on the middle two of the four streets now used will give Route 2 riders more frequent bus service.

Because no PTC lines will run on 13th and 15th sts., additional riders may be expected to use the Broad St. Subway and Route C buses on Broad st. Additional buses will run on Route C, giving more frequent service on Broad st., and free transfer privileges to and from Route C buses will be restored between Olney and Snyder avs.

MODERN BUSES FOR ROUTE 17

Modern buses will replace old streetcars now operated on Route 17. Buses will follow the present routing, with an extension south to Moyamensing av.

ROUTE 33 TO MARKET ST.

Route 33 will operate in both directions on Market st. instead of Arch st. This change will make it possible to ride to points along Market st. between 19th st. and Front st., convenient to most center-city stores and offices.

On Sunday, December 29, 1957, the Philadelphia Transportation Company combined trolley routes 20 and 23 into one trolley route, route 23, plus combined trolley route 32 with routes 2 and 21 into one bus route, route 2, on Sixteenth and Seventeenth Streets. This removed the last 8000-series Peter Witt trolley cars (which were last used on trolley routes 17 and 32) from regular service in Philadelphia. Presidents' Conference Committee trolley cars now handled all regular trolley service. The announcement noted that there would be "more frequent transit service on 11th, 12th, Broad, 16th, and 17th Streets." It also resulted in "freeing of 10th, 13th, 15th, and 18th Streets for automobile and truck traffic." (Craig Knox collection.)

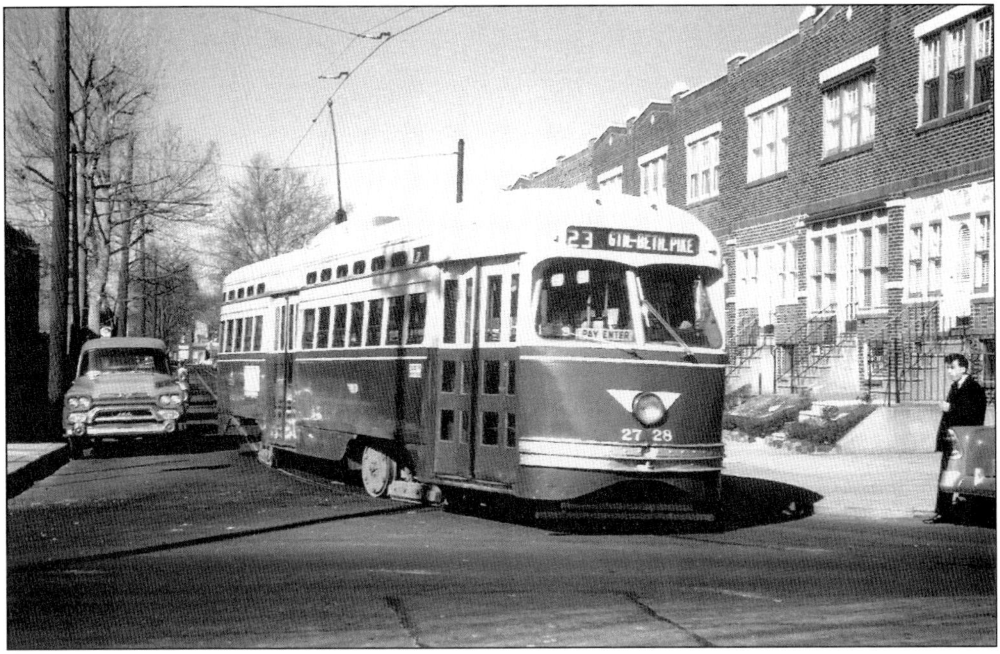

Philadelphia Transportation Company route 23 Presidents' Conference Committee car No. 2728 is turning from Marvine Street to Bigler Street on March 4, 1962. The St. Louis Car Company built this car during 1947. It was painted silver by the Southeastern Pennsylvania Transportation Authority in 1995 and in 2005 was sold to the Baltimore Streetcar Museum. (Photograph by Kenneth C. Springirth.)

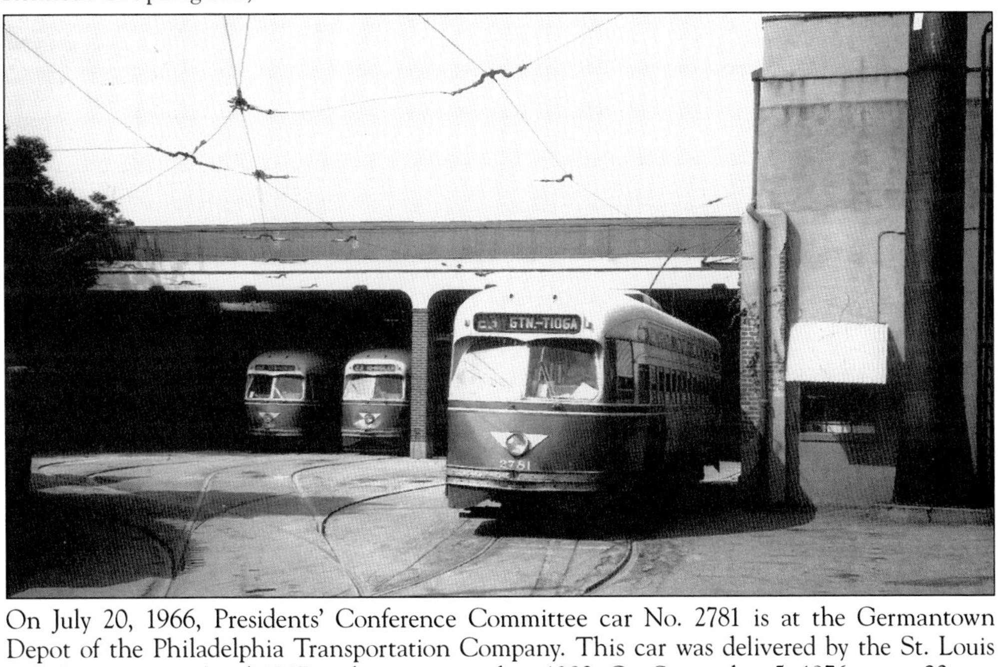

On July 20, 1966, Presidents' Conference Committee car No. 2781 is at the Germantown Depot of the Philadelphia Transportation Company. This car was delivered by the St. Louis Car Company in April 1947 and was scrapped in 1983. On September 5, 1976, route 23 was transferred to Luzerne Depot, making Germantown Depot an all-bus garage. (Photograph by Kenneth C. Springirth.)

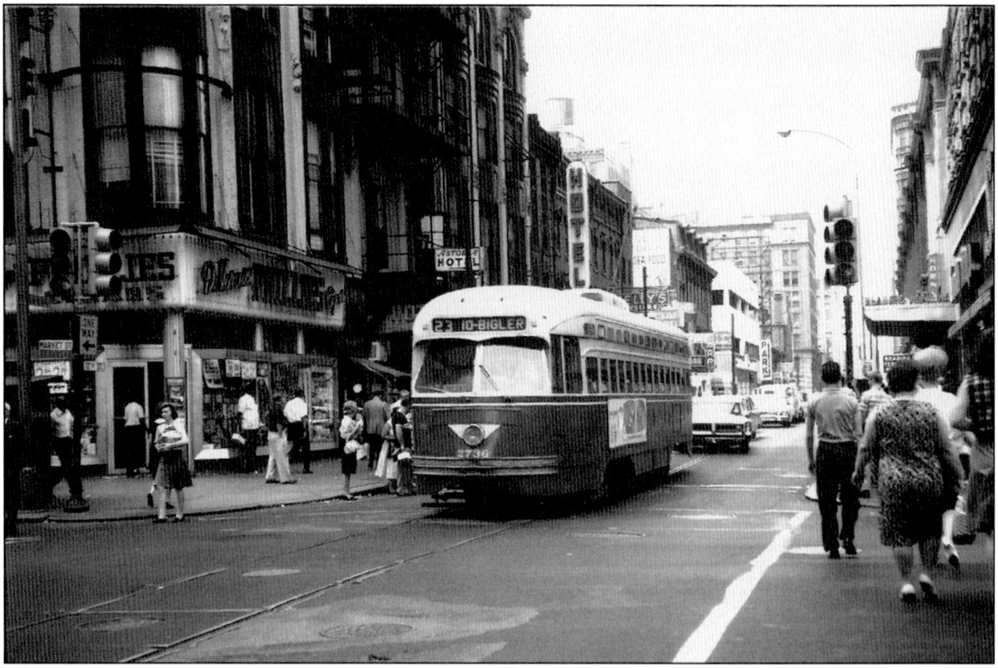

Route 23 Presidents' Conference Committee car No. 2736 is loading passengers on Twelfth Street at Market Street in busy downtown Philadelphia on July 20, 1966. The St. Louis Car Company delivered this car in March 1947 to the Philadelphia Transportation Company. It was scrapped during 1979. (Photograph by Kenneth C. Springirth.)

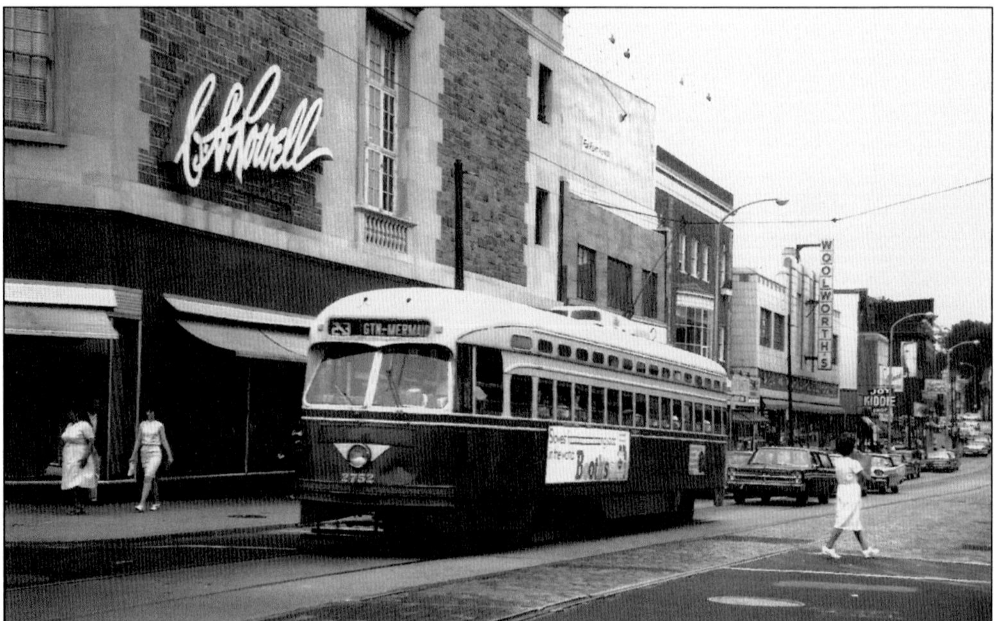

A northbound Presidents' Conference Committee route 23 Philadelphia Transportation Company car No. 2752 is on Germantown Avenue at Chelten Avenue on July 20, 1966. This car, built by the St. Louis Car Company in 1947, was destroyed in the Woodland Depot fire of October 23, 1975. (Photograph by Kenneth C. Springirth.)

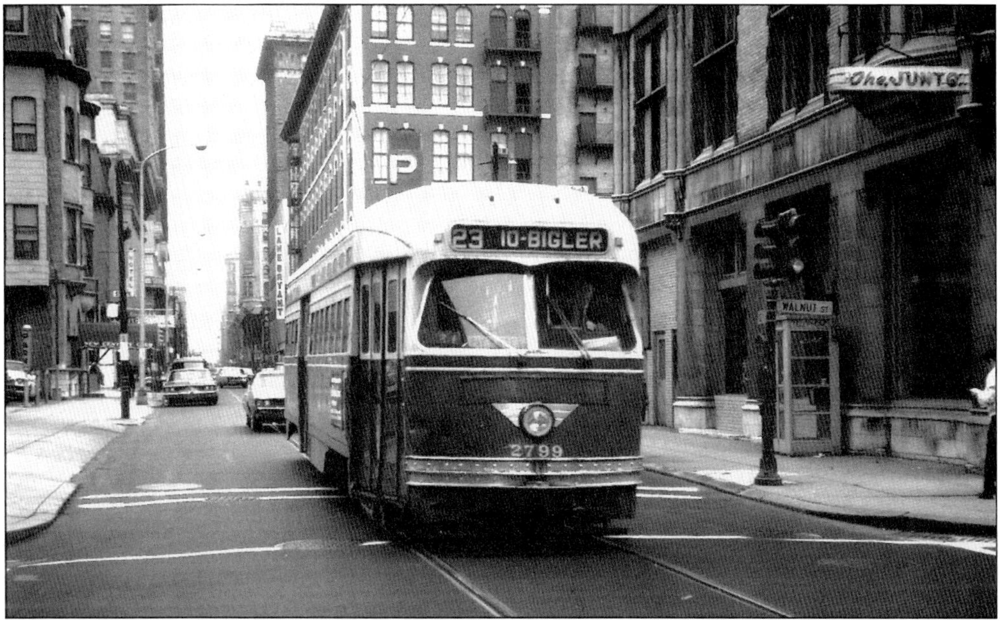

On April 27, 1968, Philadelphia Transportation Company route 23 Presidents' Conference Committee car No. 2799 is southbound on Twelfth Street at Walnut Street. Built by the St. Louis Car Company during 1947, the car was overhauled by the Southeastern Pennsylvania Transportation Authority in August 1985, painted Philadelphia Suburban Transportation Company colors in 1995, and in 2005 was sold to the Baltimore Streetcar Museum. (Photograph by Kenneth C. Springirth.)

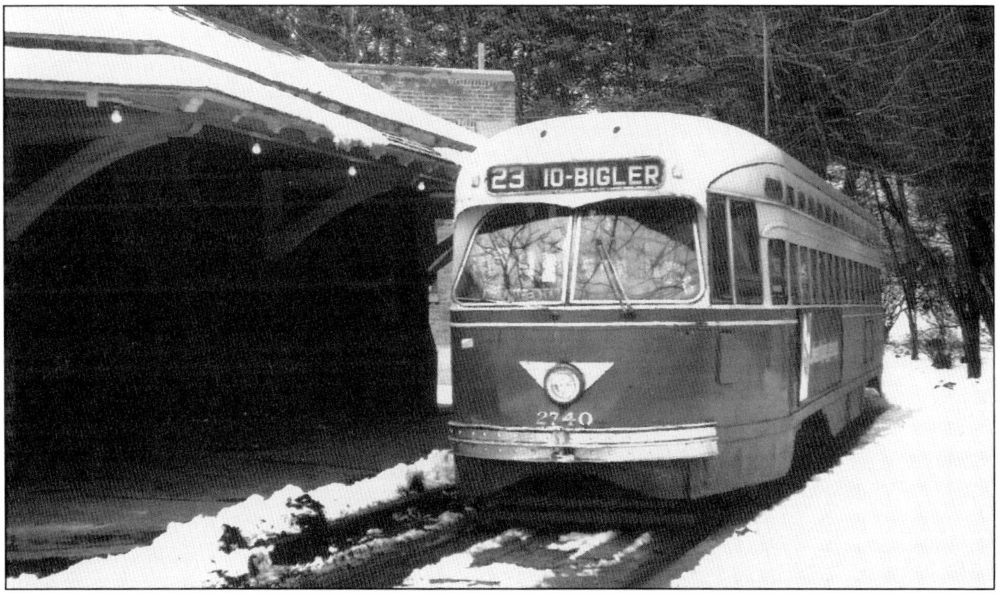

Snow-covered Mermaid Lane loop shows Presidents' Conference Committee car No. 2740 awaiting departure time for a southbound route 23 trip on February 22, 1969. Built by the St. Louis Car Company in 1947, this car was overhauled by the Southeastern Pennsylvania Transportation Authority in October 1983 and was sold to the Museum of Transportation in St. Louis during 1994. (Photograph by Kenneth C. Springirth.)

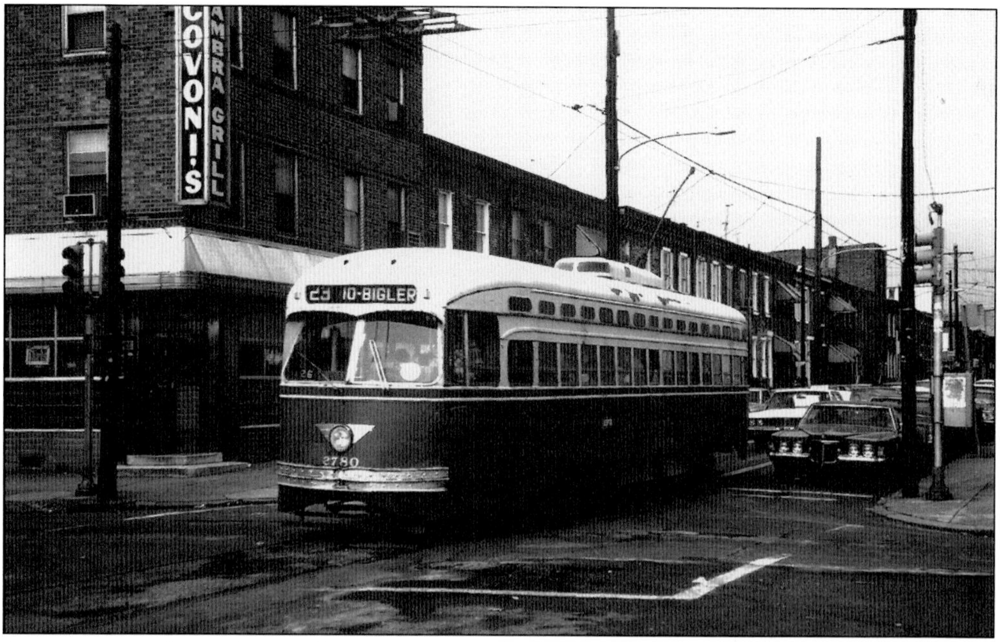

Southeastern Pennsylvania Transportation Authority route 23 Presidents' Conference Committee car No. 2780 is southbound on Twelfth Street at Morris Street, a transfer point for the route 29 trackless trolley, on December 26, 1970. Built by the St. Louis Car Company in 1947, this car was overhauled in August 1981 and was later sold to the Brookville Equipment Company. (Photograph by Kenneth C. Springirth.)

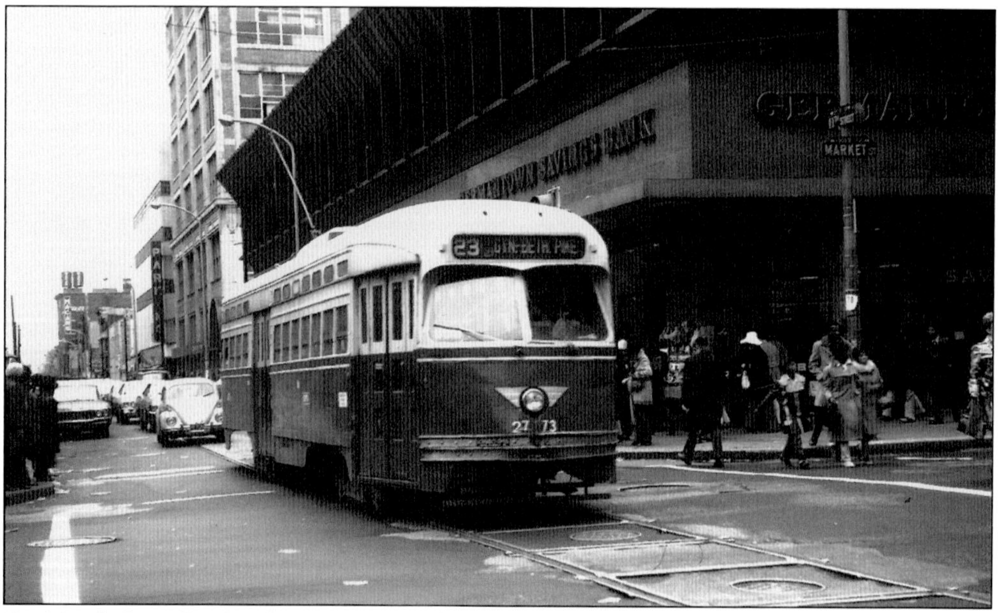

On March 31, 1972, Southeastern Pennsylvania Transportation Authority route 23 Presidents' Conference Committee car No. 2773 is in Center City Philadelphia on Eleventh Street crossing Market Street on March 31, 1972. The St. Louis Car Company delivered this car to the Philadelphia Transportation Company during April 1947. The car was scrapped during 1985. (Photograph by Kenneth C. Springirth.)

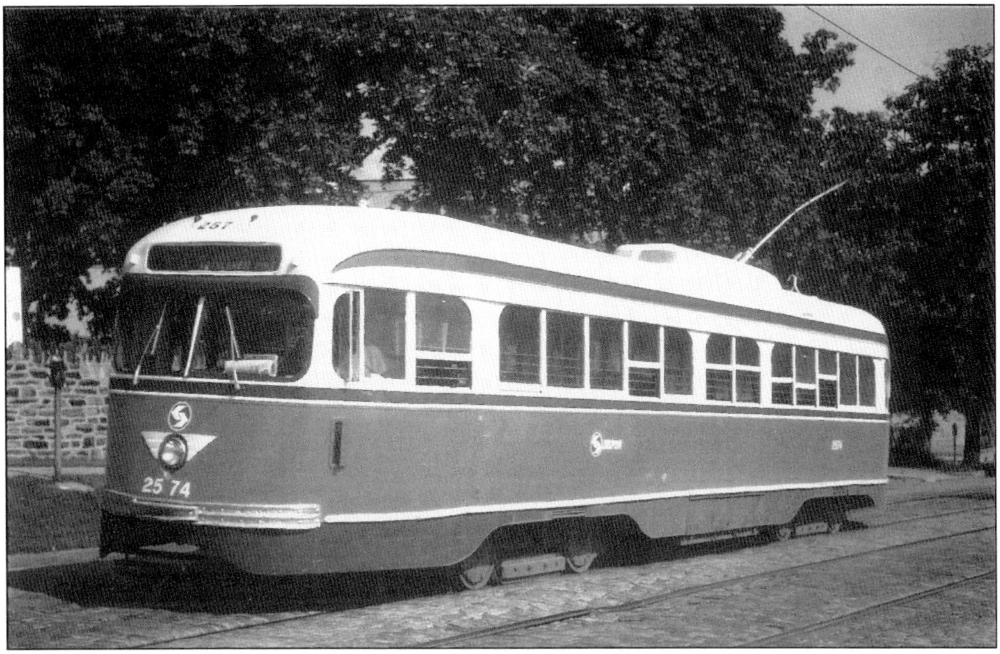

Germantown Avenue at Allen Lane in the Mount Airy section of Philadelphia finds Southeastern Pennsylvania Transportation Authority route 23 Presidents' Conference Committee car No. 2574 passing by on July 19, 1978. The St. Louis Car Company delivered this car to the Philadelphia Transportation Company during January 1941. The car was scrapped during 1982. (Photograph by Kenneth C. Springirth.)

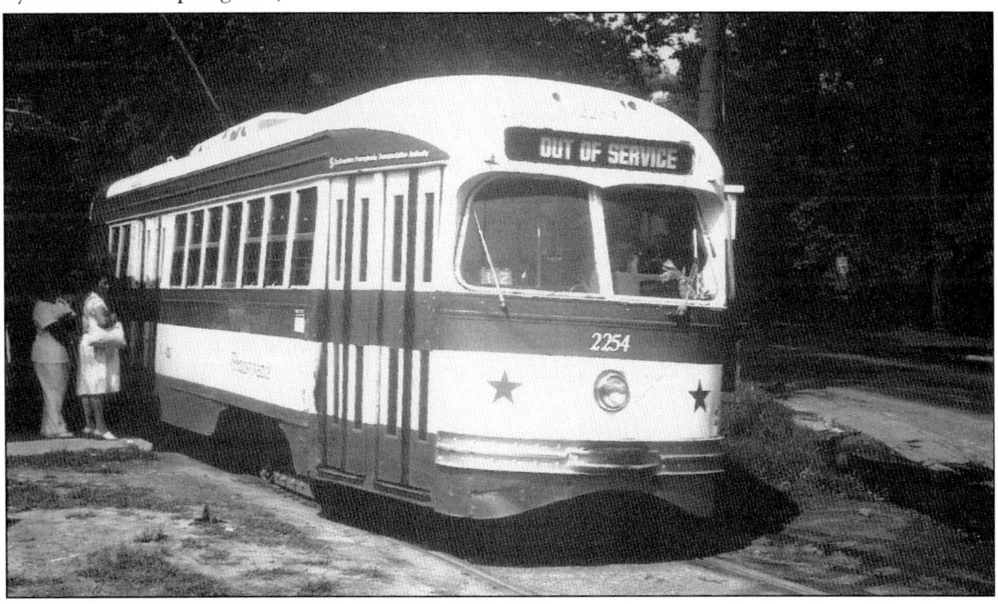

On July 19, 1978, picturesque route 23 Mermaid Lane loop is the setting for Presidents' Conference Committee car No. 2254 in a bicentennial paint scheme and lettered "Pennsylvania." Built by the St. Louis Car Company as No. 725 for the Kansas City Public Service Company in 1946, it was purchased by the Philadelphia Transportation Company during 1955. The car was scrapped in December 1982. (Photograph by Kenneth C. Springirth.)

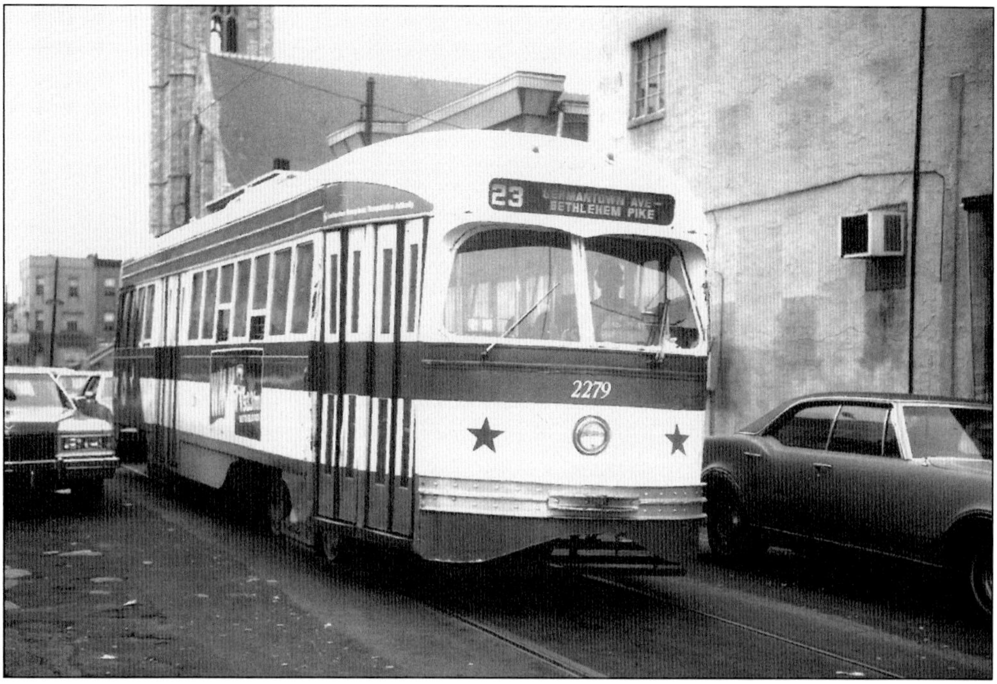

Southeastern Pennsylvania Transportation Authority route 23 Presidents' Conference Committee car No. 2279 is on Eleventh Street at Snyder Avenue on July 24, 1978. Formerly Kansas City Public Service Company car No. 731 built by the St. Louis Car Company in 1946, it was acquired by the Philadelphia Transportation Company in June 1955 and sold to Vintage Electric Streetcar Company of Windber during 1985. (Photograph by Kenneth C. Springirth.)

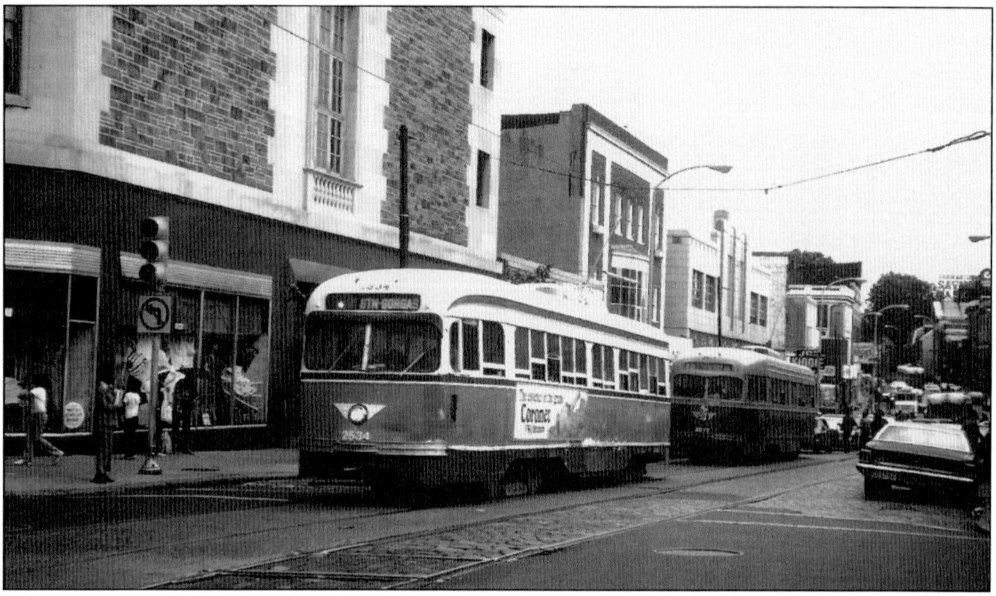

Germantown Avenue at Chelten Avenue on June 20, 1980, is the scene for Southeastern Pennsylvania Transportation Authority route 23 Presidents' Conference Committee cars Nos. 2534 and No. 2617. These cars built by the St. Louis Car Company in 1941 and 1942, respectively, were scrapped during 1982. (Photograph by Kenneth C. Springirth.)

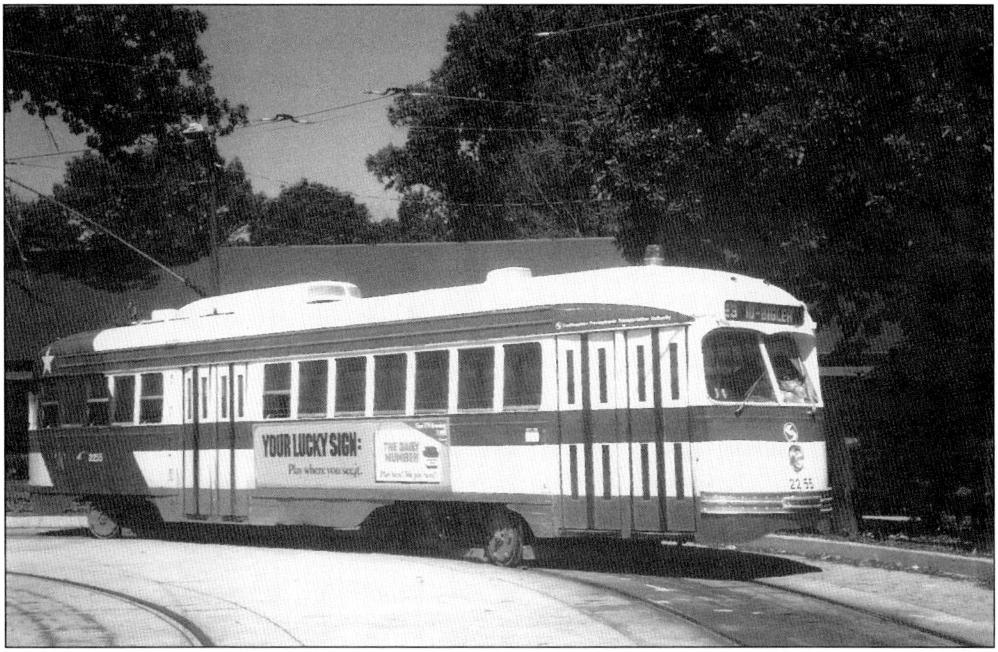

Route 23 car No. 2255 is at Germantown Avenue and Bethlehem Pike loop on June 21, 1980. This originally was car No. 753 and was one of 40 Presidents' Conference Committee cars purchased from the Kansas City Public Service Company in 1955. Conversion to bus operation created a surplus of trolley cars in Kansas City. Trolley car service ended in Kansas City during 1957. (Photograph by Kenneth C. Springirth.)

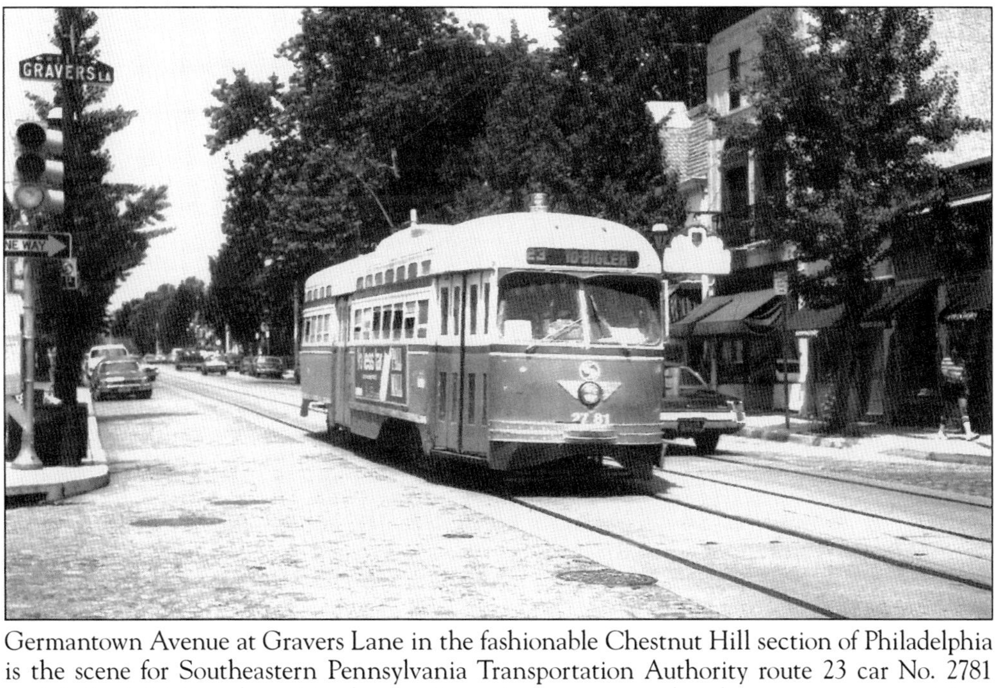

Germantown Avenue at Gravers Lane in the fashionable Chestnut Hill section of Philadelphia is the scene for Southeastern Pennsylvania Transportation Authority route 23 car No. 2781 on July 27, 1980. Presidents' Conference Committee cars were placed in service on route 23 on May 11, 1947. (Photograph by Kenneth C. Springirth.)

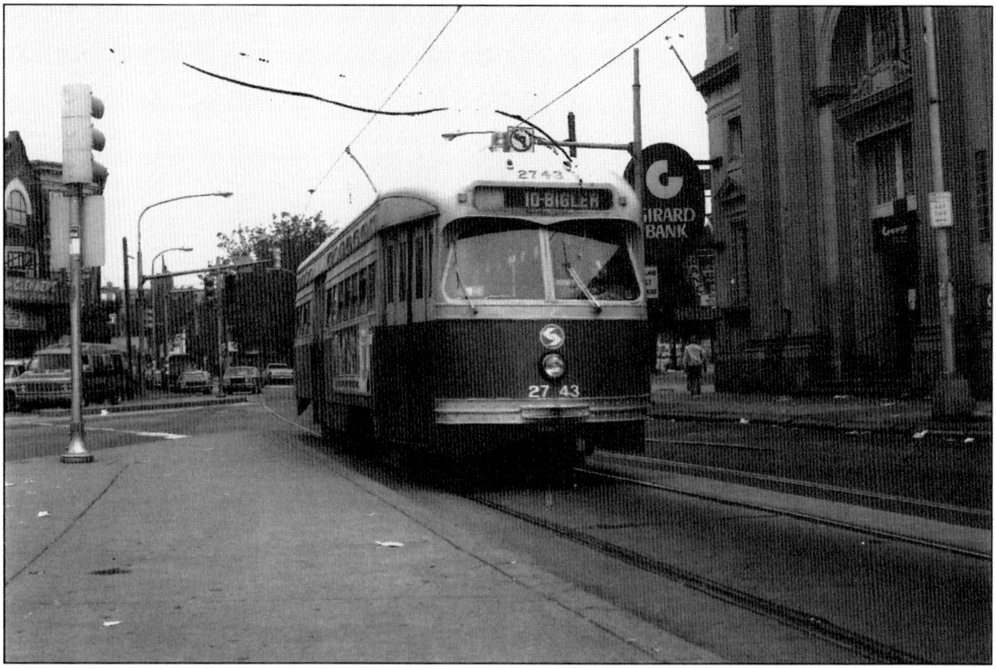

Route 23 trolley car No. 2743 is on Germantown Avenue ready to cross Erie Avenue on September 6, 1981. The St. Louis Car Company delivered this Presidents' Conference Committee car to the Philadelphia Transportation Company during March 1947. This car has been preserved in operating condition at the Rockhill Trolley Museum. (Photograph by Kenneth C. Springirth.)

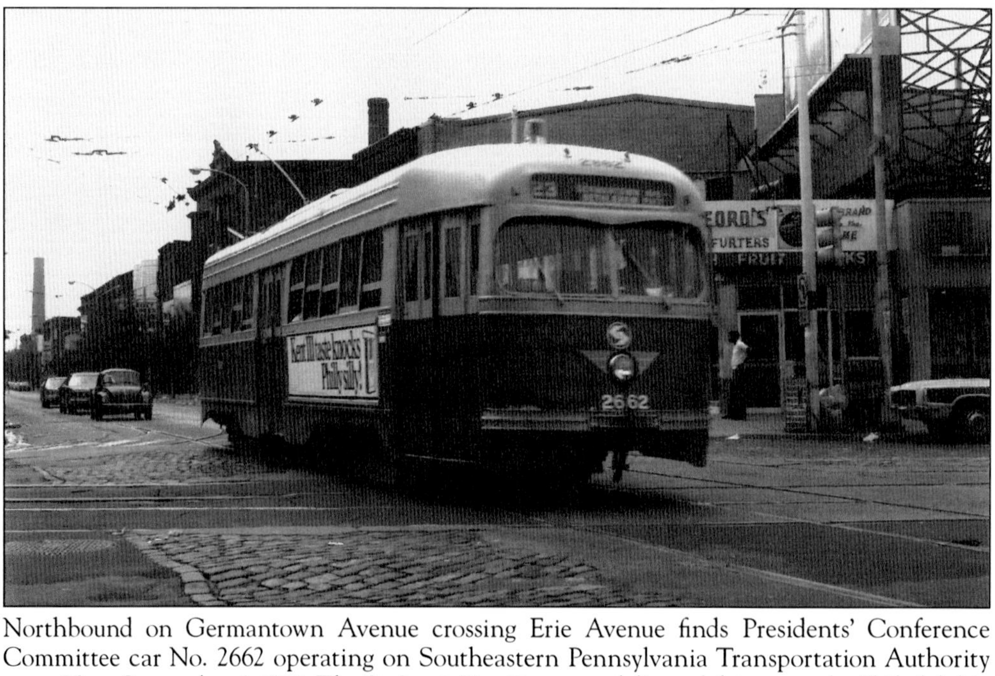

Northbound on Germantown Avenue crossing Erie Avenue finds Presidents' Conference Committee car No. 2662 operating on Southeastern Pennsylvania Transportation Authority route 23 on September 6, 1981. The St. Louis Car Company delivered this car to the Philadelphia Transportation Company during July 1942. It was scrapped during 1983. (Photograph by Kenneth C. Springirth.)

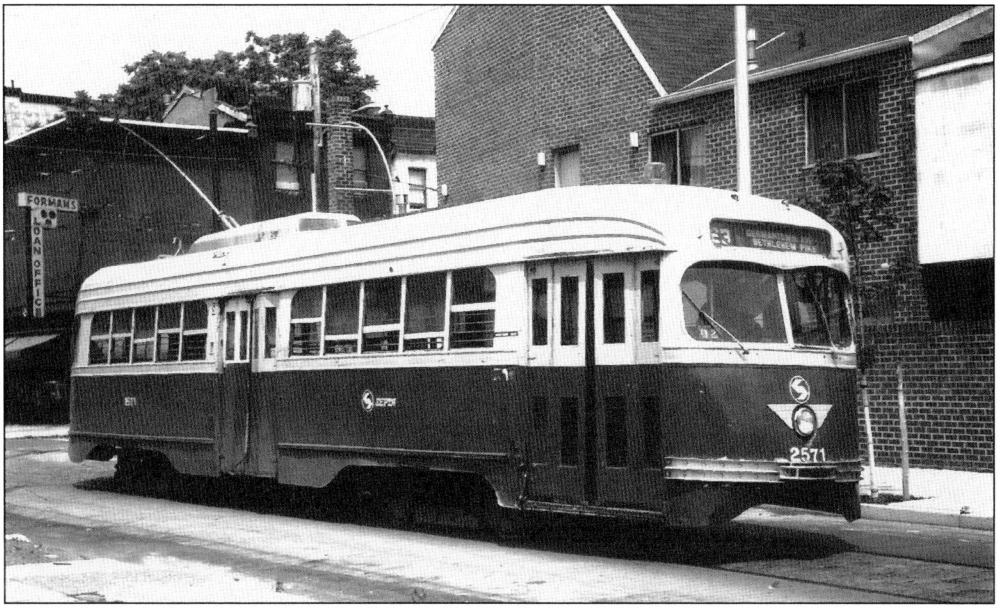

Southeastern Pennsylvania Transportation Authority route 23 car No. 2571 has just turned from Twelfth Street to Bainbridge Street on May 29, 1982. This trackage, located south of Center City Philadelphia, permitted a late-running car to head north and get back on schedule. The St. Louis Car Company built this car in 1941, and it was scrapped during 1983. (Photograph by Kenneth C. Springirth.)

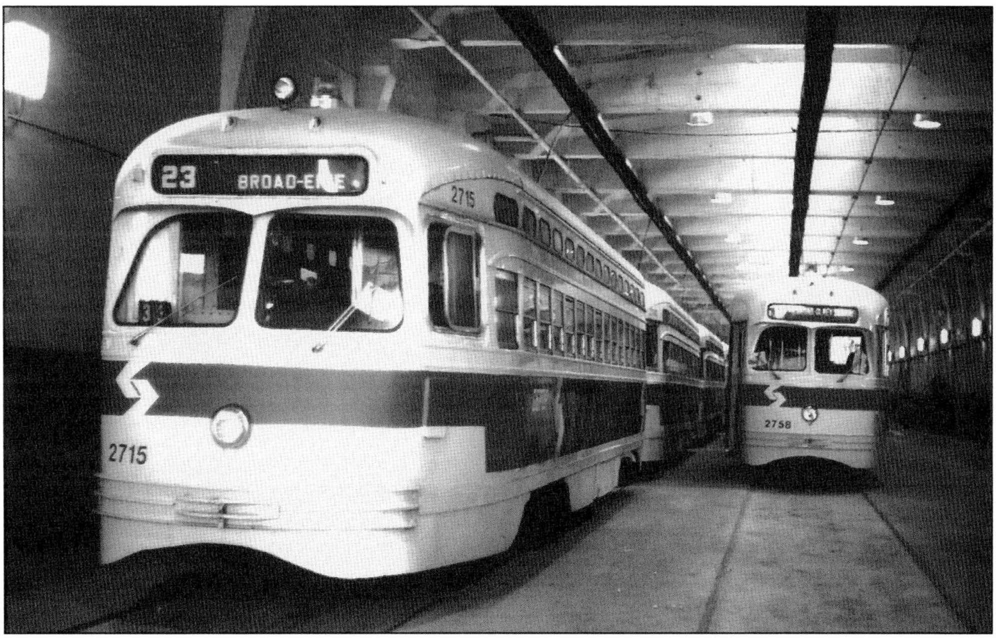

A lineup of trolleys is shown inside Luzerne Depot on January 11, 1986. Cars Nos. 2715 and 2758 were built by the St. Louis Car Company in 1947. Car No. 2715 is now in San Francisco renumbered 1060. Car 2758 was rebuilt by the Brookville Equipment Company, renumbered 2331, and delivered to the Southeastern Pennsylvania Transportation Authority on July 30, 2004. (Photograph by Kenneth C. Springirth.)

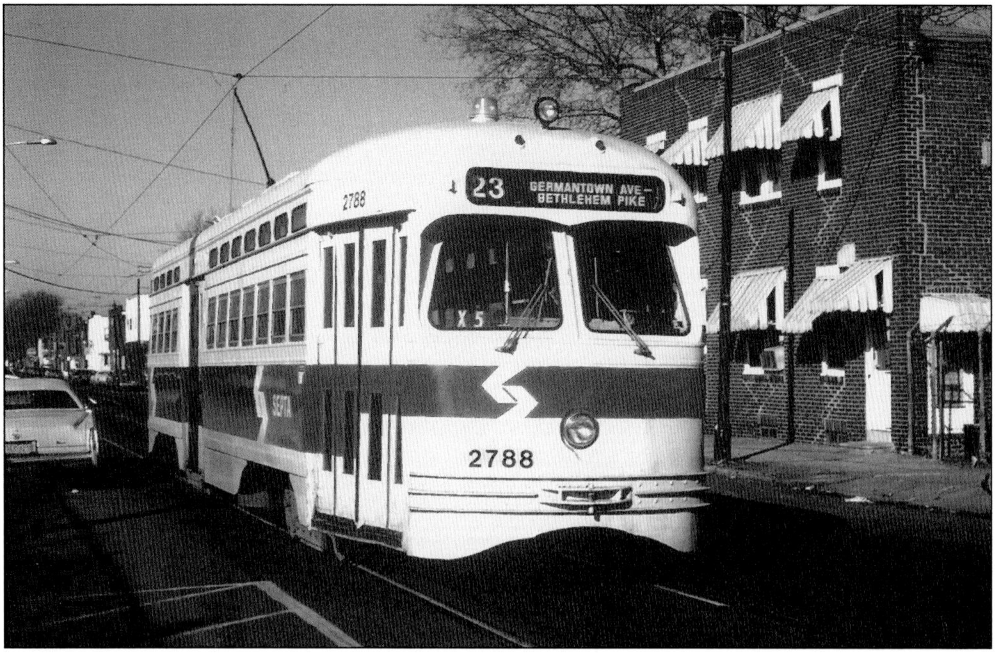

In February 1987, route 23 Presidents' Conference Committee car No. 2788 is on Bigler Street at Tenth Street. The Philadelphia Transportation Company received this car from the St. Louis Car Company in April 1947. The Southeastern Pennsylvania Transportation Authority overhauled it in May 1984. It was sold to the Regional Transit Authority of New Orleans in 1994. (Photograph by Kenneth C. Springirth.)

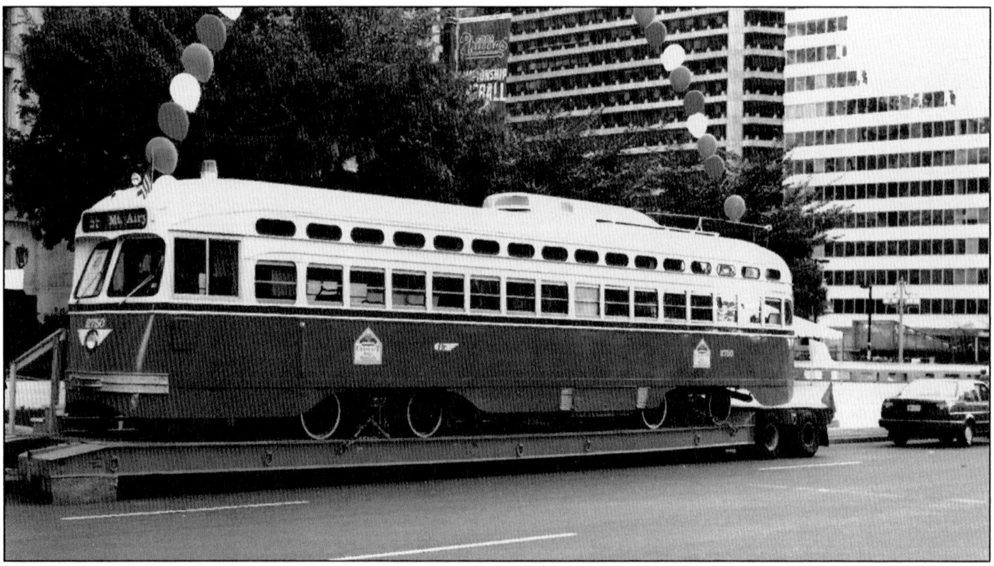

Presidents' Conference Committee car No. 2750, built by the St. Louis Car Company in 1947, is on display at Philadelphia City Hall on October 2 and 3, 1993, for the Southeastern Pennsylvania Transportation Authority's Trolley Fest 93. The St. Louis Car Company built this car for the Philadelphia Transportation Company during 1947. This car was rebuilt by the Brookville Equipment Company and renumbered as 2320 during 2003. (Photograph by Kenneth C. Springirth.)

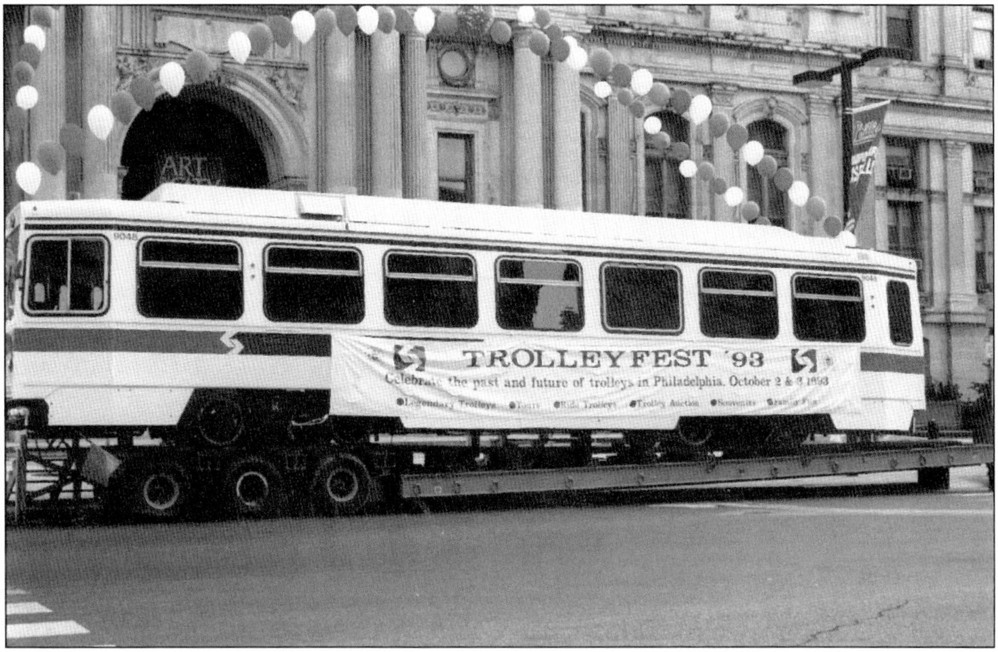

Trolley car No. 9048, built by Kawasaki Heavy Industries in 1981, is on display at Philadelphia City Hall for the October 2 and 3, 1993, Trolley Fest. The Southeastern Pennsylvania Transportation Authority conducted the event, which featured special trolley car trips, displays, and entertainment at the Fortieth Street subway portal. (Photograph by Kenneth C. Springirth.)

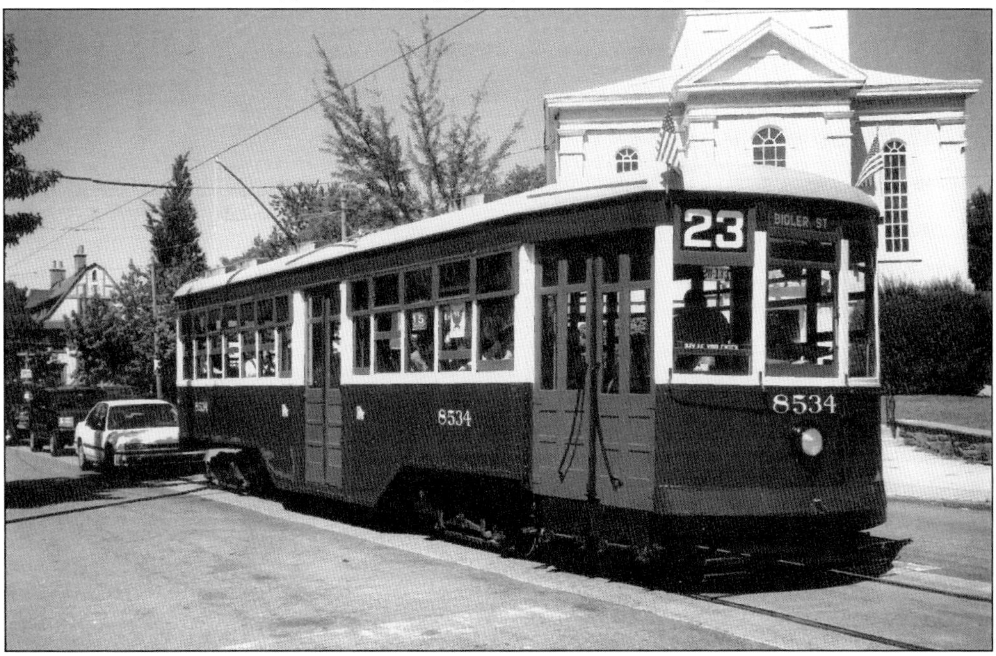

Bethlehem Pike at Germantown Avenue provides the setting for car No. 8534 on August 7, 1994. J. G. Brill Car Company built this car in 1926 for the Philadelphia Rapid Transit Company. Two General Electric model 275A motors powered this Peter Witt–type car, named for the designer. (Photograph by Kenneth C. Springirth.)

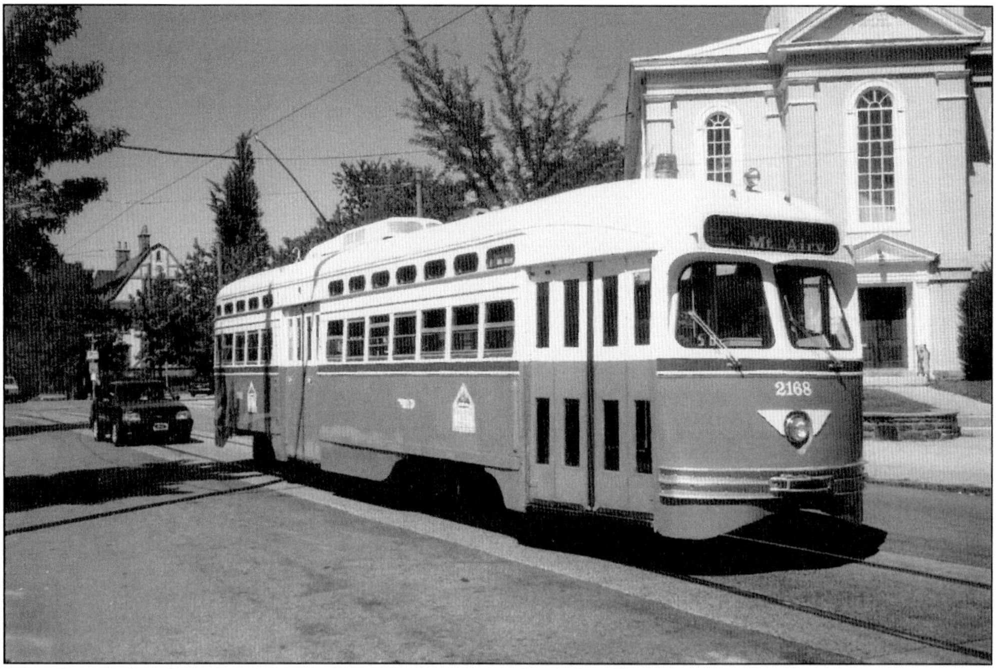

Presidents' Conference Committee car No. 2168, built by the St. Louis Car Company in 1948, is on Bethlehem Pike at Germantown Avenue on August 7, 1994. This was the Chestnut Hill trolley, which operated from 1992 to 1996 from Chestnut Hill Loop to Gorgas Lane at Germantown Depot. The Southeastern Pennsylvania Transportation Authority sold this car to the Baltimore Streetcar Museum in 2005. (Photograph by Kenneth C. Springirth.)

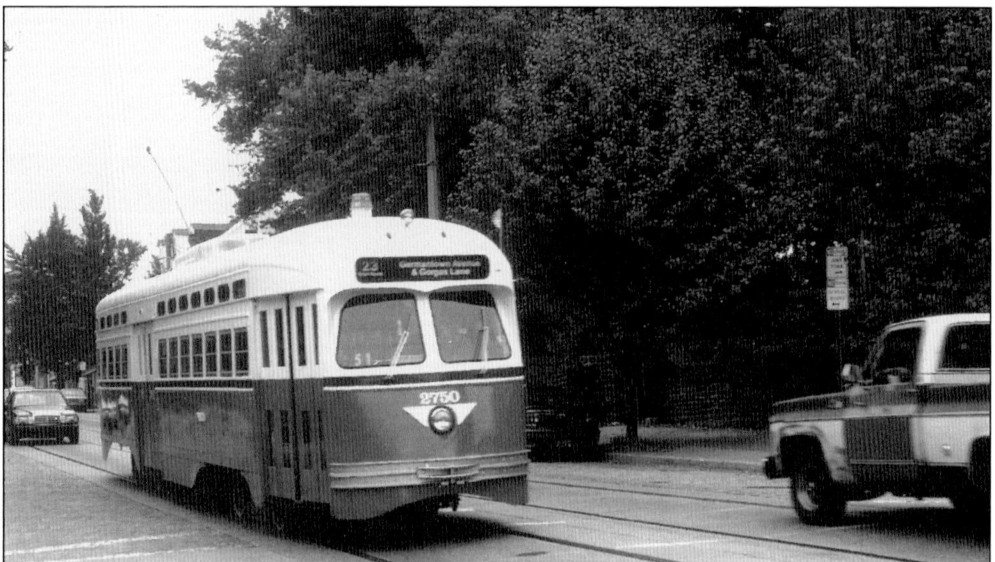

Germantown Avenue near Evergreen Avenue is the setting for Presidents' Conference Committee car No. 2750 on the Chestnut Hill trolley line on October 4, 1992. Four trolleys were repainted for this line, which required two cars for service every 20 minutes on Saturdays and Sundays except holidays. (Photograph by Kenneth C. Springirth.)

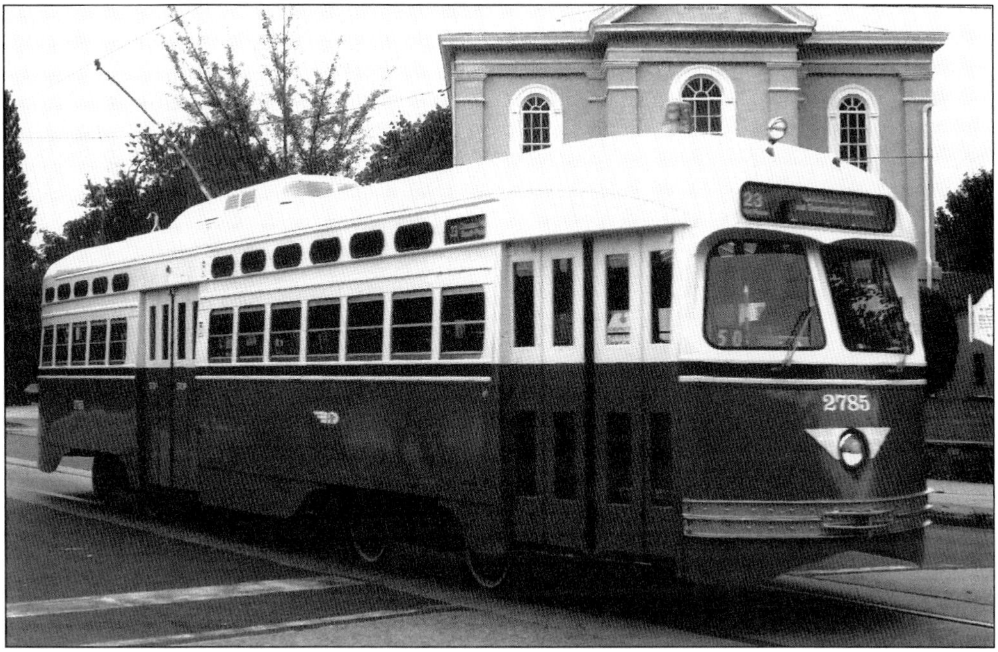

Presidents' Conference Committee car No. 2785 is on Bethlehem Pike at Germantown Avenue on October 4, 1992, operating the Chestnut Hill trolley, which was a partnership between the Southeastern Pennsylvania Transportation Authority and the Chestnut Hill Business Association. This car was delivered in April 1947 to the Philadelphia Transportation Company. It was overhauled in August 1986 and was still in existence in 2007. (Photograph by Kenneth C. Springirth.)

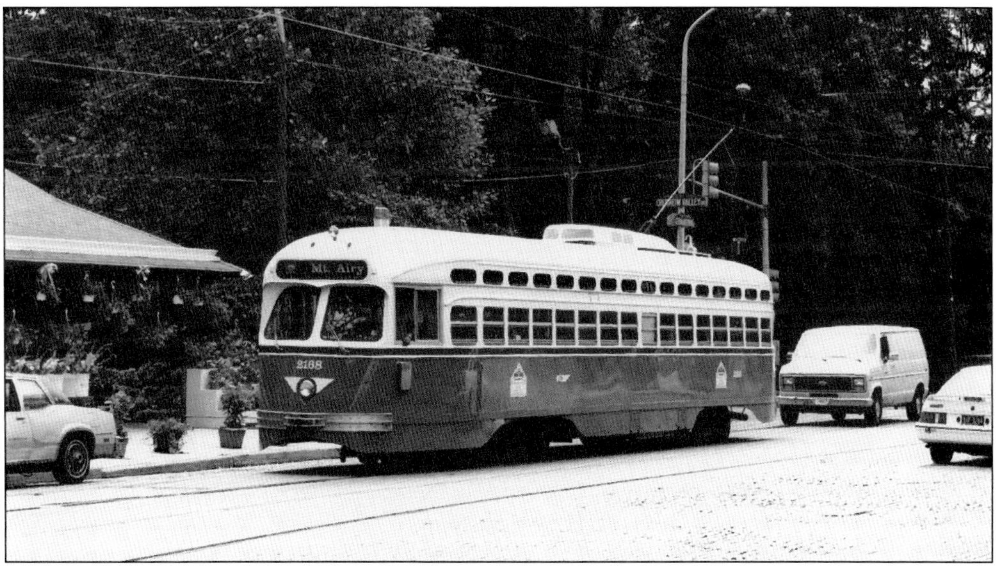

Presidents' Conference Committee car No. 2168 on Germantown Avenue has crossed Cresheim Valley Drive passing by Mermaid Lane loop on July 16, 1995. After route 23 was converted to bus operation on February 21, 1992, the Chestnut Hill trolley was inaugurated to provide a weekend trolley service between the Chestnut Hill and Mount Airy sections of Philadelphia. (Photograph by Kenneth C. Springirth.)

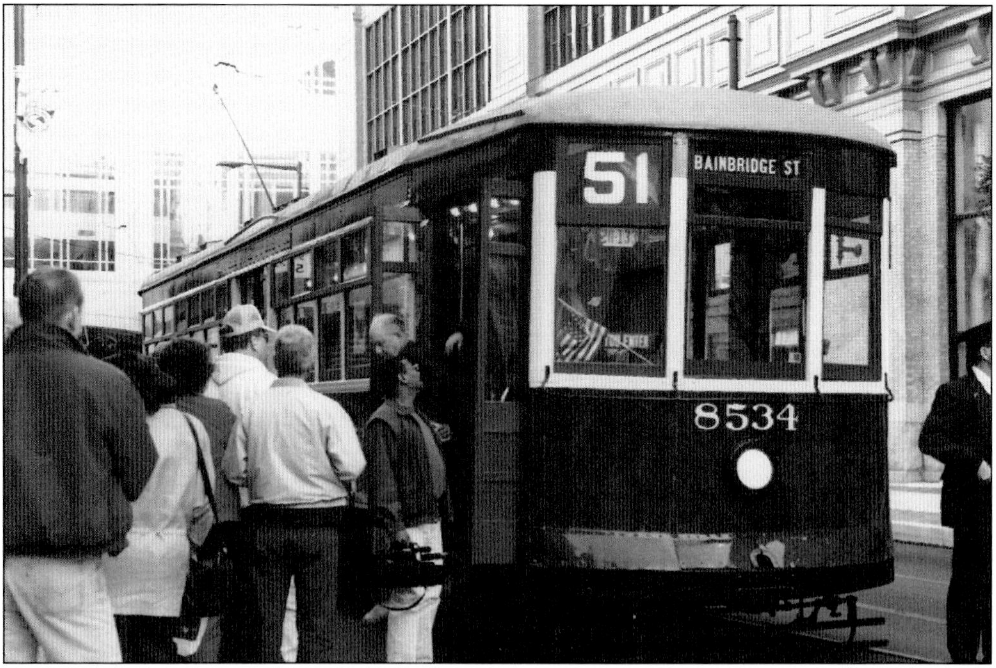

Trolley car No. 8534 is loading passengers on Twelfth Street at Filbert Street on October 22, 1995. Trolley Fest 1995, held on October 21 and 22, featured vintage trolley rides, tours of Elmwood Depot, Woodland Shop, Norristown High Speed Line Shop, and the Overbrook Maintenance Facility. (Photograph by Kenneth C. Springirth.)

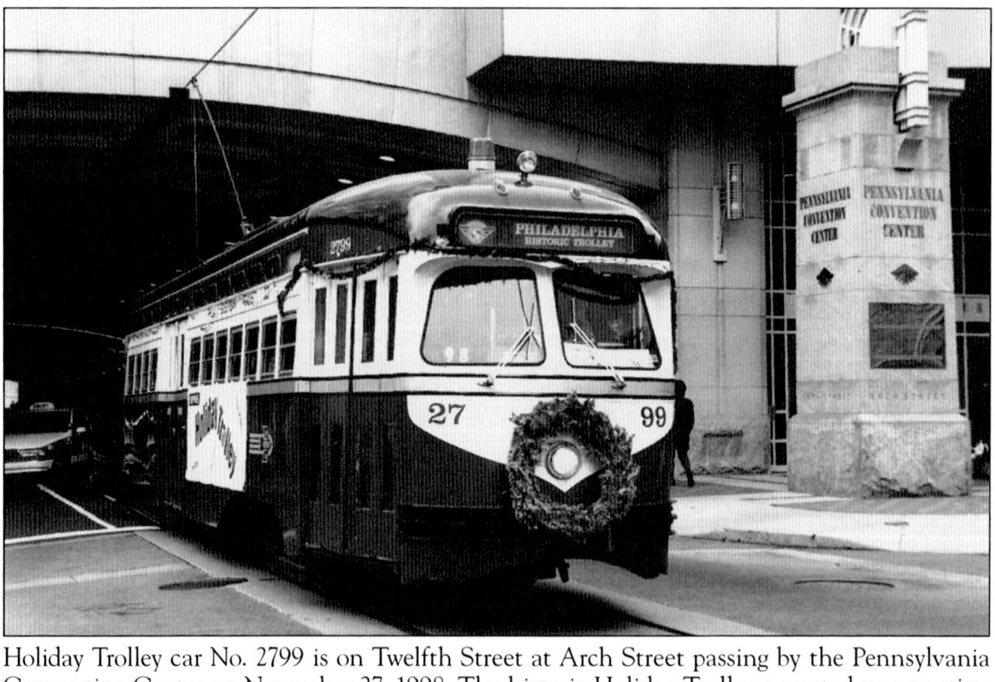

Holiday Trolley car No. 2799 is on Twelfth Street at Arch Street passing by the Pennsylvania Convention Center on November 27, 1998. The historic Holiday Trolley operated on a portion of route 23 using Eleventh and Twelfth Streets from Noble Street to Bainbridge Street. Certain trips operated into South Philadelphia. (Photograph by Kenneth C. Springirth.)

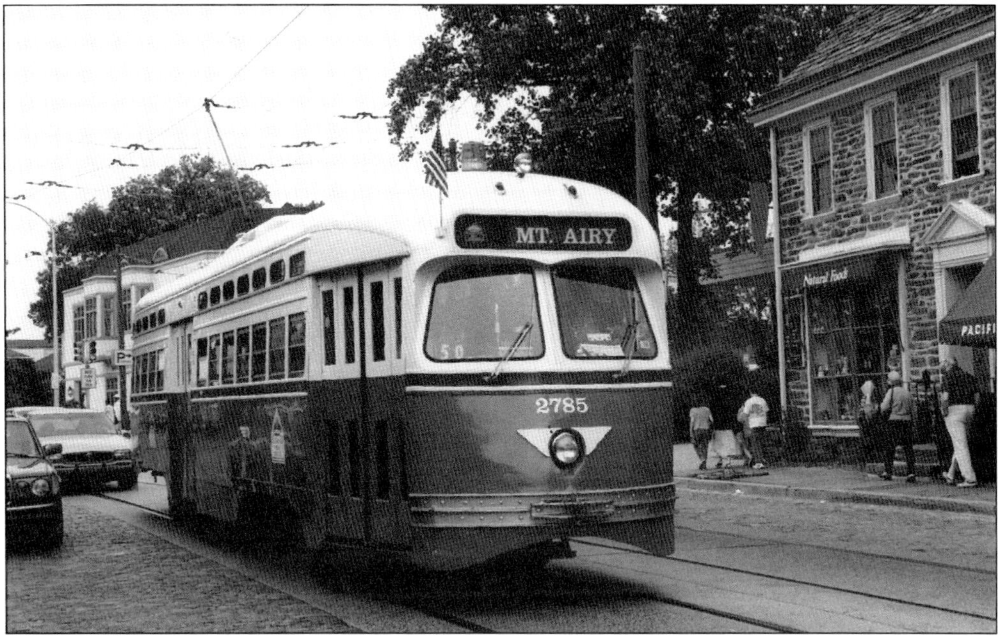

Presidents' Conference Committee car No. 2785 is on Germantown Avenue just south of Chestnut Hill Loop on May 26, 1996. This was the last year of operation for the Chestnut Hill trolley, which operated from Germantown Avenue and Bethlehem Pike loop via Germantown Avenue to Gorgas Lane, where the trolley actually looped through Germantown Depot. (Photograph by Kenneth C. Springirth.)

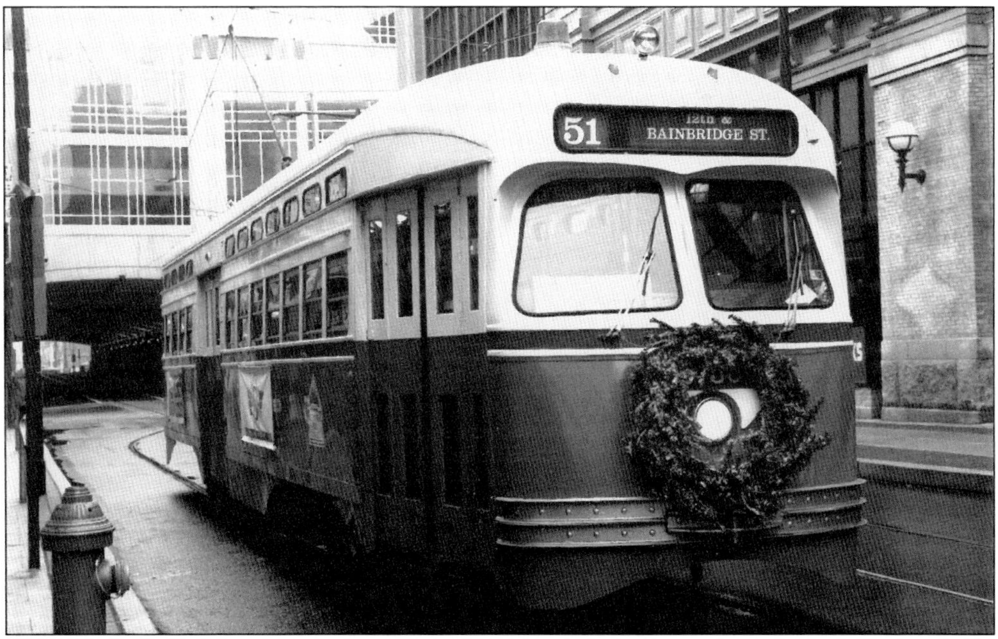

Holiday Trolley car No. 2750 is on Twelfth Street at Filbert Street on December 28, 1996. Route 51 Welcome Line was established on May 19, 1995. The Chestnut Hill trolley and route 51 were eliminated because of an operating deficit. Route 51 temporarily returned in December 1996 as the Holiday Trolley. (Photograph by Kenneth C. Springirth.)

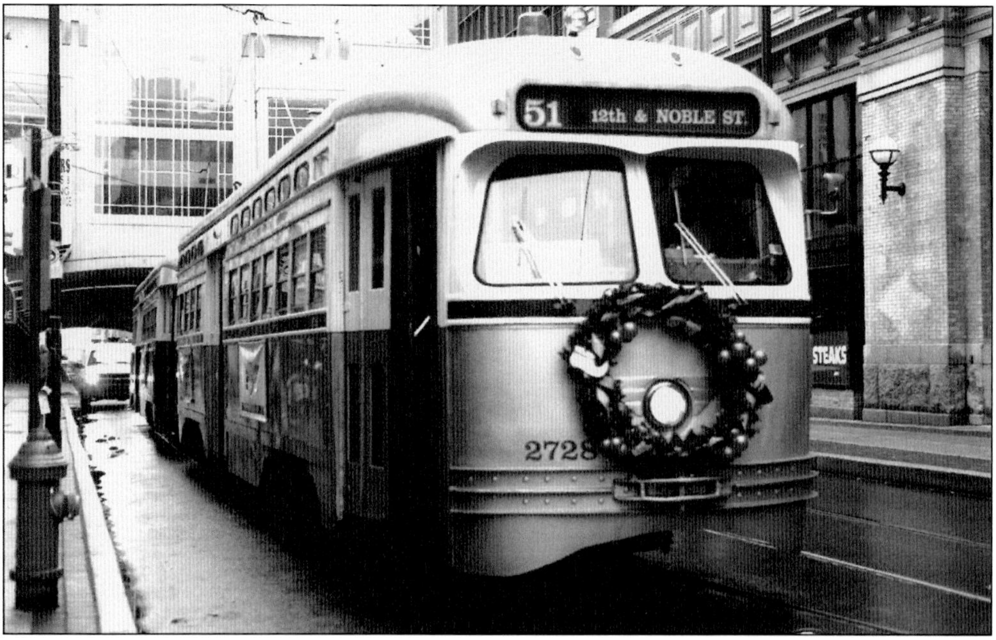

Presidents' Conference Committee car No. 2728 followed by No. 2732 are on Twelfth Street at Filbert Street on December 29, 1996, for the Holiday Trolley, which operated as the route 51 Welcome Line. The Holiday Trolley was operated during the Christmas shopping period of 1996, 1997, 1998, and 2000. It did not run in 1999. After the year 2000, it was not reinstated. (Photograph by Kenneth C. Springirth.)

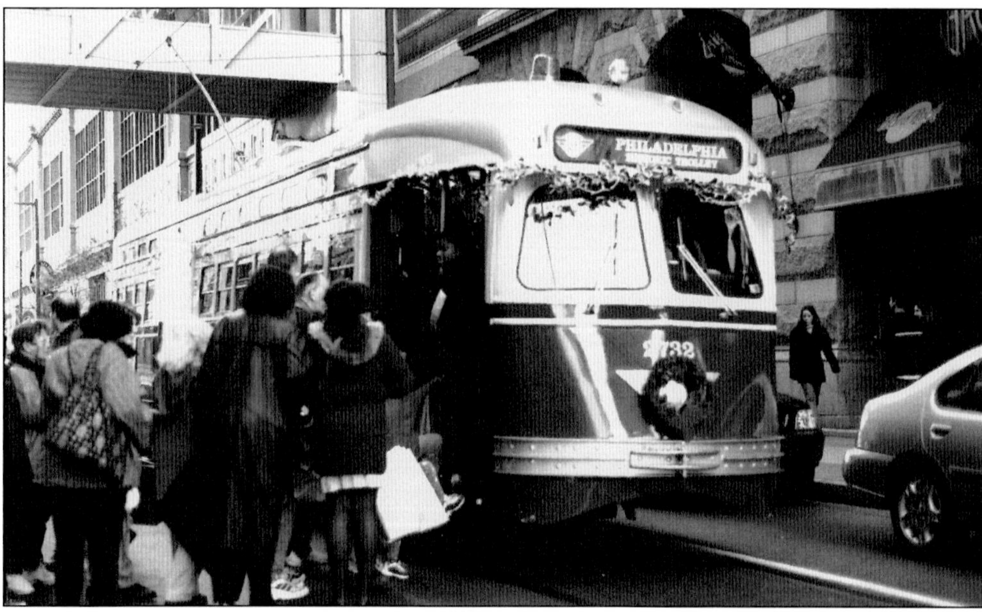

People are ready to board Presidents' Conference Committee car No. 2732, the Holiday Trolley, on November 24, 2000, on Twelfth Street at Market Street. The St. Louis Car Company delivered this car to the Philadelphia Transportation Company in March 1947. It was overhauled by the Southeastern Pennsylvania Transportation Authority during February 1985 and was sold to Glen Echo Park in 2005. (Photograph by Kenneth C. Springirth.)

Three

North to South Philadelphia Trolleys

On September 15, 1924, route 6 was established from Willow Grove to Ogontz and City Line Avenues. Service was extended via Ogontz Avenue to Broad Street and Olney Avenue on March 3, 1929. On June 8, 1958, buses replaced route 6 trolley service from Willow Grove to Ogontz and City Line Avenues. Buses replaced the remainder of route 6 on January 12, 1986.

Route 47 began as the Seventh and Ninth Streets line before 1890. On August 31, 1913, the line operated from Eighth Street and Allegheny Avenue to Eighth and Wolf Streets. The line was extended northward to Fifth Street and Green Lane on May 10, 1925, becoming the Godfrey Avenue Eighth and Ninth Street line on March 20, 1930. Buses operated the entire line beginning on June 15, 1969.

The Philadelphia and Delaware Railroad Company began horse-drawn street railway service on January 21, 1858, on Fifth and Sixth Streets from Montgomery Avenue to Morris Street on what later became route 50. By 1896, route 50 operated from Fox Chase to Sixth and Jackson Streets and on October 1, 1890, was extended southward to Porter Street via Fifth and Sixth Streets. Service reached Sixth Street and Oregon Avenue on April 5, 1953. On January 27, 1956, the northern end was cut back to Lawndale loop. Buses replaced route 50 trolleys on October 12, 1980.

Prior to 1890, the Wayne Avenue line, which became route 53, operated from Thirteenth and Locusts Streets to Wayne Avenue and Johnson Street. Effective June 16, 1929, route 53 operated from Wayne Avenue and Carpenter Lane to Eleventh Street and Erie Avenue, reaching Tenth and Luzerne Streets on September 7, 1930. Buses replaced route 53 trolleys on May 16, 1985.

Route 56 began operation on March 18, 1907, from Second and Tioga Streets via Erie Avenue to Hunting Park Avenue. The western terminus was established at Twenty-third and Venango Streets on June 29, 1926. Service was extended eastward to Torresdale and Cottman Avenues on September 2, 1928. Buses replaced route 56 trolleys on June 14, 1992.

Route 60 began operation from Richmond Street via Allegheny Avenue to Seventeenth Street on November 1, 1906. It was extended westward via Allegheny Avenue to Ridge Avenue on May 21, 1910. A new eastern loop was established at Richmond and Westmoreland Streets on February 24, 1956. Buses replaced route 60 trolleys on September 4, 1977.

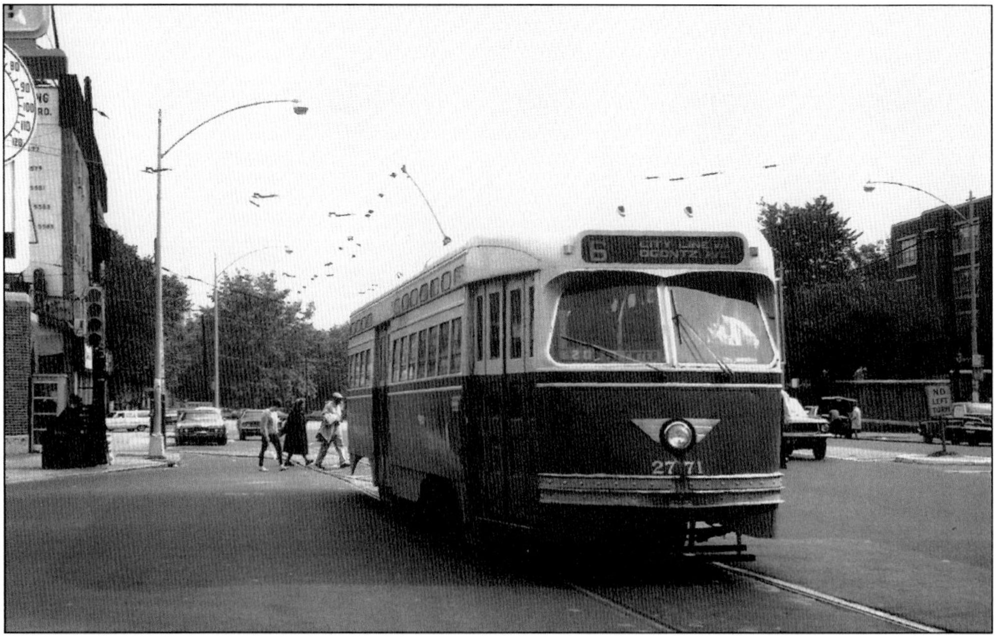

Philadelphia Transportation Company route 6 Presidents' Conference Committee car No. 2771 is on Broad Street at Olney Avenue on May 31, 1968. This car, built by the St. Louis Car Company in 1947, was destroyed in the Woodland Depot fire of October 23, 1975. Route 6 from Ogontz and City Line loop to Willow Grove was replaced by buses on June 8, 1958. (Photograph by Kenneth C. Springirth.)

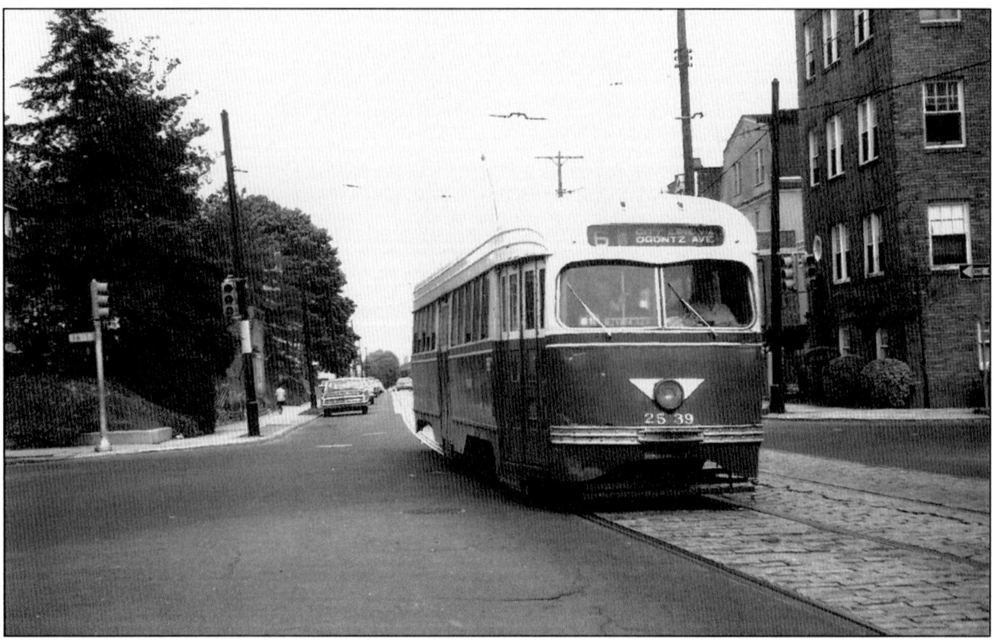

Philadelphia Transportation Company route 6 Presidents' Conference Committee car No. 2539 is on Champlost Street at Sixteenth Street and will soon turn north on Ogontz Avenue for its run to City Line loop on May 31, 1968. Delivered by the St. Louis Car Company in January 1941, this car was scrapped in 1981. (Photograph by Kenneth C. Springirth)

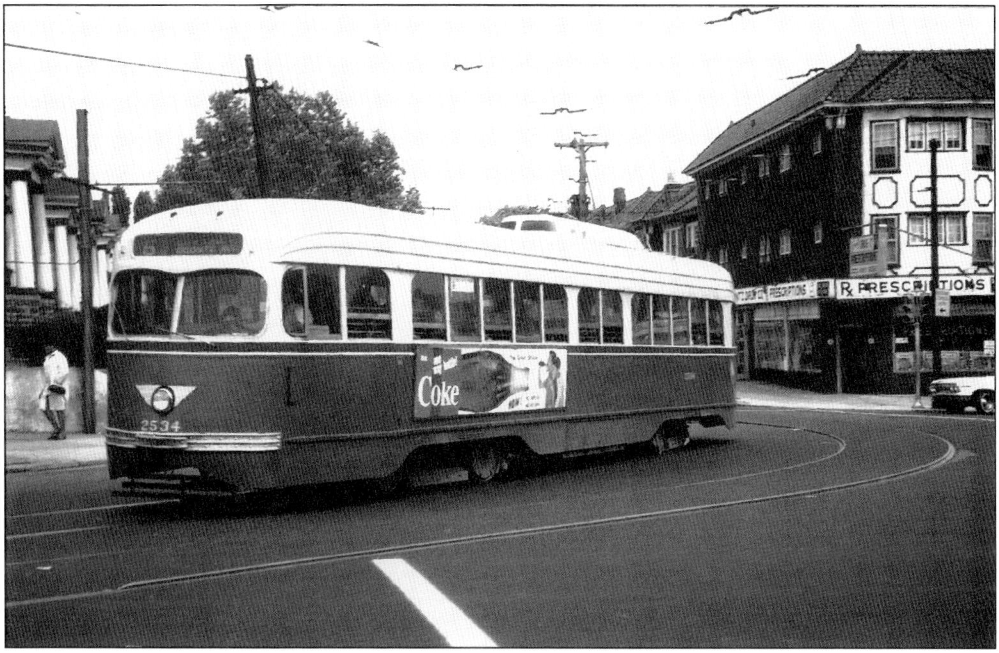

Philadelphia Transportation Company route 6 car No. 2534 is turning from Champlost Street to Ogontz Avenue on May 31, 1968. Presidents' Conference Committee cars were introduced on route 6 for Sundays on April 20, 1941, and were used full time on this line beginning on June 20, 1948. (Photograph by Kenneth C. Springirth.)

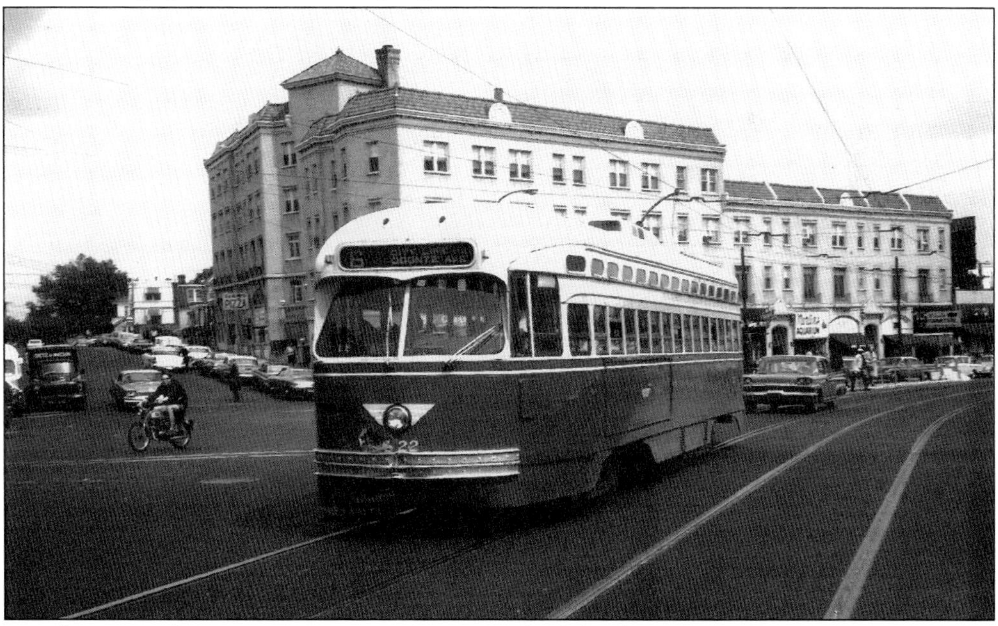

Presidents' Conference Committee car No. 2122, built by the St. Louis Car Company in 1948, is on Ogontz Avenue at Walnut Lane on Philadelphia Transportation Company route 6 on May 31, 1968. An overhaul of this car was completed on February 27, 1981. In October 1992, it was sold to the Municipal Railway of San Francisco and was refurbished and renumbered as 1055. (Photograph by Kenneth C. Springirth.)

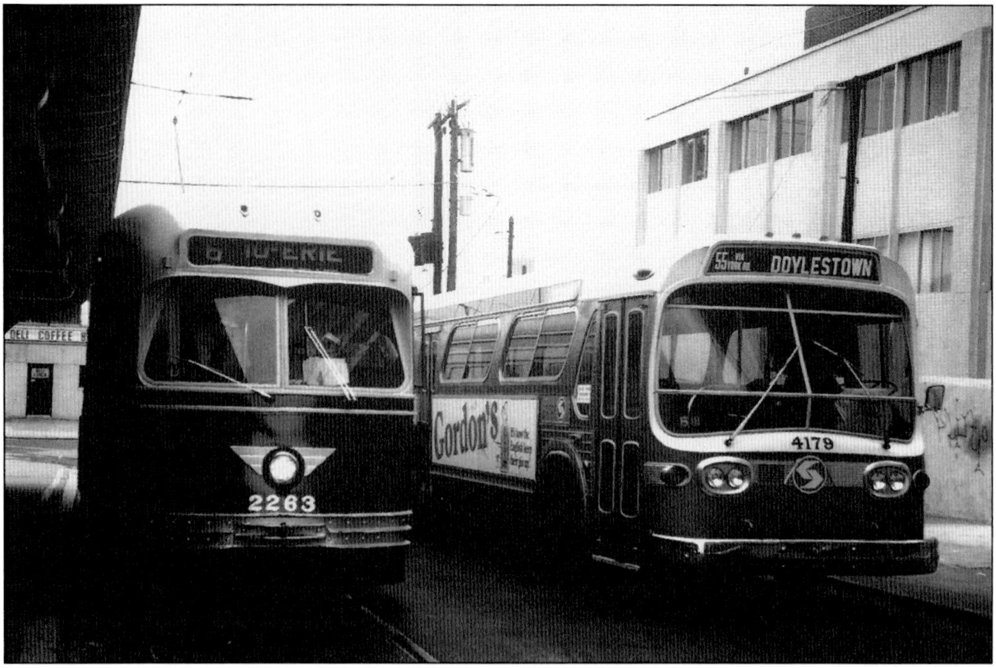

On June 13, 1971, Southeastern Pennsylvania Transportation Authority car No. 2263, built by the St. Louis Car Company in 1946 for the Kansas City Public Service Company as car No. 768, and bus No. 4179, model TDH5304 built by General Motors in 1967, are at the Broad and Olney Terminal. (Photograph by Kenneth C. Springirth.)

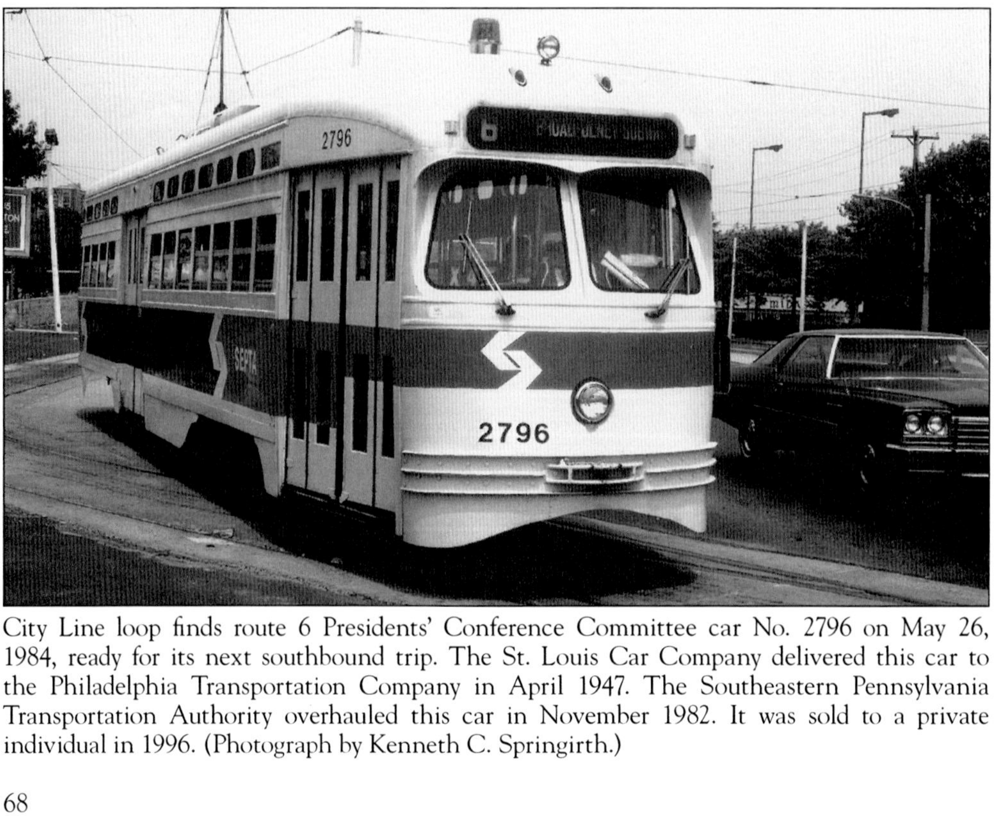

City Line loop finds route 6 Presidents' Conference Committee car No. 2796 on May 26, 1984, ready for its next southbound trip. The St. Louis Car Company delivered this car to the Philadelphia Transportation Company in April 1947. The Southeastern Pennsylvania Transportation Authority overhauled this car in November 1982. It was sold to a private individual in 1996. (Photograph by Kenneth C. Springirth.)

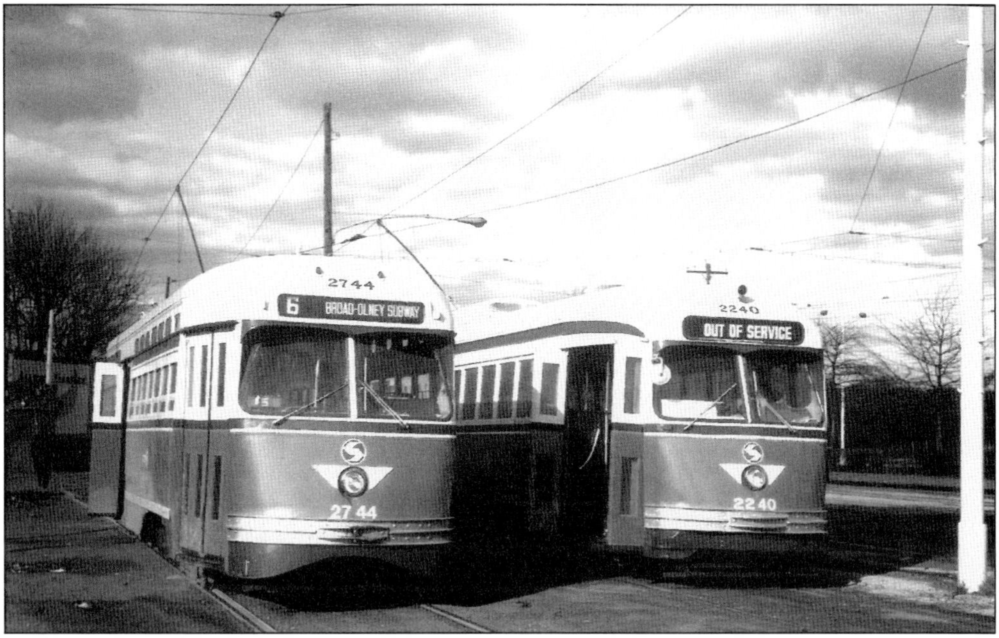

On November 24, 1978, route 6 cars built by the St. Louis Car Company are at City Line loop. Car No. 2744, built in 1947, was scrapped in 1985. Car No. 2240, built in 1946 as Kansas City Public Service Company car No. 526, became Toronto Transit Commission car No. 4750, Southeastern Pennsylvania Transportation Authority car No. 2240, and was scrapped in 1983. (Photograph by Kenneth C. Springirth.)

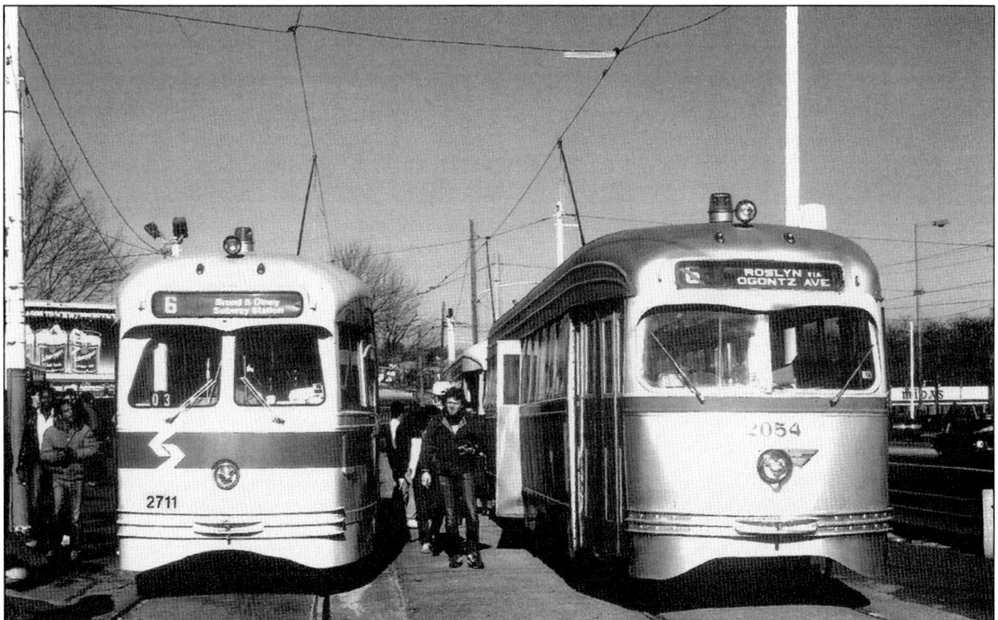

On January 11, 1986, two Presidents' Conference Committee cars Nos. 2711 and 2054 built by the St. Louis Car Company are at City Line loop on the last day of route 6 trolley car operation. Students of rail transportation came to make the last ride on the trolleys, with buses taking over the next day. (Photograph by Kenneth C. Springirth.)

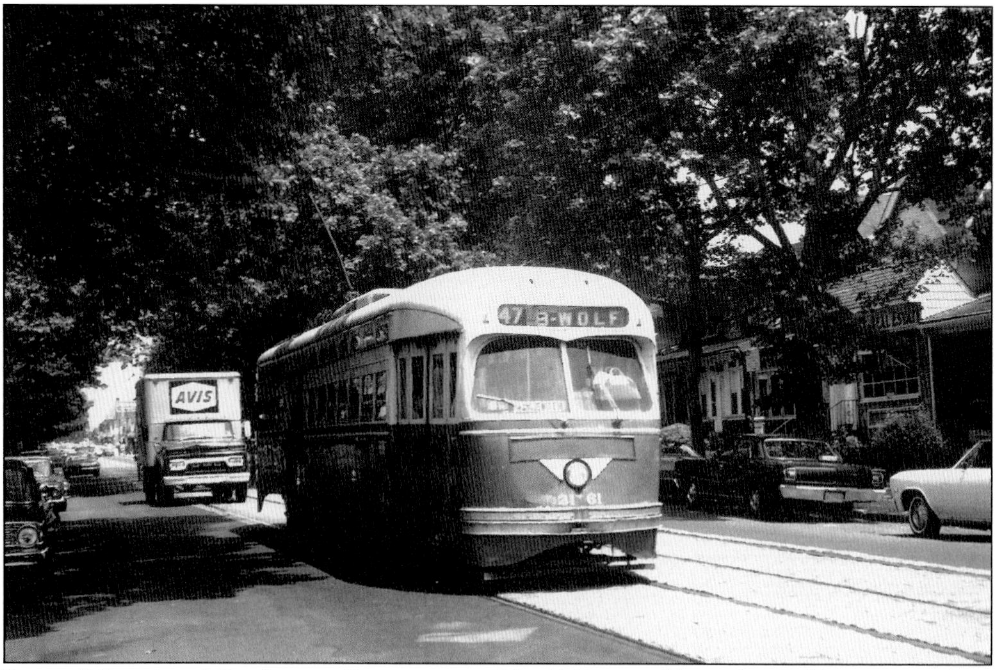

Route 47 Presidents' Conference Committee car No. 2161 is southbound on Fifth Street at Chew Avenue on May 31, 1968. The St. Louis Car Company delivered this car to the Philadelphia Transportation Company in June 1948. This car was scrapped during 1969. On August 30, 1942, Presidents' Conference Committee cars were placed in service on route 47. (Photograph by Kenneth C. Springirth.)

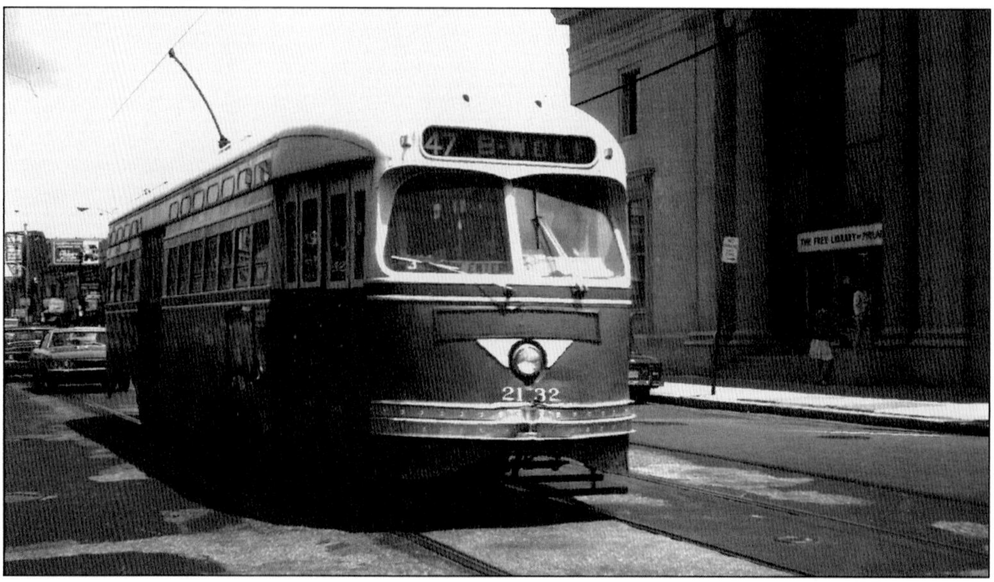

Philadelphia Transportation Company car No. 2132 is on route 47 on Fifth Street at Tabor Road on May 31, 1968. On July 9, 1967, route 47 went to bus operation south of Spring Garden Street (car No. 2132 made the last run on that portion) because of Eighth Street excavation between Market and Race Streets for subway track realignment for the Lindenwold rapid transit line. (Photograph by Kenneth C. Springirth.)

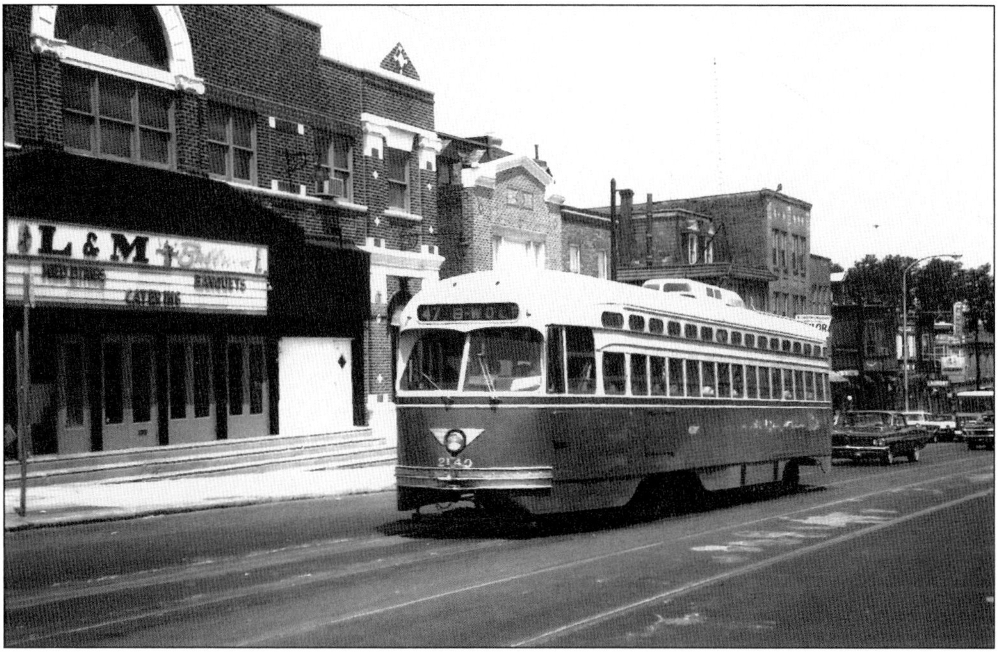

On May 31, 1968, Philadelphia Transportation Company route 47 car No. 2140 is on Fifth Street at Rockland Street. The St. Louis Car Company delivered this car to the Philadelphia Transportation Company in September 1948. This car was destroyed in the Woodland Depot fire of October 23, 1975. (Photograph by Kenneth C. Springirth.)

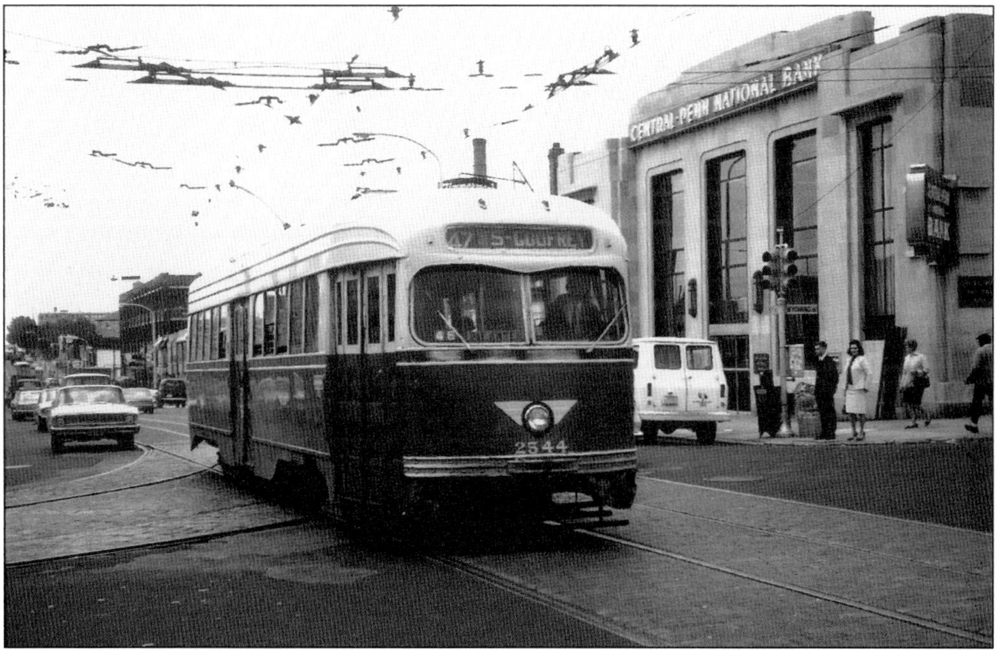

Route 47 Presidents' Conference Committee car No. 2544, built by the St. Louis Car Company for the Philadelphia Transportation Company in January 1941 and scrapped in 1982, is on Fifth Street crossing Wyoming Avenue on May 31, 1968. Wyoming Avenue was used by route 75 trackless trolleys. (Photograph by Kenneth C. Springirth.)

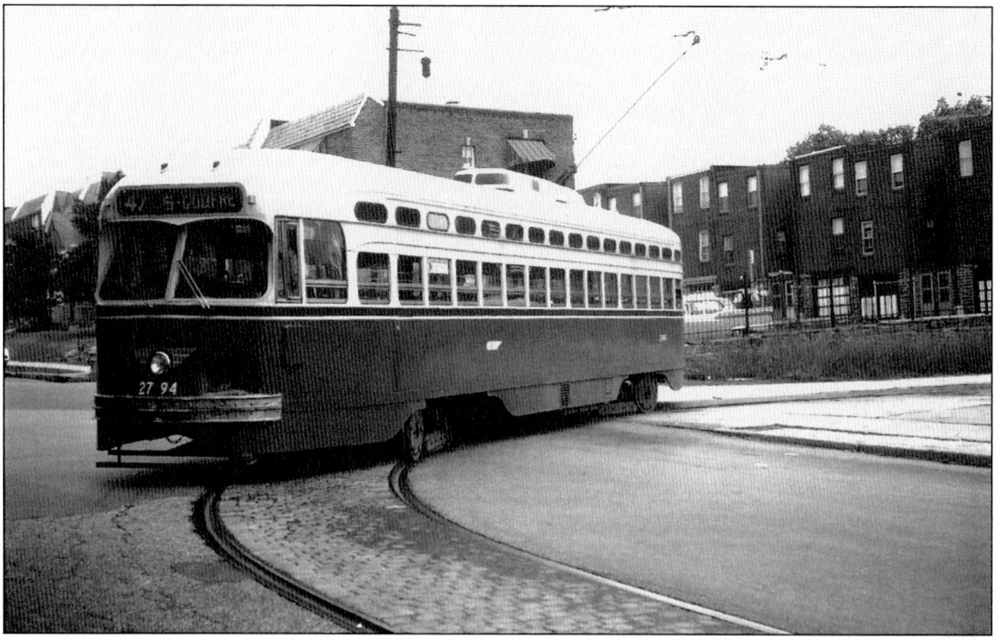

Presidents' Conference Committee car No. 2794 is leaving the Fifth Street and Godfrey Avenue terminus of route 47 on May 31, 1968. The St. Louis Car Company delivered this car in April 1947 to the Philadelphia Transportation Company. It was destroyed in the Woodland Depot fire of October 23, 1975. (Photograph by Kenneth C. Springirth.)

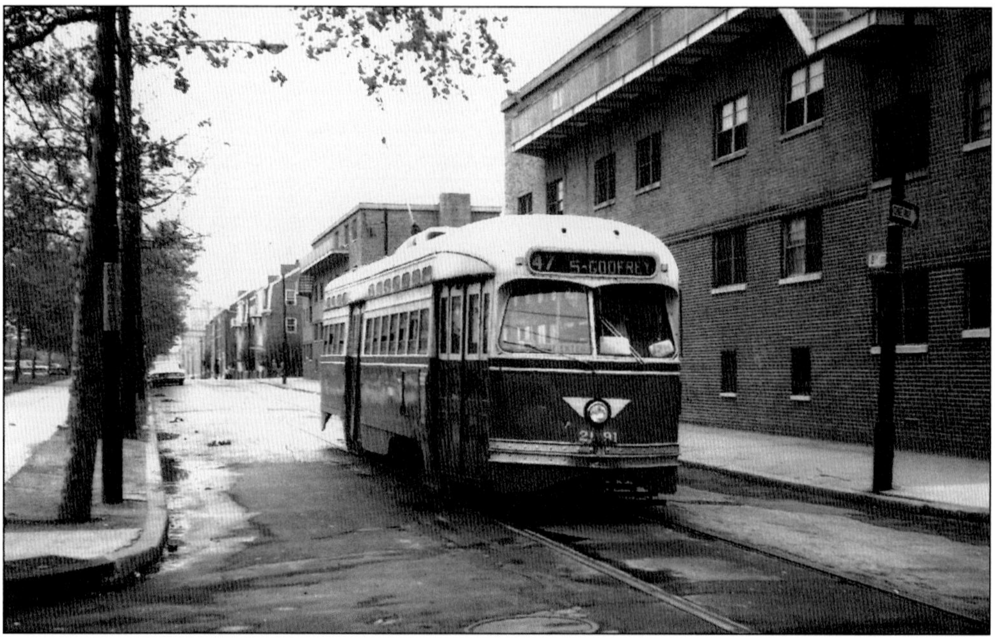

Route 47 Presidents' Conference Committee car No. 2191 is heading north on Eighth Street at Green Street on April 27, 1968. On July 9, 1967, the southern portion of route 47 from Spring Garden to Wolf Streets was converted to bus operation. The northern section of route 47 went to bus operation on June 15, 1969, making the entire route a bus line. (Photograph by Kenneth C. Springirth.)

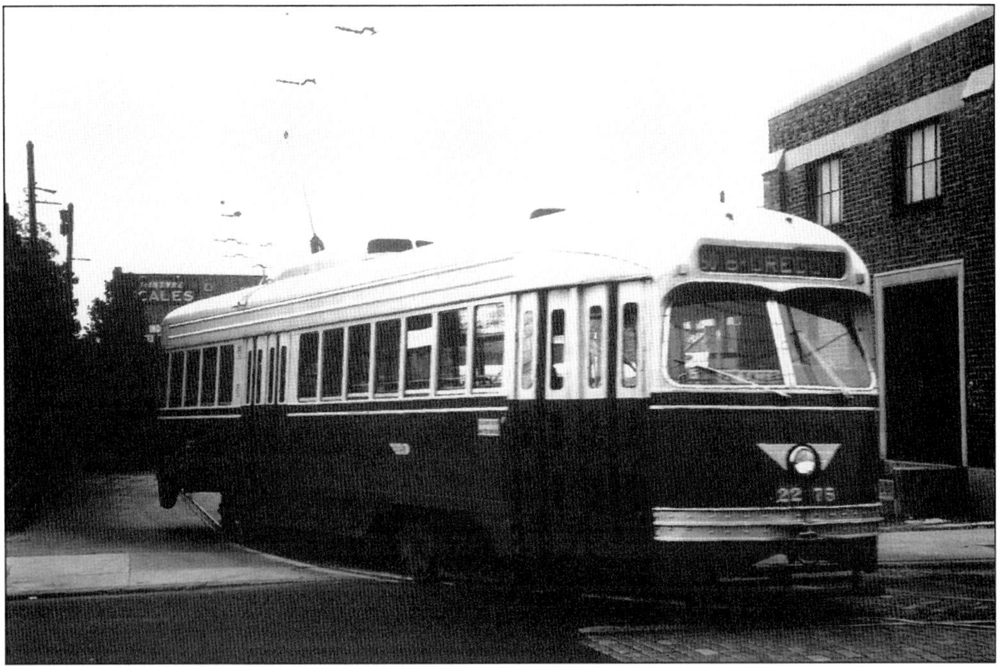

On April 20, 1962, route 50 car No. 2275 is leaving the Rising Sun Avenue and Knorr Street loop. Built by the St. Louis Car Company in 1946 as Kansas City Public Service Company car No. 774, it was purchased by the Philadelphia Transportation Company in 1955 and scrapped in 1982. (Photograph by Kenneth C. Springirth.)

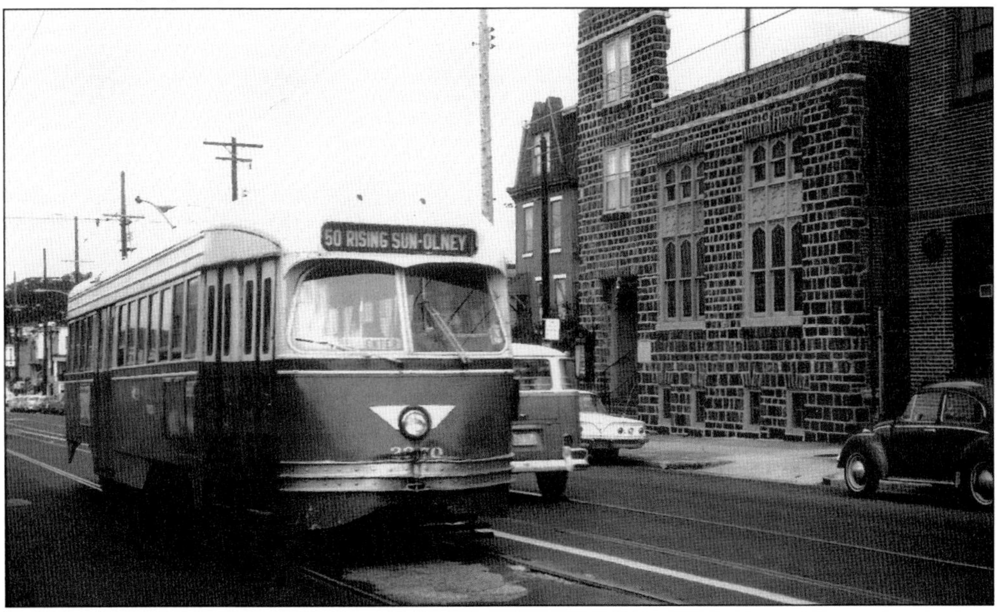

Wyoming Avenue at Third Street is the location for route 50 Presidents' Conference Committee car No. 2270 on May 31, 1968. This was Kansas City Public Service Company car No. 736, built by the St. Louis Car Company in 1946 and purchased by the Philadelphia Transportation Company in June 1955. In 1985, the Vintage Electric Streetcar Company acquired it. (Photograph by Kenneth C. Springirth.)

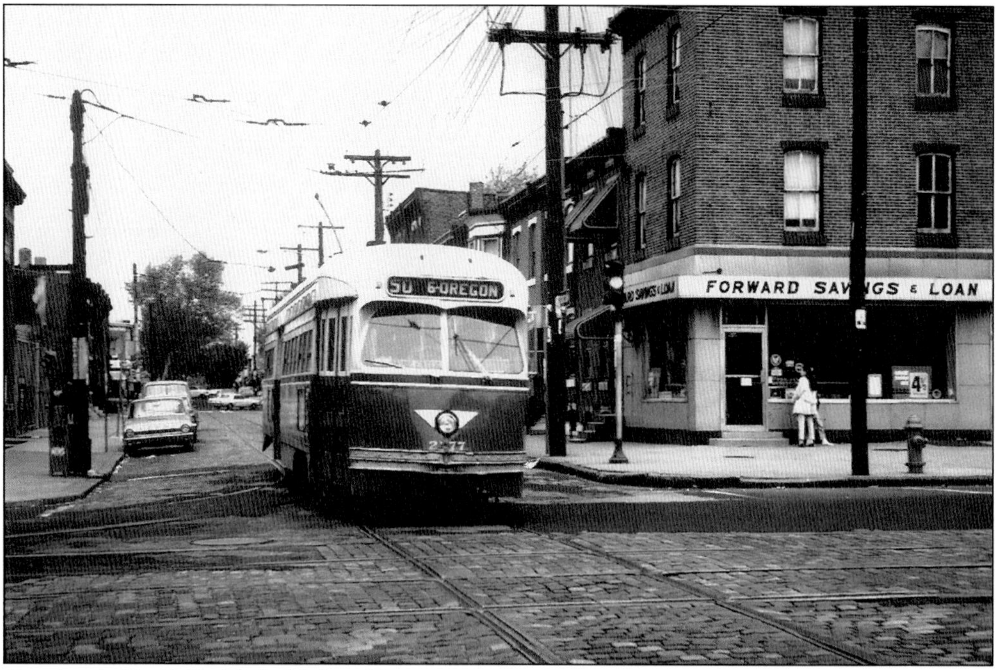

On April 27, 1968, Philadelphia Transportation Company car No. 2177 is southbound on Sixth Street crossing route 56 trolley car tracks on Erie Avenue. This Presidents' Conference Committee car, built by the St. Louis Car Company in 1948, was destroyed in the Woodland Depot fire of October 23, 1975. (Photograph by Kenneth C. Springirth.)

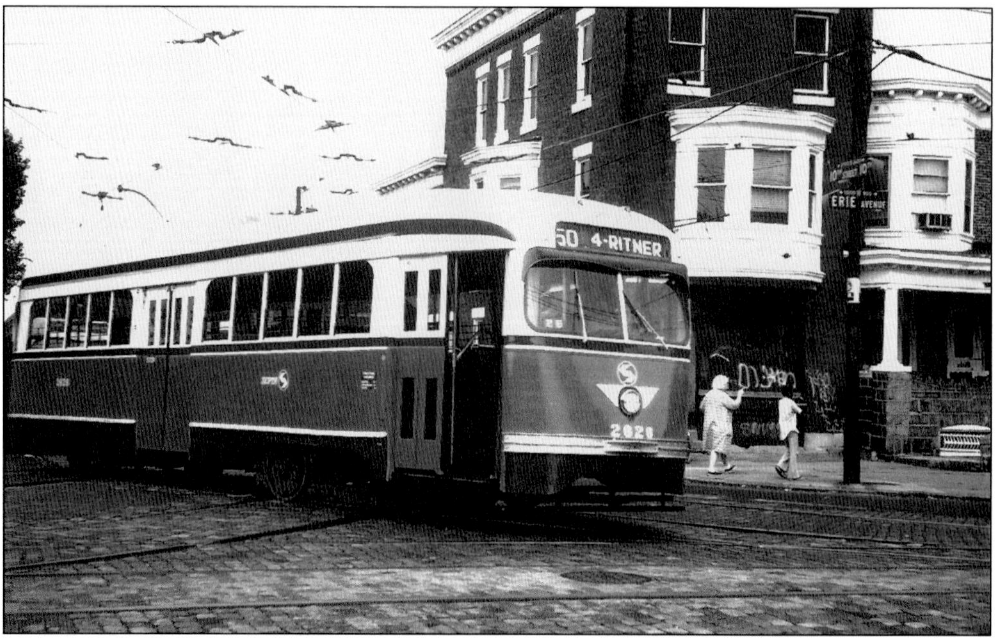

Southeastern Pennsylvania Transportation Authority car No. 2626 is turning from Tenth Street to Erie Avenue going into service for the afternoon rush hour of August 1, 1975. The Philadelphia Transportation Company received this car from the St. Louis Car Company in July 1942. It was scrapped in 1982. (Photograph by Kenneth C. Springirth.)

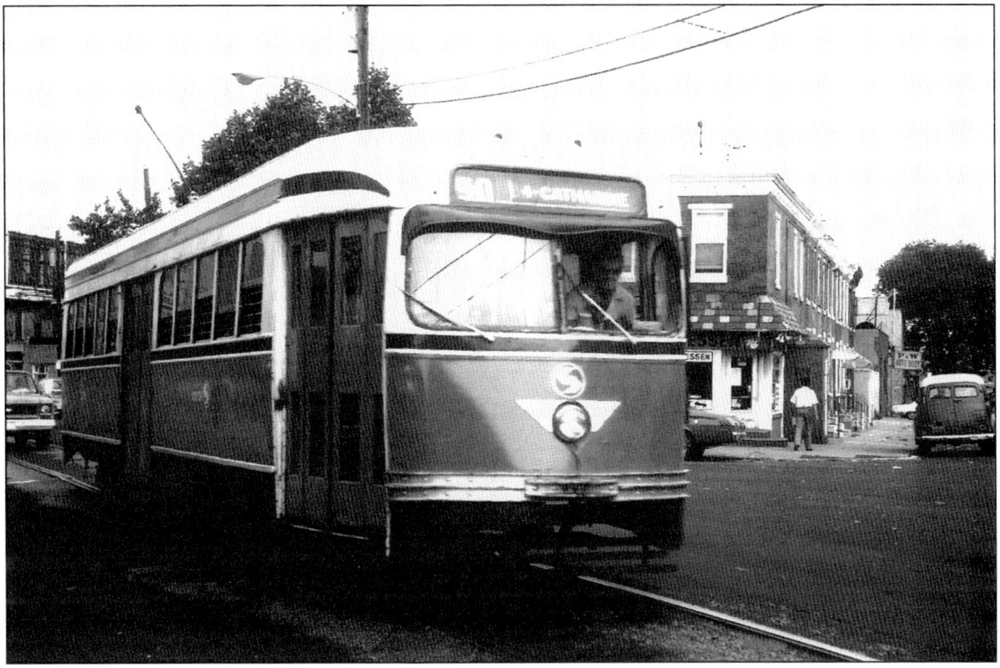

Rising Sun Avenue at Butler Street is the location for Southeastern Pennsylvania Transportation Authority route 50 car No. 2595 on August 1, 1975. The St. Louis Car Company delivered this car to the Philadelphia Transportation Company in June 1942. This car was scrapped in September 1972. (Photograph by Kenneth C. Springirth.)

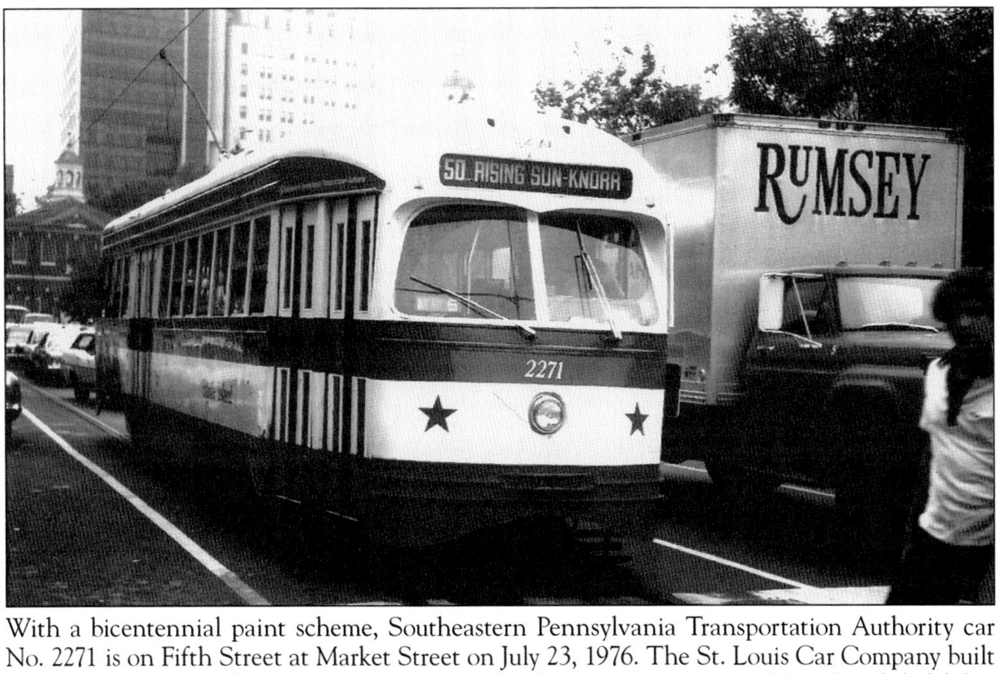

With a bicentennial paint scheme, Southeastern Pennsylvania Transportation Authority car No. 2271 is on Fifth Street at Market Street on July 23, 1976. The St. Louis Car Company built this car as number 777 for the Kansas City Public Service Company in 1946. The Philadelphia Transportation Company purchased this car in 1955. The Vintage Electric Streetcar Company acquired this car in 1985. (Photograph by Kenneth C. Springirth.)

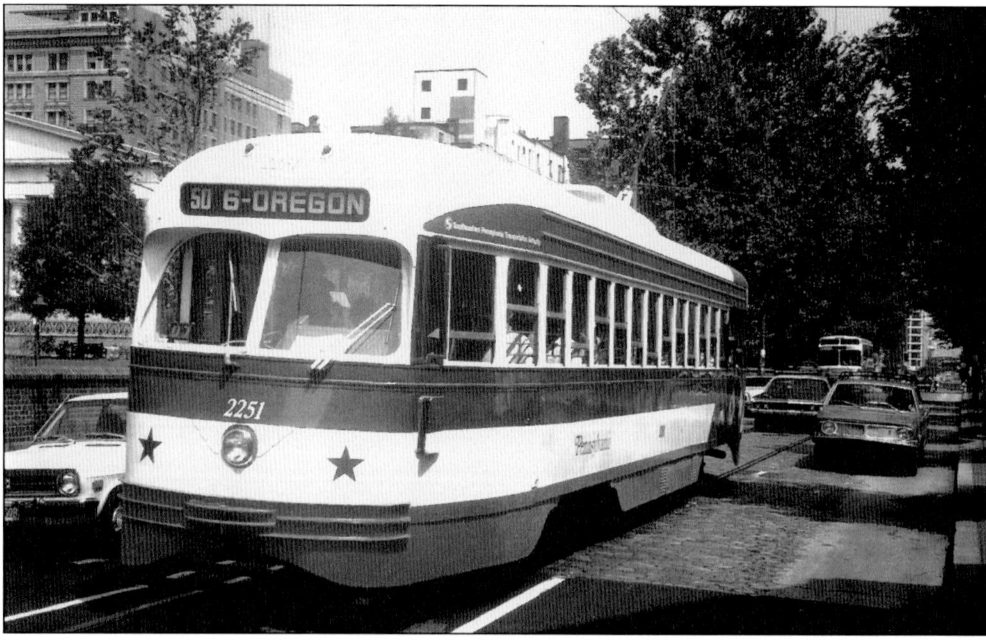

On August 14, 1976, Southeastern Pennsylvania Transportation Authority route 50 car No. 2251 is southbound on Fourth Street at Walnut Street. The St. Louis Car Company built this car in 1946 for the Kansas City Public Service Company as car No. 787. It was purchased by the Philadelphia Transportation Company during 1955 and was scrapped during March 1982. (Photograph by Kenneth C. Springirth.)

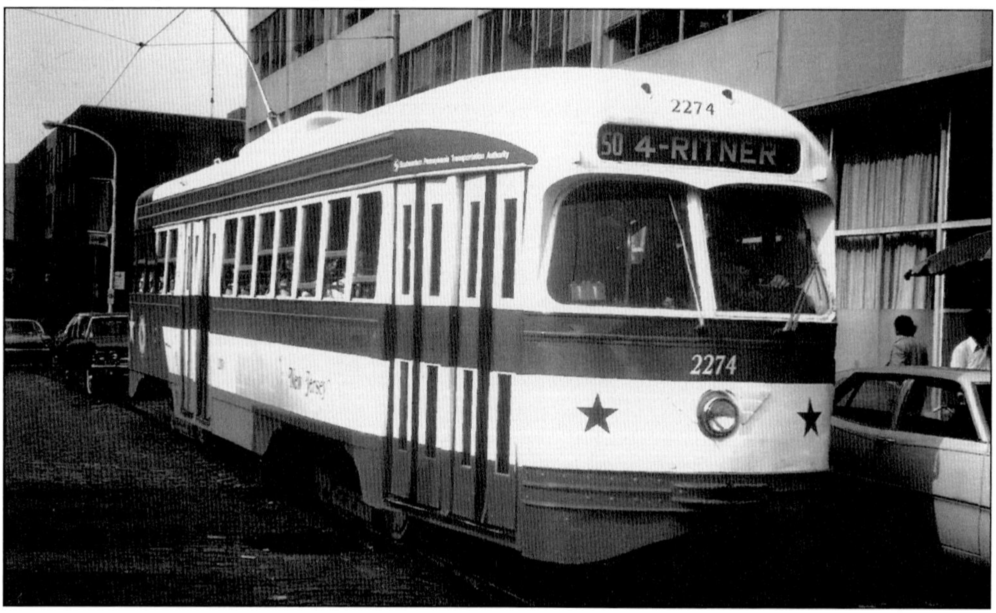

On August 13, 1976, Southeastern Pennsylvania Transportation Authority route 50 car No. 2274 is on Fourth Street at Chestnuts Street. This car, built by the St. Louis Car Company in 1946 as No. 763 for the Kansas City Public Service Company, was purchased by the Philadelphia Transportation Company during 1955 and sold in 1985 to the Vintage Electric Streetcar Company. (Photograph by Kenneth C. Springirth.)

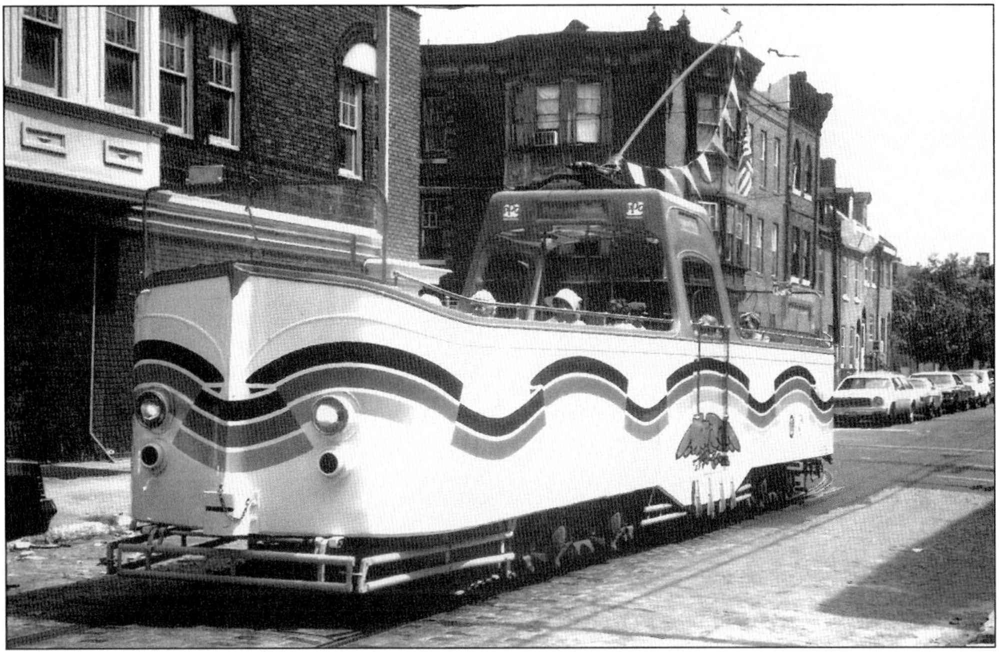

The Blackpool, England, "boat trolley," built by English Electric in 1934 and seating 56, is on Catharine Street at Fourth Street on August 14, 1976. A bicentennial loop on a portion of route 50 was established by the Southeastern Pennsylvania Transportation Authority northbound on Fifth Street and southbound on Fourth Street between Girard Avenue and Catharine Street. (Photograph by Kenneth C. Springirth.)

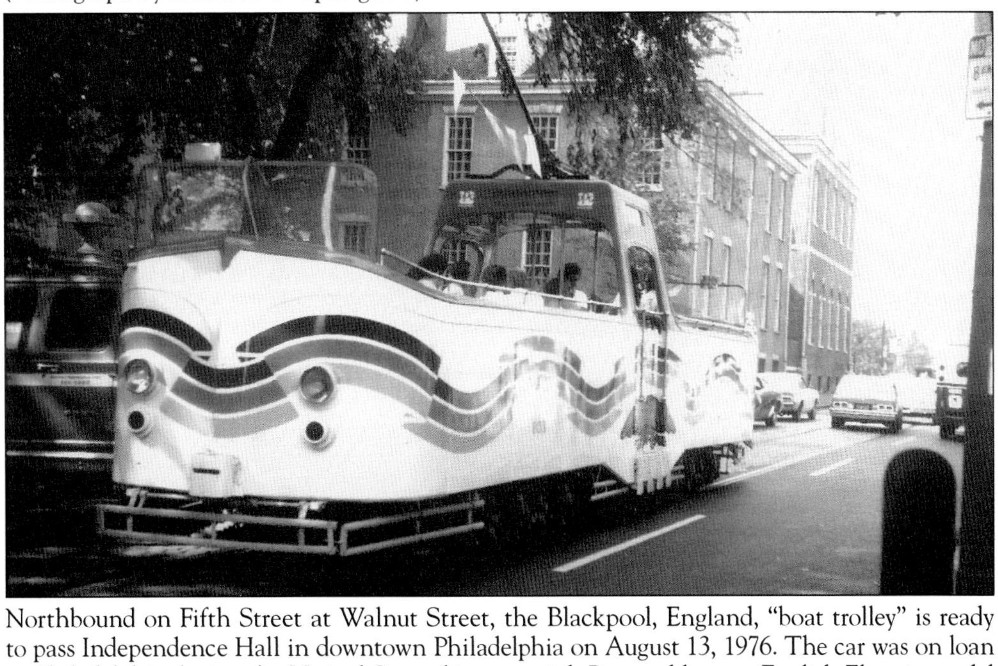

Northbound on Fifth Street at Walnut Street, the Blackpool, England, "boat trolley" is ready to pass Independence Hall in downtown Philadelphia on August 13, 1976. The car was on loan to Philadelphia during the United States bicentennial. Powered by two English Electric model 305 motors, the car was 42 feet long, 8.16 feet wide, 11.5 feet high, and weighed 20,000 pounds. (Photograph by Kenneth C. Springirth.)

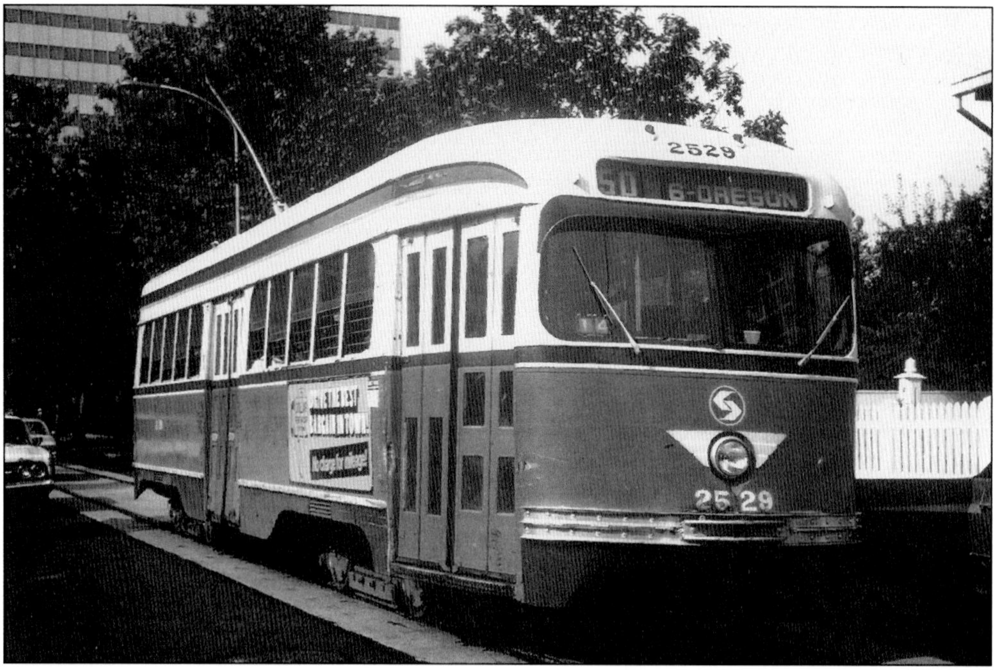

Southeastern Pennsylvania Transportation Authority route 50 Presidents' Committee car No. 2529 (painted white, orange, and blue) is on Fourth Street at Walnut Street on July 19, 1978. The St. Louis Car Company delivered this car to the Philadelphia Transportation Company in 1940. It was scrapped in March 1982. (Photograph by Kenneth C. Springirth.)

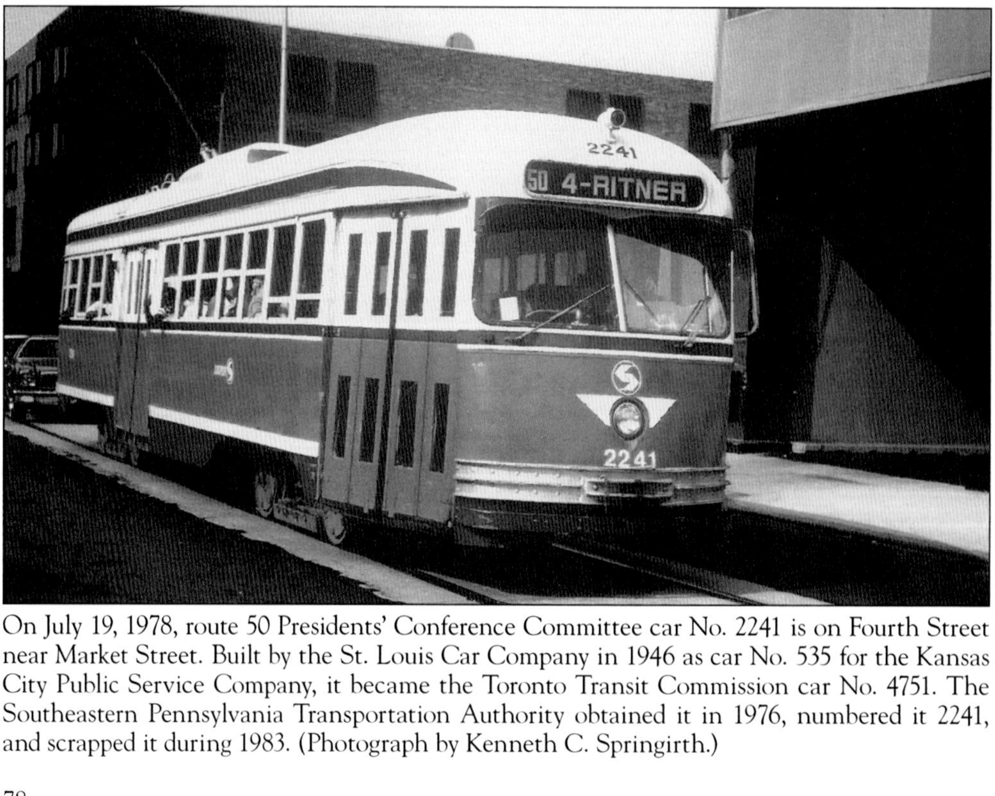

On July 19, 1978, route 50 Presidents' Conference Committee car No. 2241 is on Fourth Street near Market Street. Built by the St. Louis Car Company in 1946 as car No. 535 for the Kansas City Public Service Company, it became the Toronto Transit Commission car No. 4751. The Southeastern Pennsylvania Transportation Authority obtained it in 1976, numbered it 2241, and scrapped it during 1983. (Photograph by Kenneth C. Springirth.)

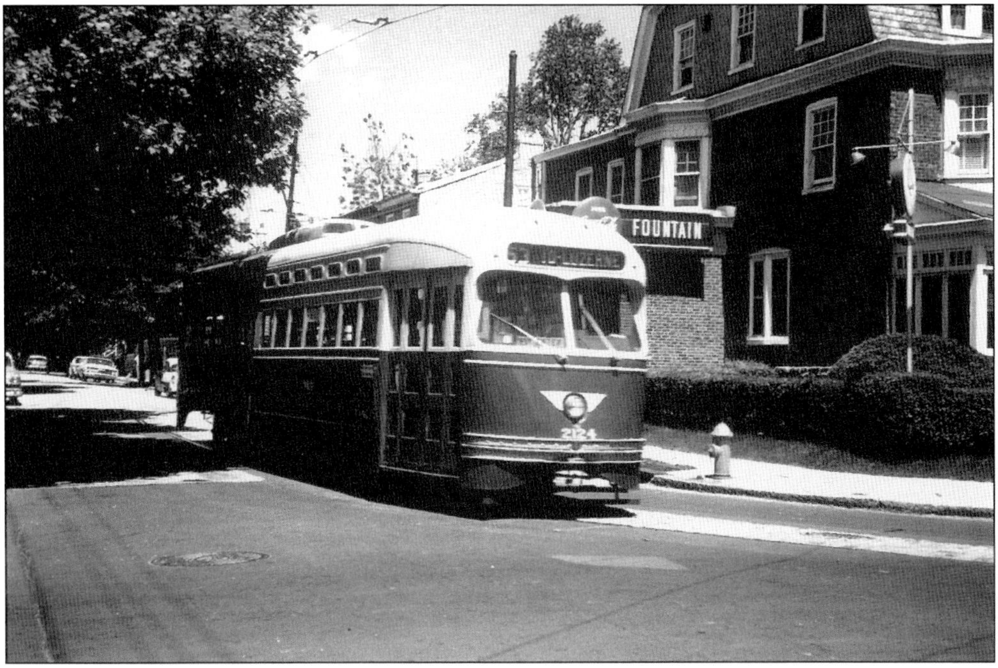

Philadelphia Transportation Company route 53 Presidents' Conference Committee car No. 2124 is on Carpenter Lane at Wayne Avenue on May 30, 1961. This car, built by the St. Louis Car Company in 1948, had an overhaul completed by the Southeastern Pennsylvania Transportation Authority on August 29, 1980. It was acquired by San Francisco Municipal Railway during 1992 and refurbished as No. 1058. (Photograph by Kenneth C. Springirth.)

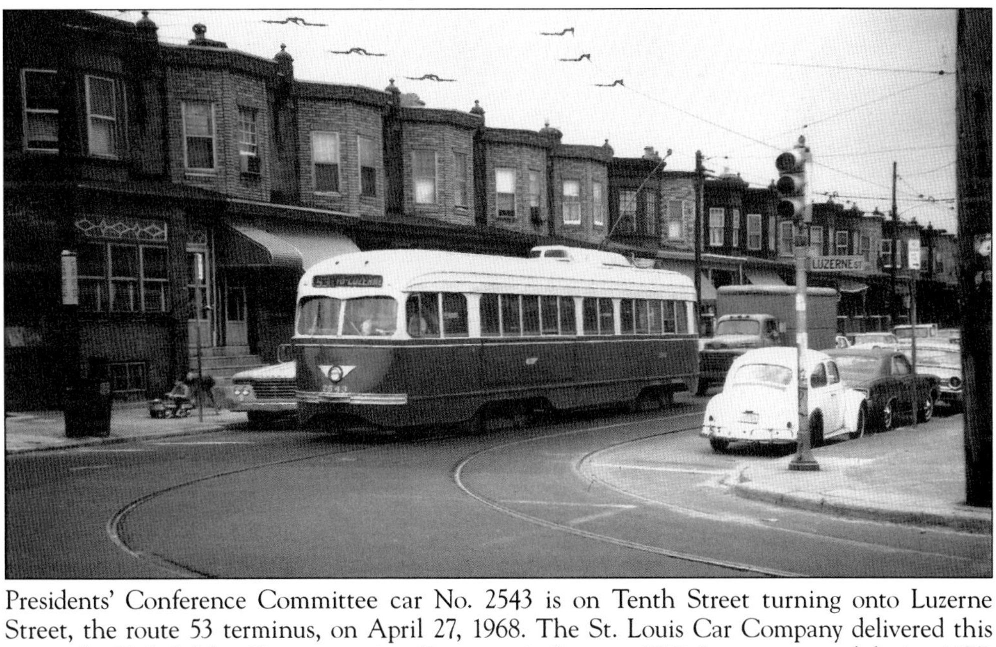

Presidents' Conference Committee car No. 2543 is on Tenth Street turning onto Luzerne Street, the route 53 terminus, on April 27, 1968. The St. Louis Car Company delivered this car to the Philadelphia Transportation Company in January 1941. It was scrapped during 1977. Philadelphia's first Presidents' Conference Committee cars were placed in service on route 53 on August 14, 1938. (Photograph by Kenneth C. Springirth.)

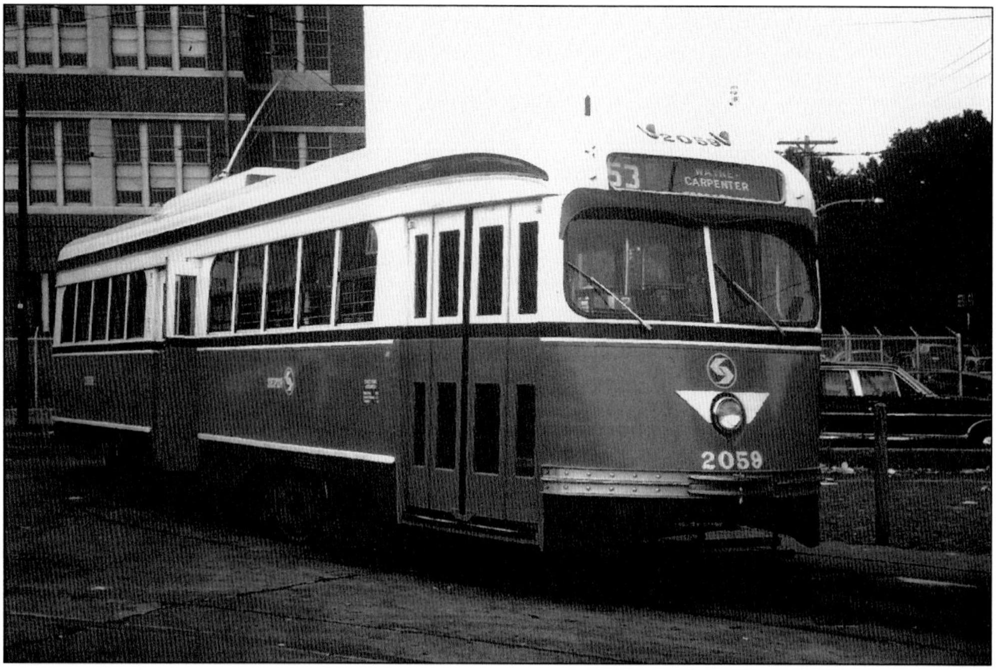

Southeastern Pennsylvania Transportation Authority route 53 Presidents' Conference Committee car No. 2059 is at the Tenth and Luzerne Streets loop at Luzerne Depot on August 1, 1975. The St. Louis Car Company delivered this car to the Philadelphia Transportation Company in February 1941. It was scrapped during 1982. (Photograph by Kenneth C. Springirth.)

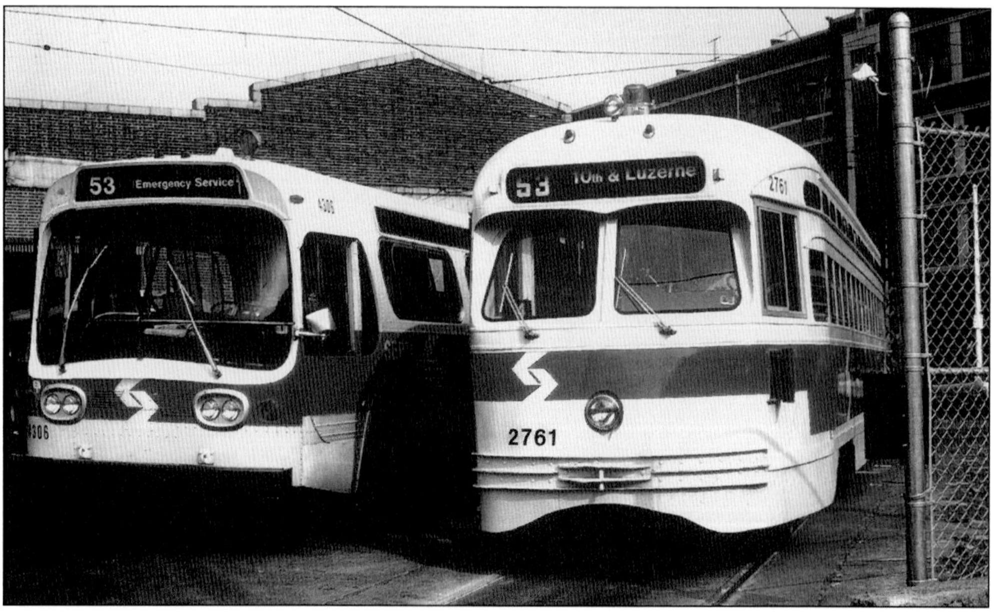

Presidents' Conference Committee car No. 2761, built by the St. Louis Car Company in 1947, and model T6H5306A bus No. 4306, built by General Motors in 1969, are at the Tenth and Luzerne Streets loop of Southeastern Pennsylvania Transportation Authority route 53 on August 7, 1984. Buses were used in emergencies to maintain service on trolley car lines. (Photograph by Kenneth C. Springirth.)

ROUTE 23

GERMANTOWN AVE.–11TH–12TH STS.

LATE-AT-NIGHT SCHEDULE

SOUTHBOUND

FROM GERMANTOWN AVE. & BETHLEHEM PIKE TO 10TH & BIGLER STS.

WEEKDAYS	SATURDAYS		SUNDAYS*
AM	AM	AM	AM
4.24	4.25	2.29	4.26
4.41	4.45	3.00	4.43
4.58	5.01	3.31	4.58
5.11	5.17	4.02	5.14
5.23	5.33		5.29
★	5.49		5.43
PM	6.02		★
11.40	6.16		PM
11.49	6.29		11.49
11.58	6.42		11.58
12.18	★		12.18
12.39	PM		12.39
1.00	11.57		1.00
1.27	12.18		1.27
1.58	12.39		1.58
2.29	1.00		2.29
3.00	1.27		3.00
3.31	1.58		3.31
4.02			4.02
AM	AM	AM	AM

★MAXIMUM INTERVALS—12 MIN.

AVERAGE RUNNING TIME—SOUTHBOUND

From Bethlehem Pike (Loop):

To Germantown & Mermaid	4 Min.
" Germantown & Westview	8 "
" Germantown & Windrim	18 "
" Germantown & Cambria	28 "
" 12th & Ridge	40 "
" 12th & Wharton	51 "
" 10th & Bigler	58 "

*Schedules similar to the Sunday schedule are operated on the following holidays: New Year's, Memorial, Independence, Labor, Thanksgiving and Christmas days.

SUBJECT TO CHANGE

9-3-61 (For Northbound Schedule see other side)

PHILADELPHIA TRANSPORTATION COMPANY

2353 2356 1649

ROUTE 47

GODFREY-8TH-9TH

NORTHBOUND

FROM 8TH & WOLF STS. TO 5TH ST. & GODFREY AVE.

WEEKDAY	SATURDAY	SUNDAY
AM	AM	AM
5.00	5.01	5.26
5.15	5.18	5.46
5.26	5.35	6.06
★	5.50	6.26
AM	6.05	6.46
1.25	6.20	7.06
1.40	★	7.21
1.56	AM	7.36
2.26	1.25	7.51
2.56	1.40	8.06
3.26	1.56	8.20
3.56	2.26	★
4.26	2.56	AM
4.46	3.26	1.20
	3.56	1.37
	4.26	1.55
	4.56	2.25
		2.55
		3.25
		3.55
		4.25
		4.45
AM	AM	AM

★MAXIMUM INTERVALS 15 MIN.

AVERAGE RUNNING TIME—NORTHBOUND

From 8th & Wolf

To 9th & Pine	8 Min.
" 8th & Spring Garden	16 "
" 5th & Erie	34 "
" 5th & Godfrey	46 "

Schedules similar to the Sunday schedule are operated on the following holidays: New Year's, Memorial, Independence, Labor, Thanksgiving and Christmas days.

SUBJECT TO CHANGE

1-22-61 (For Southbound Schedule see other side)

PHILADELPHIA TRANSPORTATION COMPANY

1838 1958 1984

ROUTE 50

LAWNDALE-4TH-5TH

SOUTHBOUND

FROM RISING SUN & OLNEY AVES. TO 6TH ST. & OREGON AVE.

WEEKDAY	SATURDAY	SUNDAY	
AM	AM	AM	PM
B4.34	4.58	5.14	11.18
AB5.04	5.08	5.34	11.33
AB5.19	5.18	5.54	11.48
AB5.33	★	6.14	12.03
★	AM	6.34	12.23
AM	12.10	6.47	12.43
12.11	12.24	★	1.04
12.24	12.41	PM	1.49
12.41	1.04	9.49	2.35
1.04	1.49	10.03	3.20
1.49	2.34	10.18	4.06
2.34	3.20	10.33	4.50
3.20	4.06	10.48	
4.06	4.50	11.03	
4.49			
AM	AM	PM	AM

★MAXIMUM INTERVALS 15 MIN.

AFrom Lawndale "Loop" 6 min. earlier.
BTo 4th & Ritner Sts.

AVERAGE RUNNING TIME—SOUTHBOUND

From Rising Sun & Knorr

To Rising Sun & Olney	6 Min.
" 5th & Wyoming	12 "
" 6th & Erie	17 "
" 4th & Girard	29 "
" 4th & Arch	34 "
" 6th & Oregon	48 "

To 4th & Ritner from 4.34 A.M. to 8.24 A.M. and 2.12 P.M. to 6.04 P. M. weekdays only.

Schedules similar to the Sunday schedule are operated on the following holidays: New Year's, Memorial, Independence, Labor, Thanksgiving and Christmas days.

SUBJECT TO CHANGE

1-22-61 (For Northbound Schedule see other side)

PHILADELPHIA TRANSPORTATION COMPANY

ROUTE 53

WAYNE AVE.—ERIE AVE.

LATE-AT-NIGHT SCHEDULE

SOUTHBOUND

FROM WAYNE AVE. & CARPENTER ST. TO 10TH & LUZERNE STS.

WEEKDAYS	SATURDAYS	SUNDAYS*	
AM	AM	AM	AM
5.41	5.40	5.40	1.27
5.56	5.55	5.56	2.12
6.08	6.08	6.15	2.57
6.21	6.20	6.31	3.42
★	★	6.46	4.27
AM	AM	7.01	5.12
12.02	12.00	7.14	
12.15	12.14	★	
12.31	12.31	PM	
12.51	12.51	11.17	
1.27	1.27	11.31	
2.12	2.12	11.46	
2.57	2.57	12.01	
3.42	3.42	12.16	
4.27	4.27	12.31	
5.13	5.12	12.50	
AM	AM	AM	AM

★MAXIMUM INTERVALS—15 MIN.

AVERAGE RUNNING TIME—SOUTHBOUND

From Wayne & Carpenter:

To Wayne & Manheim	8 Min.
" 10th & Luzerne	20 "

*Schedules similar to the Sunday schedule are operated on the following holidays: New Year's, Memorial, Independence, Labor, Thanksgiving and Christmas days.

SUBJECT TO CHANGE

1-22-62 (For Northbound Schedule see other side)

PHILADELPHIA TRANSPORTATION COMPANY

2553 2136 2443

ROUTE 56

ERIE AVE.-TORRESDALE AVE.

WESTBOUND

FROM TORRESDALE & COTTMAN AVES. TO 23RD & VENANGO STS.

WEEKDAY	SATURDAY	SUNDAY	
AM	AM	AM	AM
5.21	5.20	5.34	12.31
5.31	5.35	5.53	12.47
5.40	5.47	6.14	1.03
★	★	6.33	1.22
AM	AM	6.51	1.40
1.01	12.57	7.10	2.05
1.15	1.08	7.28	2.35
1.30	1.20	7.43	3.05
1.45	1.35	7.58	3.35
2.05	1.50	8.13	4.05
2.35	2.05	8.28	4.35
3.05	2.35	8.43	5.05
3.35	3.05	8.58	
4.05	3.35	9.13	
4.35	4.05	9.28	
5.05	4.35	★	
	5.05		
AM	AM	AM	AM

★MAXIMUM INTERVALS 15 MIN.

AVERAGE RUNNING TIME—WESTBOUND

From Torresdale & Cottman

To Kensington & Erie	15 Min.
" Front & Erie	22 "
" 10th & Erie	27 "
" 23rd & Venango	35 "

Schedules similar to the Sunday schedule are operated on the following holidays: New Year's, Memorial, Independence, Labor, Thanksgiving and Christmas days.

SUBJECT TO CHANGE

1-22-61 (For Eastbound Schedule see other side)

PHILADELPHIA TRANSPORTATION COMPANY

1862 1978 1943

ROUTE 60

ALLEGHENY AVE.

EASTBOUND

FROM 35TH ST. & ALLEGHENY AVE. TO RICHMOND & WESTMORELAND STS.

WEEKDAY	SATURDAY	SUNDAY	
AM	AM	AM	AM
5.25	5.31	5.36	10.54
5.39	5.44	5.52	11.10
5.49	5.57	6.07	11.25
★	★	6.22	11.40
AM	AM	6.37	★
12.48	12.48	6.52	AM
1.06	1.06	7.07	12.04
1.24	1.24	7.22	12.18
1.42	1.42	7.37	12.32
2.12	2.12	7.53	12.48
2.42	2.42	8.08	1.12
3.12	3.12	8.23	1.42
3.42	3.42	8.38	2.12
4.12	4.12	8.53	2.42
4.42	4.42	9.08	3.12
5.12	5.12	9.23	3.42
		9.38	4.12
		9.54	4.42
		10.09	5.12
		10.24	
		10.39	
AM	AM	AM	AM

★MAXIMUM INTERVALS 15 MIN.

AVERAGE RUNNING TIME—EASTBOUND

From 35th & Allegheny

To 22nd & Allegheny	5 Min.
" 5th & Allegheny	14 "
" Kensington & Allegheny	21 "
" Richmond & Westmoreland	28 "

Schedules similar to the Sunday schedule are operated on the following holidays: New Year's, Memorial, Independence, Labor, Thanksgiving and Christmas days.

SUBJECT TO CHANGE

1-22-61 (For Westbound Schedule see other side)

PHILADELPHIA TRANSPORTATION COMPANY

1709 1651 1484

In the 1961 to 1962 time period, Philadelphia Transportation Company trolley car schedules for routes 23, 47, 50, 53, 56, and 60 were mainly used for late-night and early-morning service. Route 23 was the busiest Philadelphia trolley car line, as evidenced by service intervals of 12 minutes or less from early morning to late evening. In the very early morning, route 23 operated every 31 minutes while routes 47, 56, and 60 operated every 30 minutes and routes 50 and 53 operated every 45 minutes.

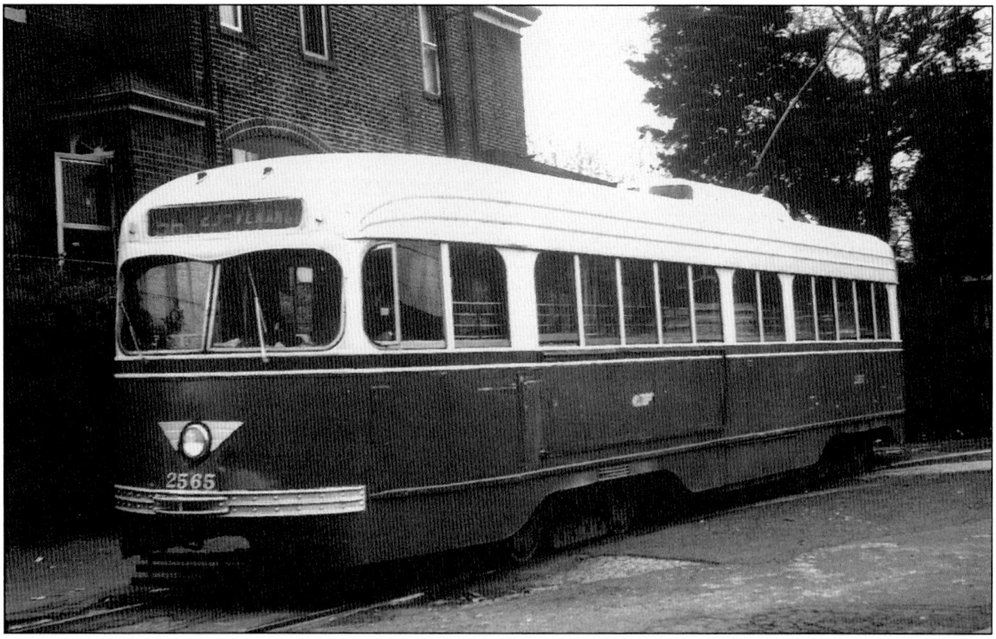

Presidents' Conference Committee car No. 2565 is at the Philadelphia Transportation Company route 56 Torresdale and Cottman Avenues loop on April 27, 1968. This car, built by the St. Louis Car Company in 1941, was scrapped in 1982. In 1941, 50 new Presidents' Conference Committee cars were assigned to route 56. (Photograph by Kenneth C. Springirth.)

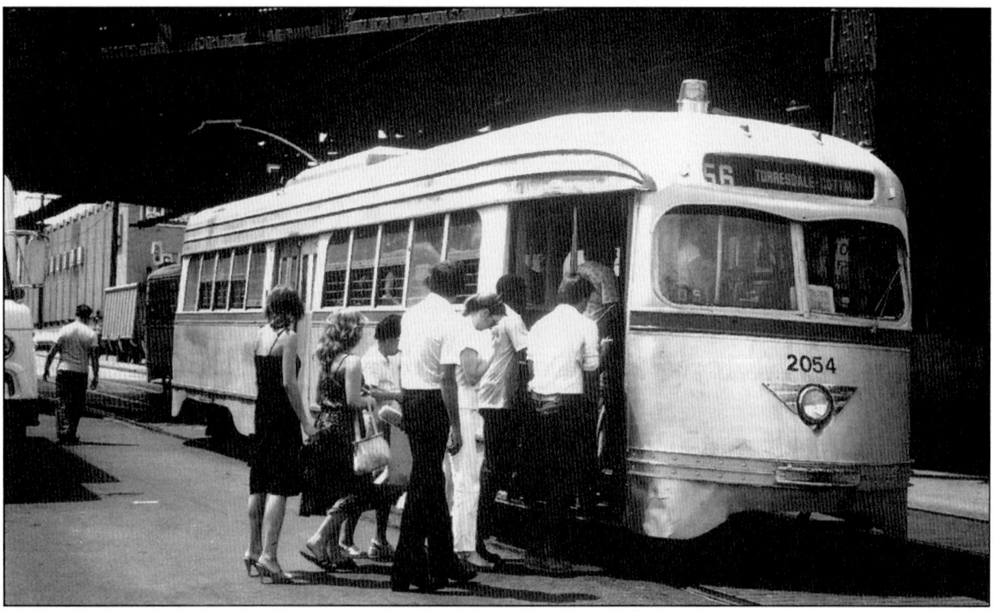

On July 28, 1980, Southeastern Pennsylvania Transportation Authority route 56 Presidents' Conference Committee car No. 2054 is loading passengers on Erie Avenue at Kensington Avenue. The St. Louis Car Company built this car in 1941 for the Philadelphia Transportation Company. This car had been repainted and rededicated at ceremonies at Wayne and Chelten Avenues according to the *Philadelphia Evening Bulletin* newspaper of September 30, 1978. (Photograph by Kenneth C. Springirth.)

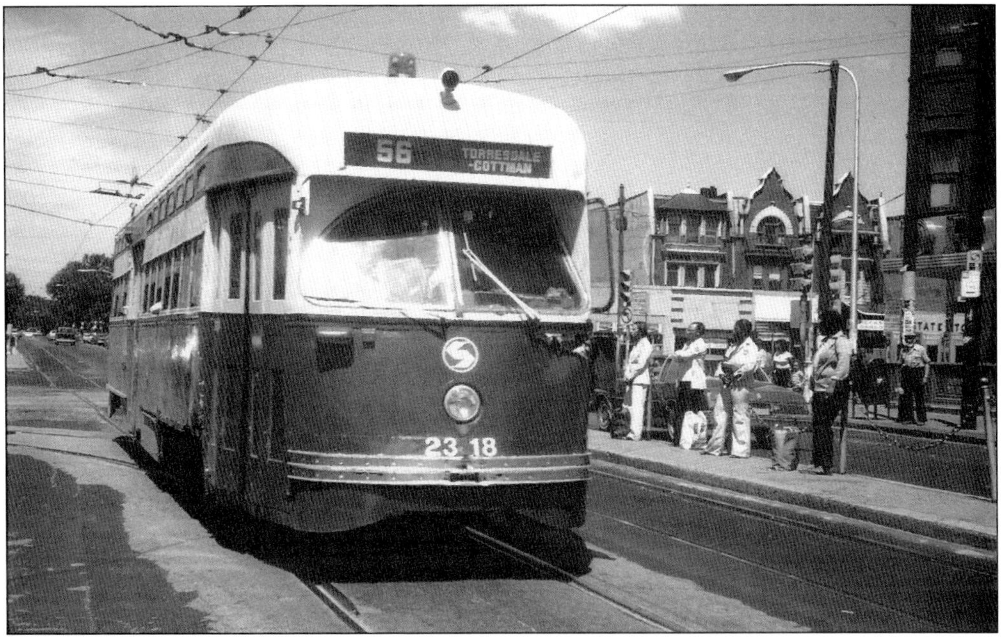

Route 56 Presidents' Conference Committee car No. 2318 is on Erie Avenue at Broad Street on June 21, 1980. Built by the Pullman Standard Company in 1946 for the Birmingham Transit Company as car No. 846, it became Toronto Transit Commission car No. 4746. In 1976, it became Southeastern Pennsylvania Transportation Authority car No. 2318 and was scrapped in September 1981. (Photograph by Kenneth C. Springirth.)

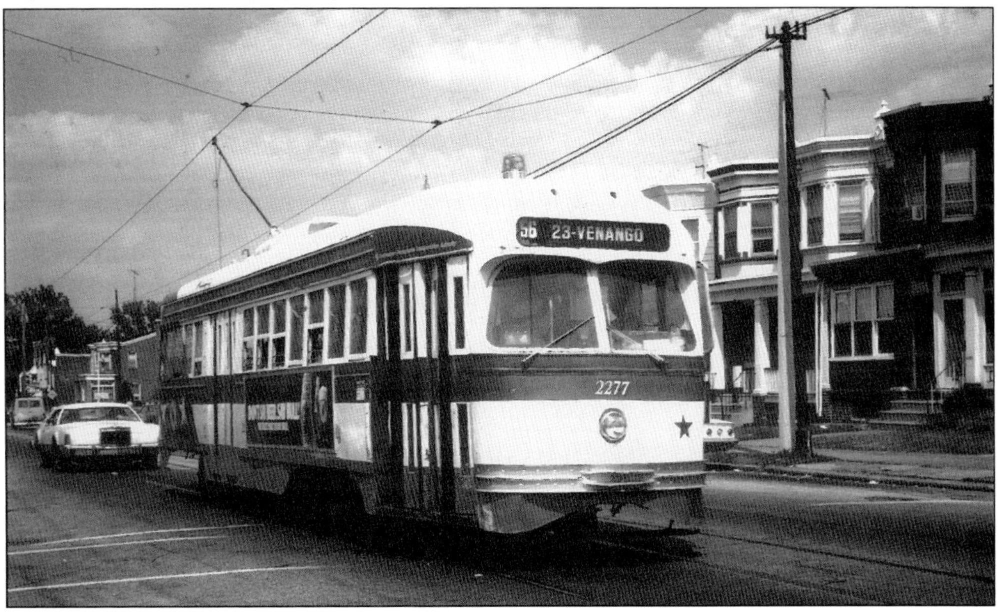

Presidents' Conference Committee car No. 2277 is on route 56 on Torresdale Avenue at Benner Street on June 19, 1980. Built by the St. Louis Car Company in 1946 for the Kansas City Public Service Company as car No. 729, it was sold to the Philadelphia Transportation Company in 1955. The Southeastern Pennsylvania Transportation Authority scrapped it in 1983. (Photograph by Kenneth C. Springirth.)

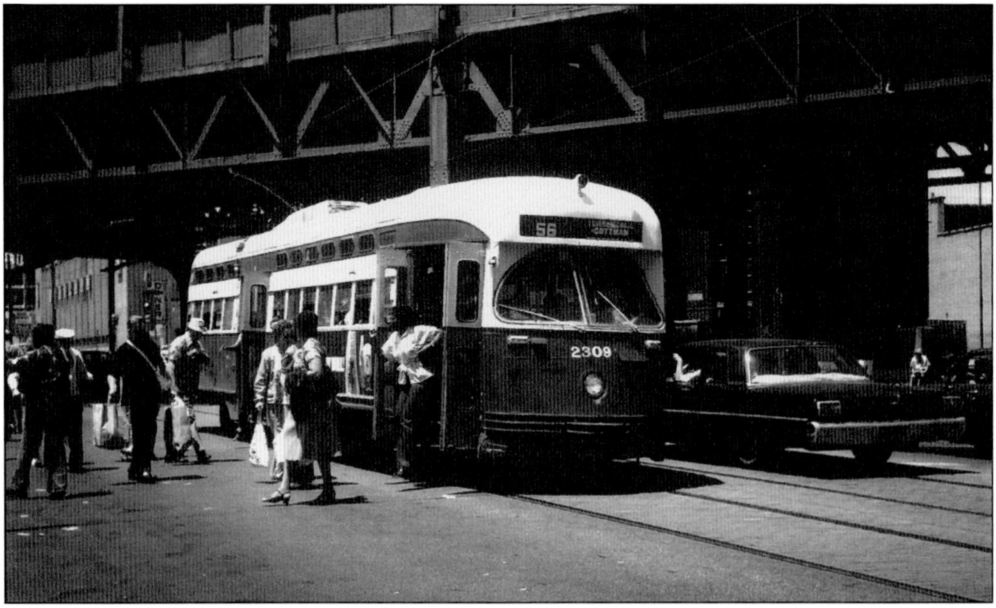

On June 21, 1980, route 56 Presidents' Conference Committee car No. 2309 is on Torresdale Avenue at Kensington Avenue. The Pullman Standard Company built this car in 1946 for the Birmingham Transit Company as car No. 828. It became Toronto Transit Commission car No. 4727. It was acquired by the Southeastern Pennsylvania Transportation Authority in 1976 and was scrapped in August 1981. (Photograph by Kenneth C. Springirth.)

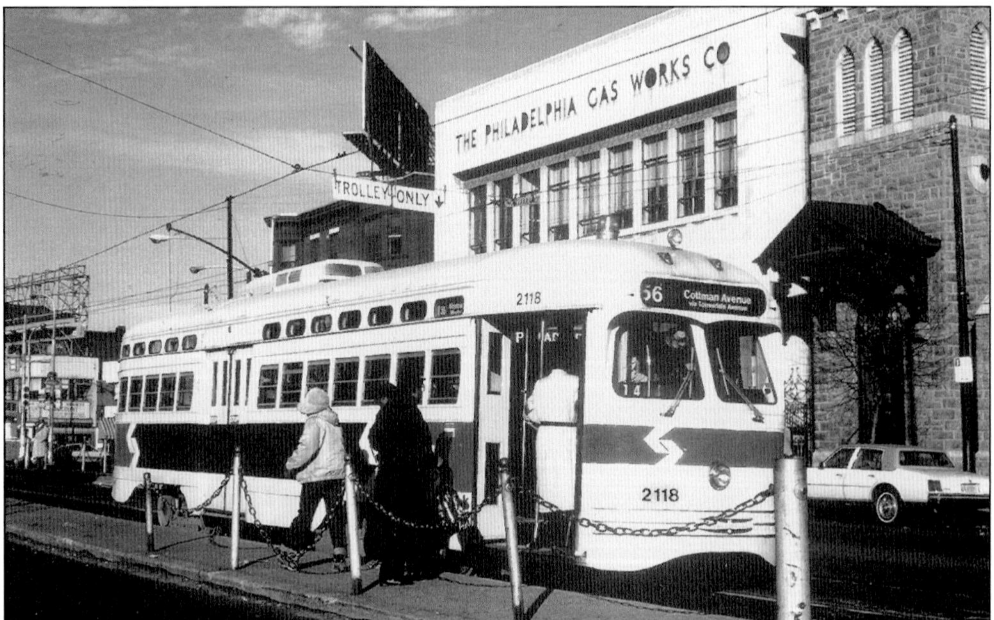

Erie Avenue at Broad Street is the location for route 56 Presidents' Conference Committee car No. 2118 in its attractive white, blue, and red paint scheme on November 23, 1984. Delivered by the St. Louis Car Company in August 1948, this car was overhauled by the Southeastern Pennsylvania Transportation Authority in 1982 and in 2004 was acquired by the Brookville Equipment Company. (Photograph by Kenneth C. Springirth.)

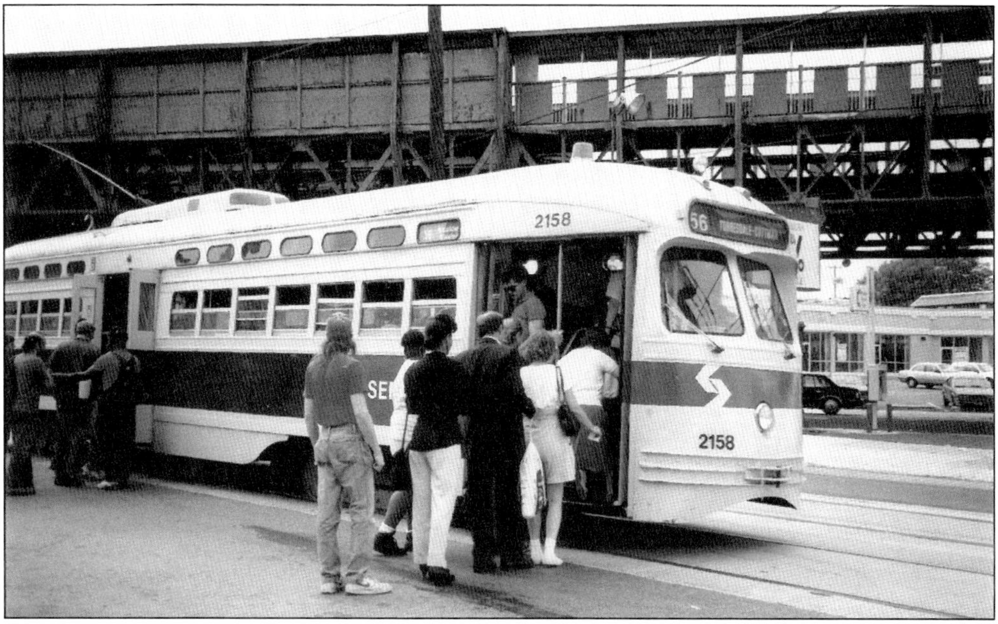

On August 4, 1991, route 56 Presidents' Conference Committee car No. 2158 is loading passengers on Torresdale Avenue at Kensington Avenue. Built by the St. Louis Car Company for the Philadelphia Transportation Company in 1948, it was overhauled by the Southeastern Pennsylvania Transportation Authority in 1984. Rebuilt by the Brookville Equipment Company as car No. 2335, it was delivered on October 19, 2004, for route 15 service. (Photograph by Kenneth C. Springirth.)

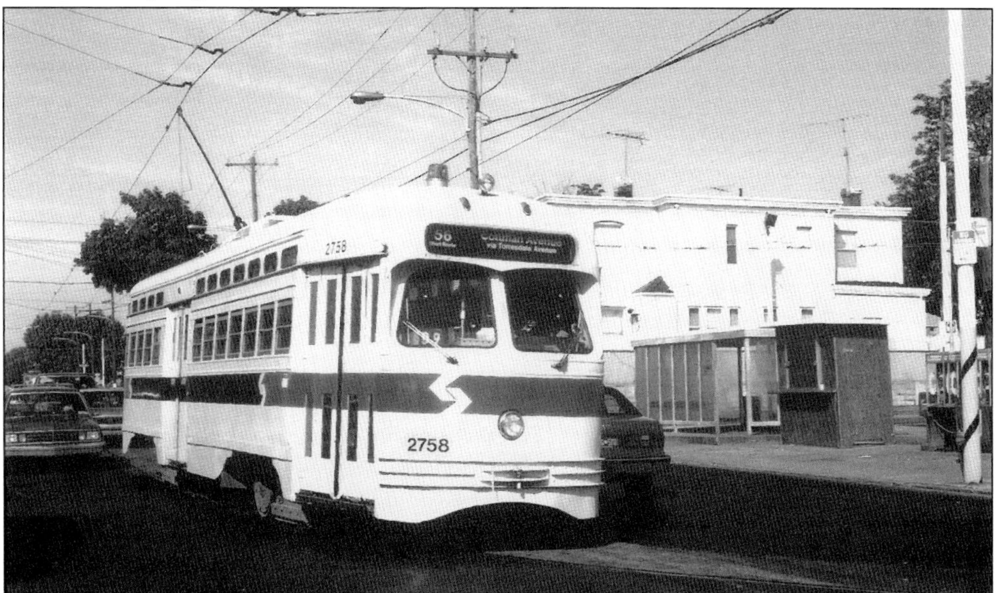

Route 56 Presidents' Conference Committee car No. 2758 is ready to turn from Torresdale Avenue into the loop at Cottman Avenue on May 29, 1992. The Southeastern Pennsylvania Transportation Authority overhauled this car in 1985. It was rebuilt by the Brookville Equipment Company as car No. 2331 and was delivered on July 30, 2004. (Photograph by Kenneth C. Springirth.)

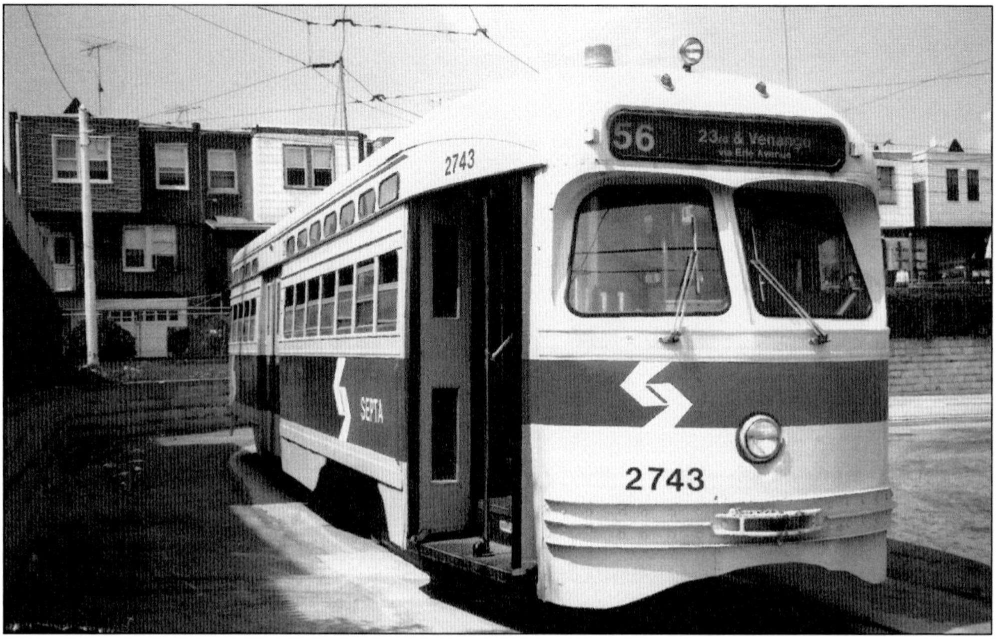

At the route 56 Torresdale and Cottman Avenues loop, Southeastern Pennsylvania Transportation Authority car No. 2743 is awaiting departure time on August 4, 1991. The car was overhauled in 1984 and was in service until 1993. The small windows above the main windows were called standee windows. (Photograph by Kenneth C. Springirth.)

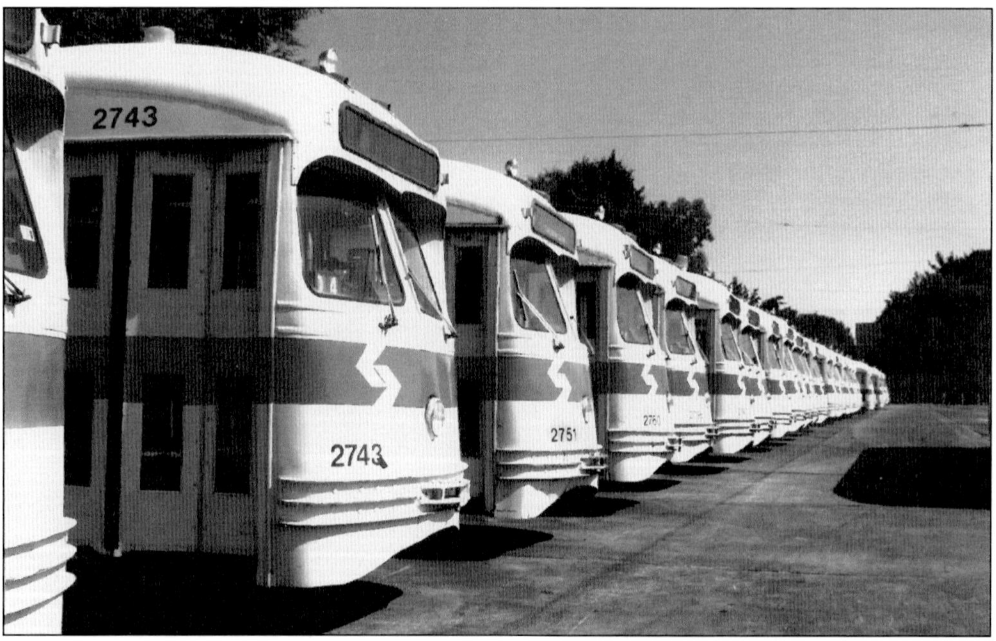

On August 22, 1993, Southeastern Pennsylvania Transportation Authority car No. 2743 is with other cars taken out of service and stored at Germantown Depot. The Rockhill Trolley Museum acquired this car in May 1994. Museum volunteers regauged this car from 5 feet, 2.25 inches to the museum's 4-foot, 8.5-inch track gauge. It was placed in service at the museum in 1998. (Photograph by Kenneth C. Springirth.)

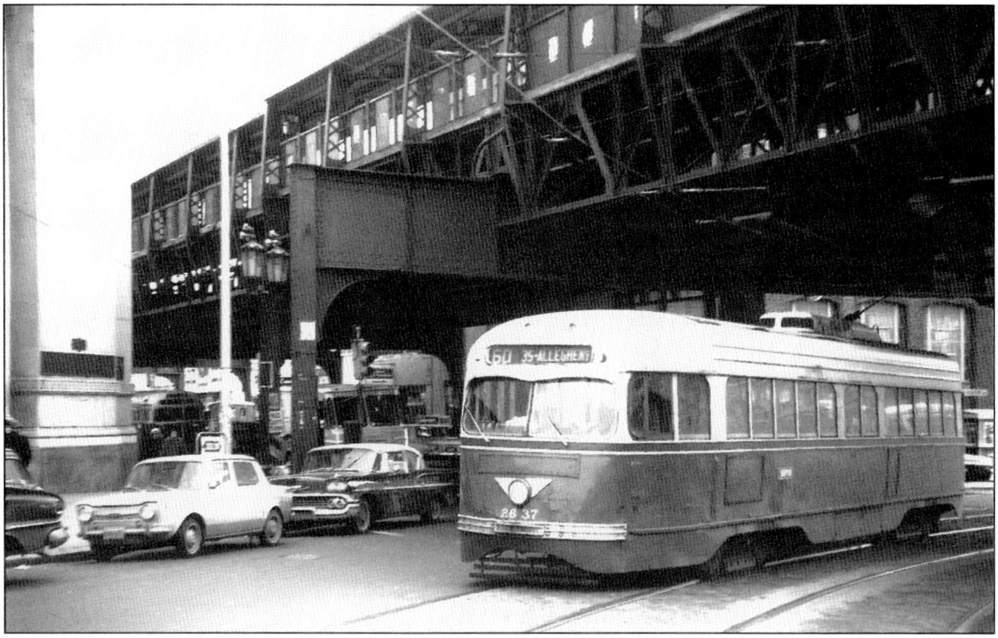

Southeastern Pennsylvania Transportation Authority route 60 Presidents' Conference Committee car No. 2637 is westbound on Allegheny Avenue at Kensington Avenue passing under the Market-Frankford Subway-Elevated Line on February 28, 1969. The Philadelphia Transportation Company received this car from the St. Louis Car Company in July 1942, and it was scrapped in March 1982. (Photograph by Kenneth C. Springirth.)

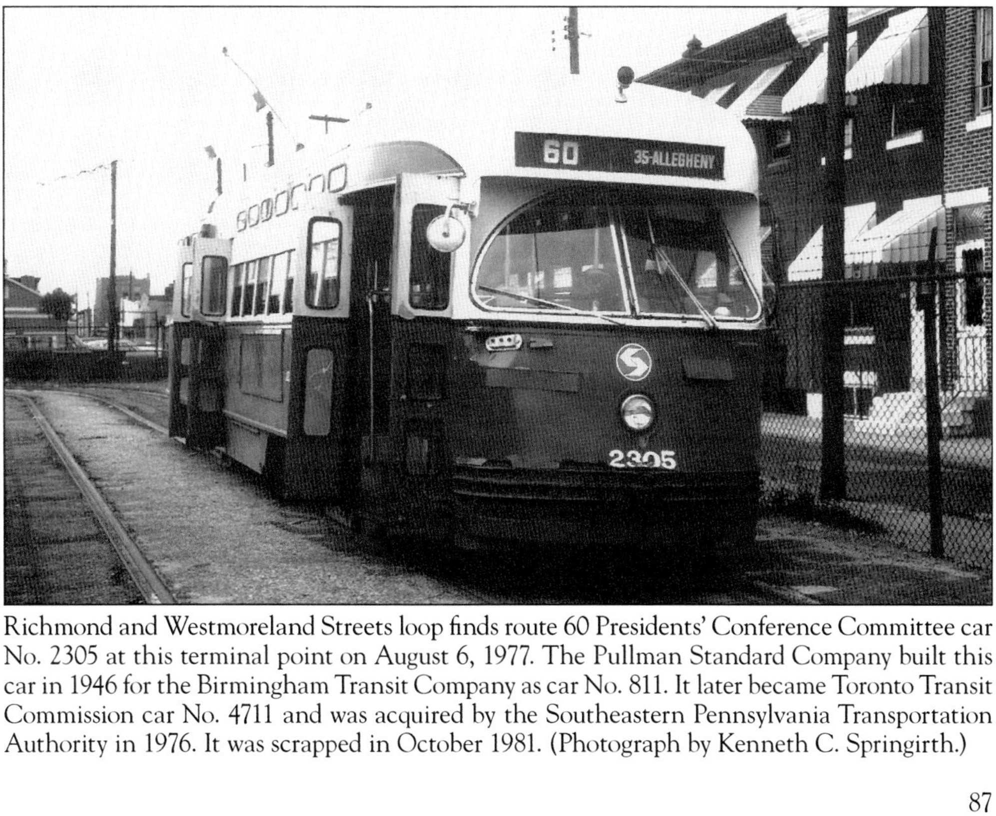

Richmond and Westmoreland Streets loop finds route 60 Presidents' Conference Committee car No. 2305 at this terminal point on August 6, 1977. The Pullman Standard Company built this car in 1946 for the Birmingham Transit Company as car No. 811. It later became Toronto Transit Commission car No. 4711 and was acquired by the Southeastern Pennsylvania Transportation Authority in 1976. It was scrapped in October 1981. (Photograph by Kenneth C. Springirth.)

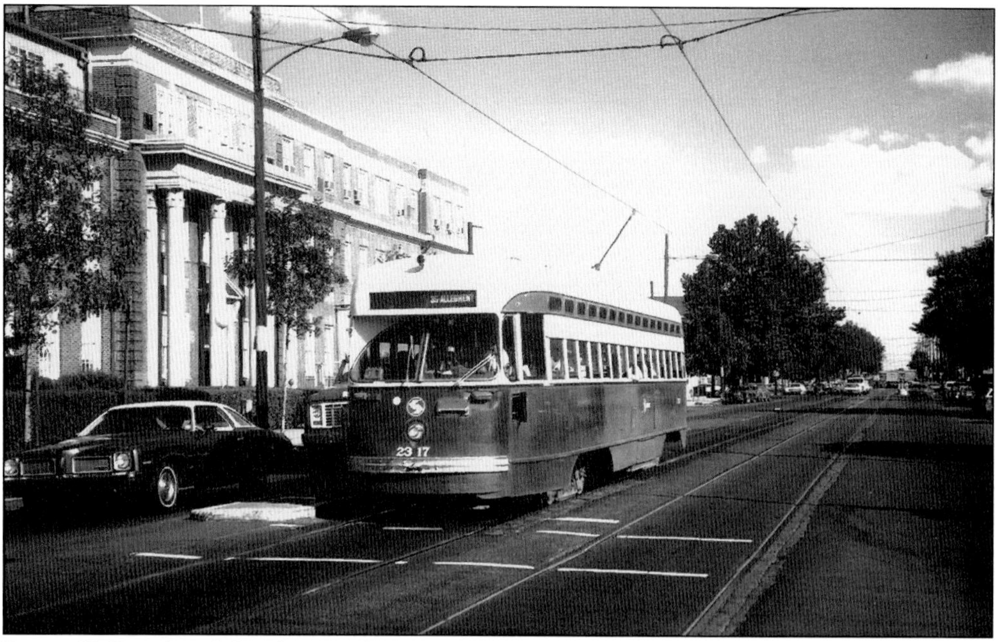

Route 60 Presidents' Conference Committee car No. 2317 is on Allegheny Avenue at Tulip Street on July 29, 1977. The Pullman Standard Company built this car as No. 844 for the Birmingham Transit Company in 1946. It became Toronto Transit Commission car No. 4744 and was delivered to the Southeastern Pennsylvania Transportation Authority in March 1976. It was scrapped in February 1982. (Photograph by Kenneth C. Springirth.)

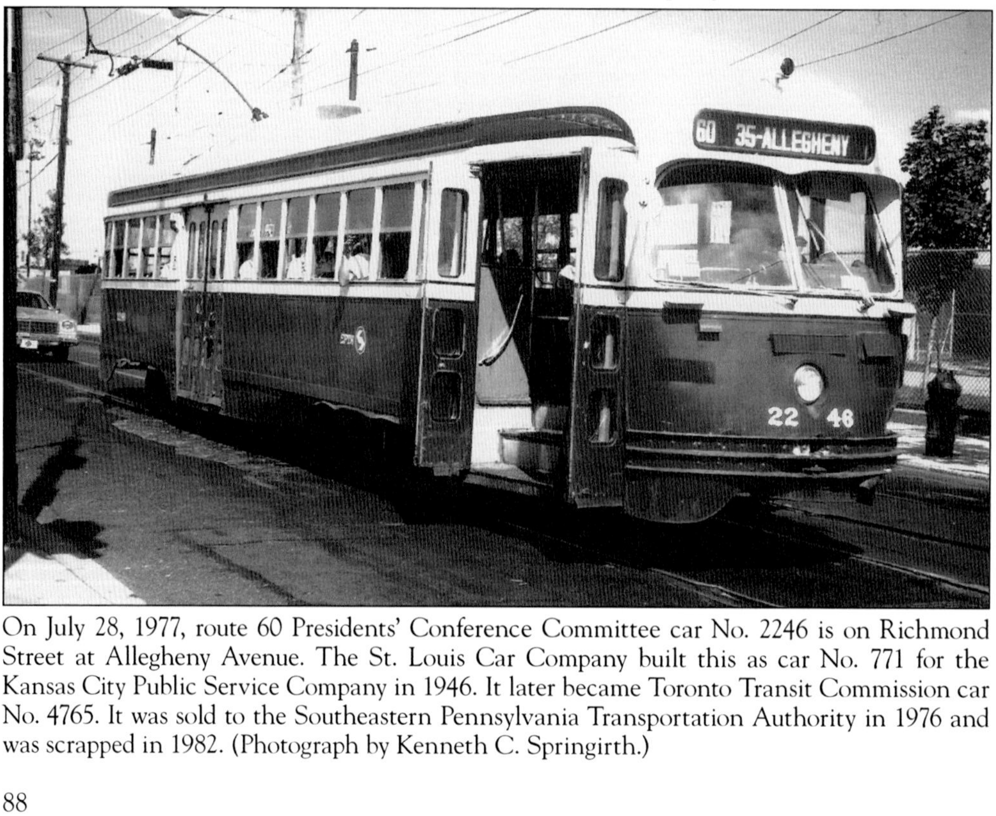

On July 28, 1977, route 60 Presidents' Conference Committee car No. 2246 is on Richmond Street at Allegheny Avenue. The St. Louis Car Company built this as car No. 771 for the Kansas City Public Service Company in 1946. It later became Toronto Transit Commission car No. 4765. It was sold to the Southeastern Pennsylvania Transportation Authority in 1976 and was scrapped in 1982. (Photograph by Kenneth C. Springirth.)

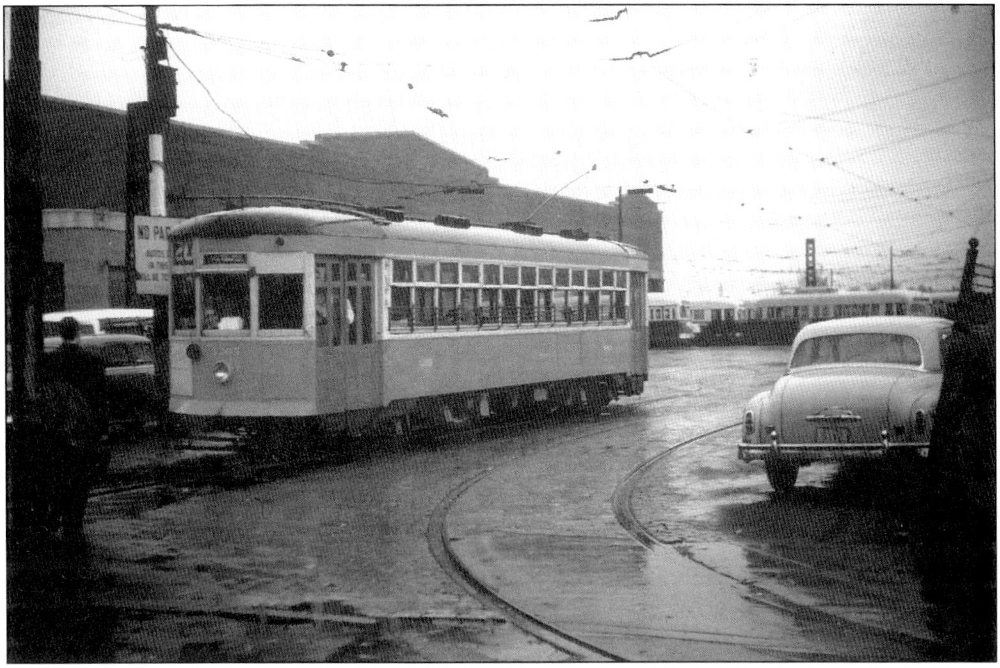

Car No. 5205 is at Luzerne Depot around 1958. This was one of 135 double-end cars, numbered 5200 to 5334, ordered in 1923 from the J. G. Brill Car Company by the Philadelphia Rapid Transit Company. Luzerne Depot, built in 1913, housed 335 trolley cars with space for 115 trolley cars in the outside yard. (Photograph by Craig Knox.)

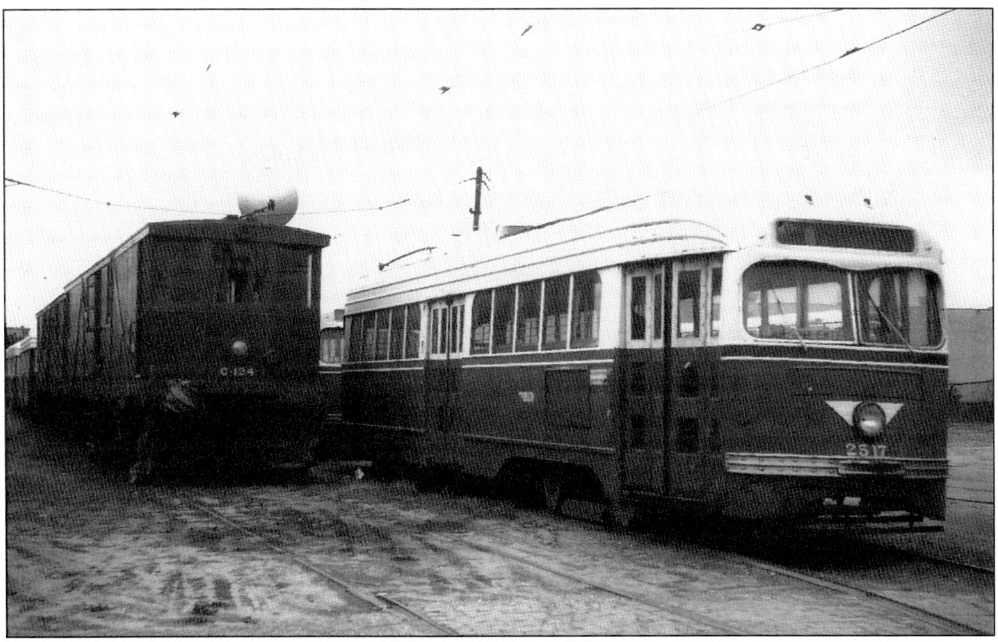

Philadelphia Transportation Company snow sweeper No. C-124 and Presidents' Conference Committee car No. 2517 are at the large outside yard at Luzerne Depot on April 27, 1968. Car No. 2517 was built by the St. Louis Car Company in 1940 and was scrapped in 1970. (Photograph by Kenneth C. Springirth.)

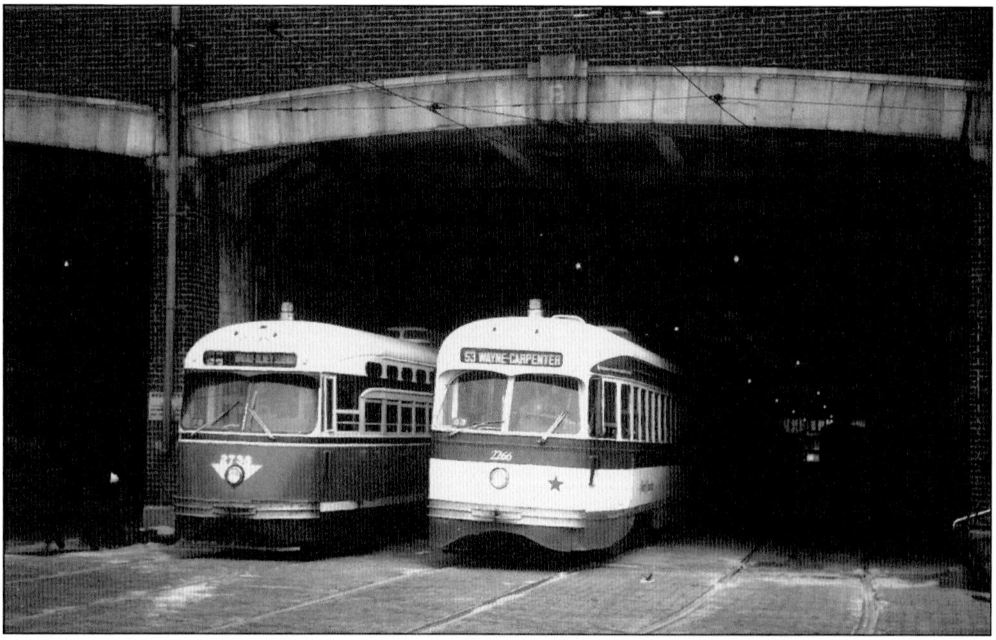

Presidents' Conference Committee cars built by the St. Louis Car Company are at Luzerne Depot on July 22, 1979. Car No. 2738, built in 1947, was overhauled in 1986 and rebuilt by the Brookville Equipment Company as car No. 2321 in 2003. Kansas City Public Service Company car No. 758, built in 1946, became Philadelphia Transportation Company car No. 2266 in 1955 and was scrapped during 1982. (Photograph by Kenneth C. Springirth.)

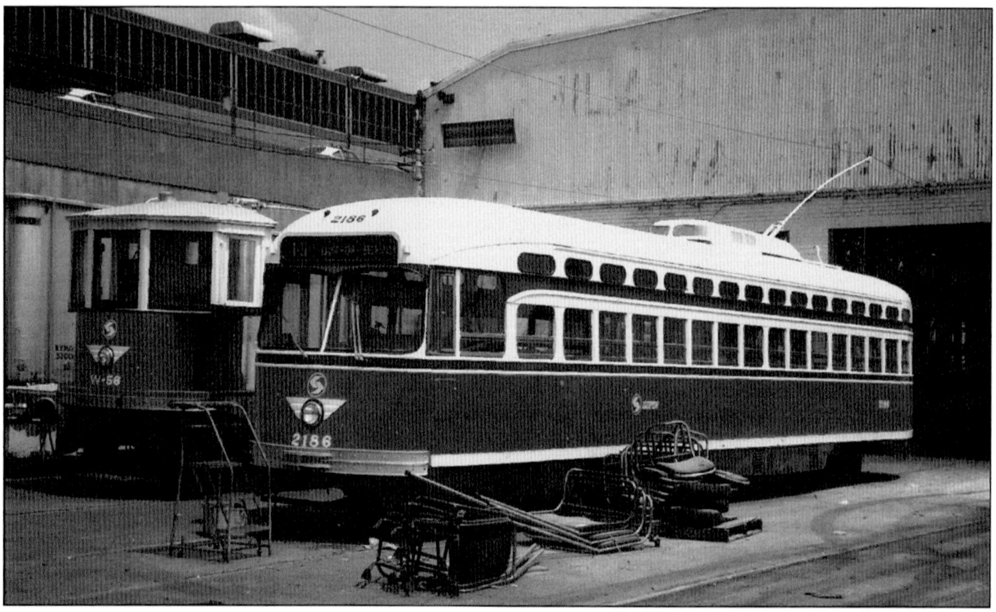

Work car W-56 and Presidents' Conference Committee car No. 2186 are at the Third and Courtland Streets shop on August 1, 1975. Car No. 2186, delivered by the St. Louis Car Company to the Philadelphia Transportation Company in July 1948, was overhauled by Southeastern Pennsylvania Transportation Authority in 1983 and was sold to the Museum of Transportation at St. Louis in November 1994. (Photograph by Kenneth C. Springirth.)

Four

Philadelphia's Subway Surface Trolleys

By 1887, the Lancaster Avenue line, which became route 10, operated from Belmont Avenue and Jefferson Street to Front and Walnut Streets. On December 15, 1906, the line operated into the subway. On June 20, 1926, route 10 was extended to Sixty-third Street and Malvern Avenue. Prior to 1887, the Darby line, which became route 11, operated from Forty-ninth Street and Woodland Avenue to Ninth and Main Streets in Darby. On December 15, 1906, route 11 operated into the subway.

On June 1, 1907, route 13 began operation as an extension of the Chestnut Street line operating from Ninth and Main Streets in Darby to Sixty-fifth Street and Kingsessing Avenue. On May 25, 1913, the two lines were consolidated operating from Ninth and Main Streets to Front and Chestnut Streets. On September 9, 1956, route 13 was rerouted into the subway.

Prior to 1890, the Baltimore Avenue line, which became route 34, operated from Twenty-fifth and South Streets to Fortieth Street and Baltimore Avenue. In 1896, route 34 was rerouted to operate from Sixty-first Street and Baltimore Avenue to Chestnut and Front Streets. On December 15, 1906, route 34 operated into the subway. On August 3, 1908, routes 10 and 11 began serving the Juniper Street subway station followed by route 34 on August 24, 1908. On October 17, 1955, eastbound service on route 10 entered the new extended subway at Thirty-sixth Street just south of Market Street, while eastbound service on routes 11 and 34 entered the new extended subway at Fortieth Street between Baltimore and Woodland Avenues. Westbound service on routes 10, 11, and 34 used the new extended subway beginning on November 7, 1955.

Route 36 was established on March 15, 1904, from Island Road and Elmwood Avenue to Paschall and Grays Ferry Avenues. On May 18, 1905, route 36 was extended to Ninth and Arch Streets. Route 36 was changed on November 6, 1955, to operate from Westinghouse Loop via Eastwick Avenue, Island Road, and Elmwood Avenue to the subway at Fortieth Street. On September 9, 1956, route 36 was cut back from Westinghouse Loop to Ninety-fourth Street and Eastwick Avenue, with a cutback to Eighty-eighth Street and Eastwick Avenue on August 15, 1962, and a cutback to Eightieth Street and Eastwick Avenue on May 9, 1975.

ROUTE 10

LANCASTER AVE.

LATE-AT-NIGHT SCHEDULE

EASTBOUND

FROM 63RD ST. & MALVERN AVE.
TO JUNIPER ST. STATION

WEEKDAYS		SATURDAYS	SUNDAYS*
AM	AM	AM	AM
4.48	Thur.	4.52	4.52
5.07	Oper-	5.07	5.12
5.20	ates to	5.22	5.29
★	40th &	5.37	5.45
PM	Filbert	★	★
11.18	Sts.	PM	PM
11.31		11.26	11.17
11.44		11.44	11.33
12.01		12.01	11.48
12.27		12.27	12.03
12.57		12.57	12.27
1.27	1.29	1.27	12.57
1.57	1.59	1.57	1.27
2.27	2.29	2.27	1.57
2.57	2.59	2.57	2.27
3.27	3.29	3.27	2.57
3.57	3.59	3.57	3.27
4.27	4.29	4.27	3.57
			4.27
AM	AM	AM	AM

★MAXIMUM INTERVALS 15 MIN.

AVERAGE RUNNING TIME—EASTBOUND

From 63rd & Malvern		Thur. AM
To 60th & Lansdowne	4 Min.	4 Min.
" Lancaster & Girard	10 "	10 "
" 40th & Filbert	—	18 "
" 36th St. Portal	19 "	—
" Juniper Station	28 "	—

*Schedules similar to the Sunday schedule are operated on the following holidays: New Year's, Memorial, Independence, Labor, Thanksgiving and Christmas days.

SUBJECT TO CHANGE

9-3-61 (For Westbound Schedule see other side)

PHILADELPHIA TRANSPORTATION COMPANY

2344-5 2386 2290

ROUTE 11

WOODLAND AVE.

LATE-AT-NIGHT SCHEDULE

EASTBOUND

FROM 9TH & MAIN STS. (DARBY)
TO JUNIPER ST. STATION

WEEKDAYS		SATURDAYS	SUNDAYS*	
AM	AM	AM	AM	AM
5.14	Thur.	5.14	5.14	12.44
5.26	Oper-	5.27	5.26	12.59
5.36	ates	5.36	5.58	1.27
★	To	★	6.14	1.54
AM	40th &	AM	6.30	2.25
12.08	Mar-	12.21	6.46	2.55
12.21	ket	12.32	7.02	3.25
12.37	Sts.	12.44	7.18	3.54
12.59		12.59	7.34	4.24
1.27	1.21	1.27	7.50	4.52
1.54	1.51	1.54	8.06	
2.25	2.21	2.25	8.22	
2.55	2.51	2.55	★	
3.25	3.21	3.25	PM	
3.54	3.51	3.54	11.59	
4.24	4.21	4.24	12.14	
4.52	4.52	4.52	12.29	
AM	AM	AM	AM	AM

★MAXIMUM INTERVALS—13 MIN.

AVERAGE RUNNING TIME—EASTBOUND

From 9th & Main		Thur. AM
To 49th & Woodland	15 Min.	15 Min.
" 42nd & Baltimore	—	19 "
" 40th St. Portal	19 "	—
" 40th & Market	—	23 "
" Juniper Station	29 "	—

*Schedules similar to the Sunday schedule are operated on the following holidays: New Year's, Memorial, Independence, Labor, Thanksgiving and Christmas days.

SUBJECT TO CHANGE

1-22-62 (For Westbound Schedule see other side)

PHILADELPHIA TRANSPORTATION COMPANY

2370-1-2 2556 2306

ROUTE 13

CHESTER AVE.

LATE-AT-NIGHT SCHEDULE

EASTBOUND

FROM YEADON LOOP
TO JUNIPER ST. STATION

WEEKDAYS		SATURDAYS	SUNDAYS*
AM	AM	AM	AM
4.59	Thur.	4.59	4.59
5.15	Oper-	5.15	5.29
5.30	ates	5.30	5.58
★	To	★	6.13
PM	40th &	PM	6.28
11.57	Mar-	11.36	6.43
12.09	ket	11.51	★
12.21	Sts.	12.07	AM
12.33		12.25	12.14
12.48		12.44	12.29
12.59		12.59	12.44
1.29	1.27	1.29	12.59
1.59	1.56	1.59	1.29
2.29	2.26	2.29	1.59
2.59	2.56	2.59	2.29
3.29	3.26	3.29	2.59
3.59	3.56	3.59	3.29
4.29	4.26	4.29	4.29
AM	AM	AM	AM

★MAXIMUM INTERVALS—15 MIN.

AVERAGE RUNNING TIME—EASTBOUND

From Yeadon Loop:		Thur. AM
To Mt. Moriah Loop	4 Min.	4 Min.
" 49th & Chester	10 "	10 "
" 40th St. Portal	14 "	—
" 40th & Market	—	21 "
" Juniper Station	24 "	—

*Schedules similar to the Sunday schedule are operated on the following holidays: New Year's, Memorial, Independence, Labor, Thanksgiving and Christmas days.

SUBJECT TO CHANGE

9-3-61 (For Westbound Schedule see other side)

PHILADELPHIA TRANSPORTATION COMPANY

2373-4 1938 2307

ROUTE 15

GIRARD AVE.

LATE-AT-NIGHT SCHEDULE

EASTBOUND

FROM 63RD ST. & GIRARD AVE.
TO RICHMOND & WESTMORELAND STS.

WEEKDAY	SATURDAY	SUNDAY
AM	AM	AM
4.00	A4.02	4.10
A4.14	4.15	4.30
4.24	A4.32	4.50
4.36	4.44	5.09
4.47	4.58	5.28
5.07	5.11	5.47
5.22	5.25	6.06
★	★	6.21
PM	PM	6.34
11.56	11.55	★
12.06	12.05	PM
12.17	12.15	11.55
12.29	12.29	12.10
12.43	12.43	12.25
12.57	12.57	12.42
1.12	1.12	1.12
1.42	1.42	1.42
2.12	2.12	2.12
2.42	2.42	2.42
3.12	3.12	3.12
3.42	3.42	3.42
AM	AM	AM

★MAXIMUM INTERVALS—15 MIN.

From 59th & Girard.

AVERAGE RUNNING TIME—EASTBOUND

From 63rd & Girard:	
To 59th & Girard	2 Min.
" 40th & Girard	10 "
" Ridge & Girard	21 "
" Front & Girard	31 "
" Richmond & Westmoreland	42 "

Schedules similar to the Sunday schedule are operated on the following holidays: New Year's, Memorial, Independence, Labor, Thanksgiving and Christmas days.

SUBJECT TO CHANGE

27-61 (For Westbound Schedule see other side)

PHILADELPHIA TRANSPORTATION COMPANY

1687 1684 1949

ROUTE 34

BALTIMORE AVE.

EASTBOUND

FROM 61ST ST. & BALTIMORE AVE.
TO JUNIPER ST. STATION

WEEKDAY		SATURDAY	SUNDAY	
AM	Thur.	AM	AM	AM
4.52	AM	4.56	4.56	3.01
5.12	Oper-	5.14	5.26	3.31
5.27	ates	5.30	5.56	4.01
5.42	To	5.45	6.14	4.31
5.55	40th &	6.00	6.30	
★	Market	★	6.46	
AM	1.30	AM	7.02	
12.20	2.00	12.18	7.17	
12.33	2.30	12.31	7.35	
12.46	3.00	12.46	7.51	
1.01	3.30	1.01	8.07	
1.31	4.00	1.31	8.23	
2.01	4.30	2.01	8.39	
2.31		2.31	8.56	
3.01		3.01	★	
3.31		3.31	AM	
4.01		4.01	12.16	
4.31		4.31	12.31	
			12.46	
			1.01	
			1.31	
			2.01	
			2.31	
AM	AM	AM	AM	AM

★MAXIMUM INTERVALS 15 MIN.

AVERAGE RUNNING TIME—EASTBOUND

From 61st & Baltimore		Thur. AM
To 49th & Baltimore	7 Min.	7 Min.
" 42nd & Baltimore	11 "	11 "
" 40th St. Portal	12 "	—
" 40th & Market	—	17 "
" Juniper Station	22 "	

Schedules similar to the Sunday schedule are operated on the following holidays: New Year's, Memorial, Independence, Labor, Thanksgiving and Christmas days.

SUBJECT TO CHANGE

1-22-61 (For Westbound Schedule see other side)

PHILADELPHIA TRANSPORTATION COMPANY

1677-8 1937 1935

ROUTE 36

ELMWOOD AVE.

EASTBOUND

FROM 94TH ST. & EASTWICK AVE.
TO JUNIPER ST. STATION

WEEKDAY		SATURDAY	SUNDAY
AM	Thur.	AM	AM
4.34	AM	4.32	4.34
4.55	Oper-	4.55	5.06
5.18	ates	5.16	5.26
5.30	To	5.36	5.46
5.42	40th &	5.56	6.06
5.52	Market	6.16	6.26
★	1.14	6.35	6.45
PM	1.44	6.52	7.04
11.38	2.14	7.08	7.22
11.50	2.43	7.23	7.35
12.06	3.14	7.38	★
12.21	3.44	★	AM
12.36	4.14	AM	12.08
12.51		12.19	12.22
1.02		12.34	12.39
1.32		12.51	12.51
2.02		1.02	1.02
2.32		1.32	1.32
3.02		2.02	2.02
3.32		2.32	2.32
4.02		3.02	3.02
		3.32	3.32
		4.02	4.02
AM	AM	AM	AM

★MAXIMUM INTERVALS 15 MIN.

AVERAGE RUNNING TIME—EASTBOUND

From 94th & Eastwick		Thur. AM
To Island Rd. & Elmwood	9 Min.	9 Min.
" 49th & Woodland	22 "	22 "
" 40th St. Portal	26 "	
" 40th & Market	—	32 "
" Juniper Station	36 "	

Schedules similar to the Sunday schedule are operated on the following holidays: New Year's, Memorial, Independence, Labor, Thanksgiving and Christmas days.

SUBJECT TO CHANGE

1-22-61 (For Westbound Schedule see other side)

PHILADELPHIA TRANSPORTATION COMPANY

1996-7 1999 2000

Philadelphia Transportation Company schedules for trolley car routes 10, 11, 13, 15, 34, and 36, during the 1961 to 1962 time period, had daytime service intervals of 15 minutes or less. Each of these lines operated 24 hours a day. The schedules were primarily used for the late-night and early-morning service period, which had 30-minute service intervals.

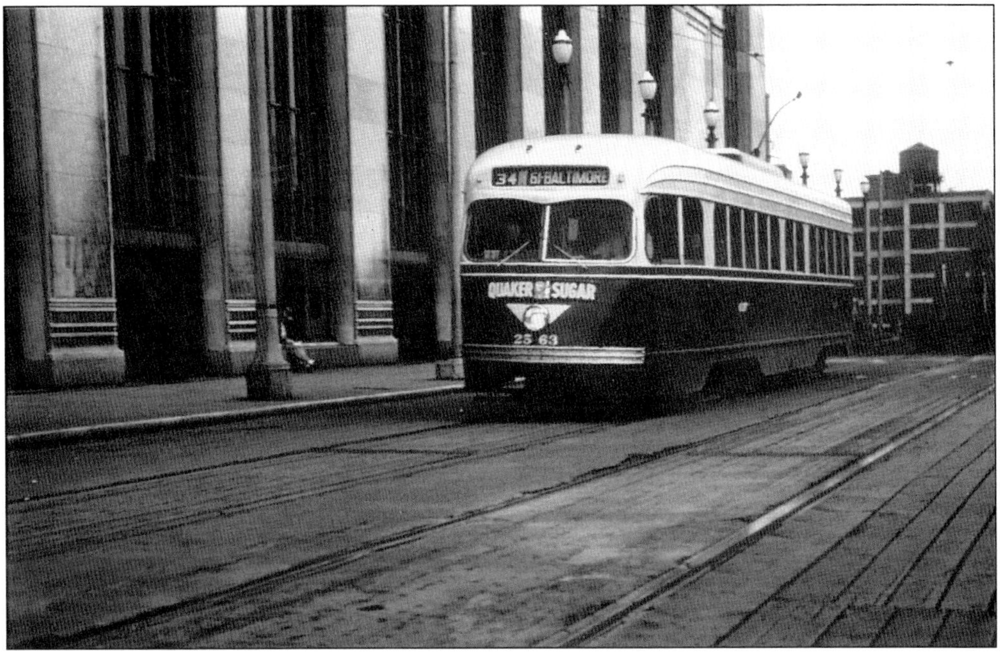

Philadelphia Transportation Company route 34 Presidents' Conference Committee car No. 2563 is gliding past the Pennsylvania Railroad Thirtieth Street Station shortly after these cars were assigned to route 34 on September 11, 1955. This car, built by the St. Louis Car Company in 1941, was scrapped during 1973. (Craig Knox collection.)

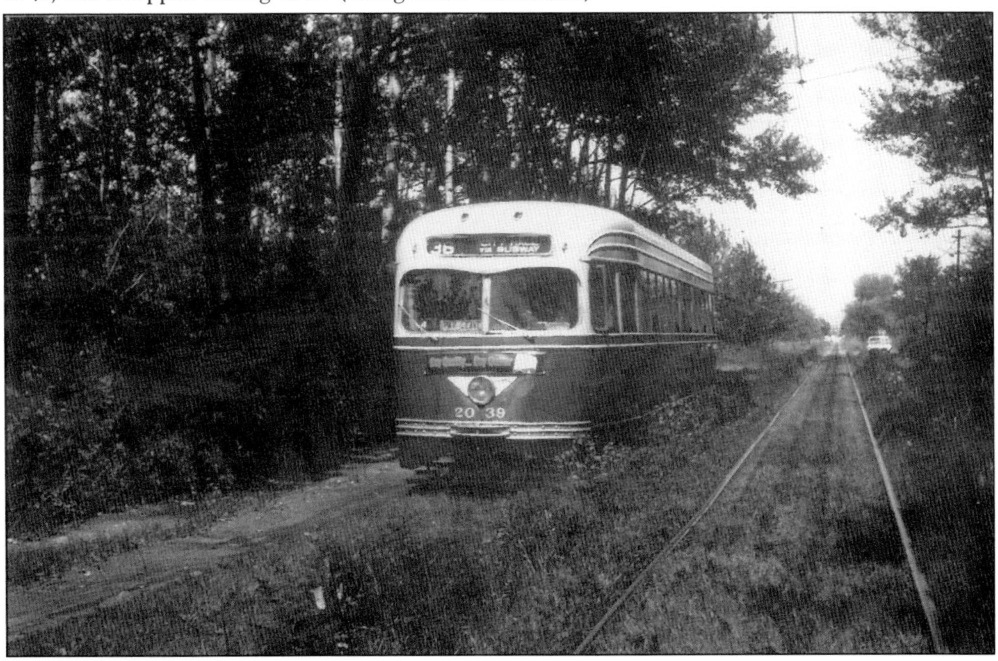

Presidents' Conference Committee car No. 2039 is on the Philadelphia Transportation Company route 36 private right-of-way in the Eastwick section of Philadelphia around 1957. This car, built by the St. Louis Car Company in 1941, was destroyed in the Woodland Depot fire of October 23, 1975. (Photograph by Craig Knox.)

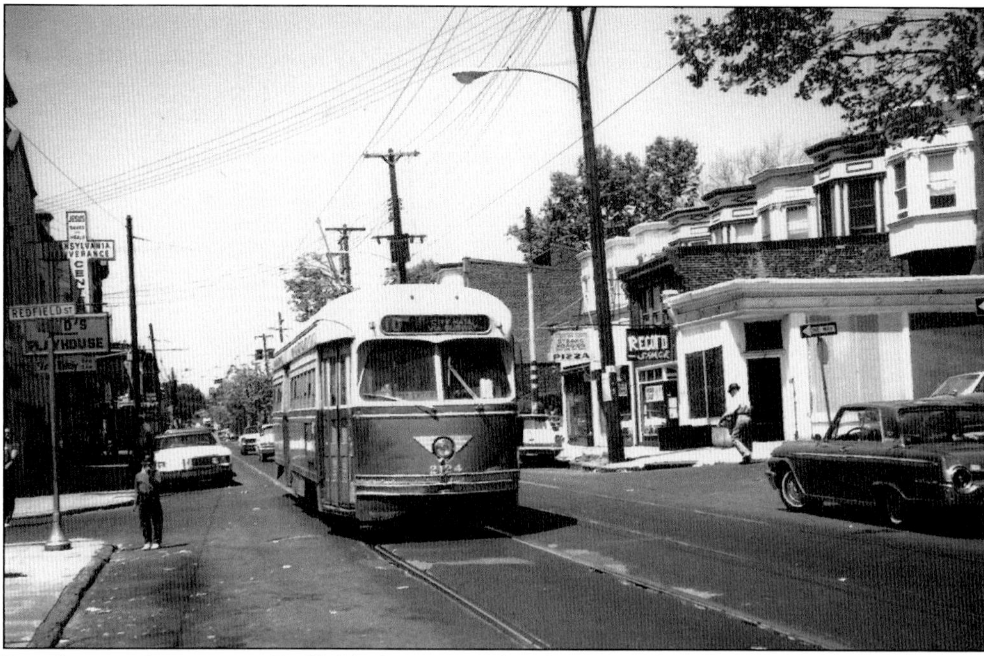

Lansdowne Avenue at Redfield Street is the location for Southeastern Pennsylvania Transportation Authority route 10 Presidents' Conference Committee car No. 2124 on May 31, 1969. This car was still in the Philadelphia Transportation Company paint scheme, with a green lower section, cream upper section, and maroon stripe below the windows. (Photograph by Kenneth C. Springirth.)

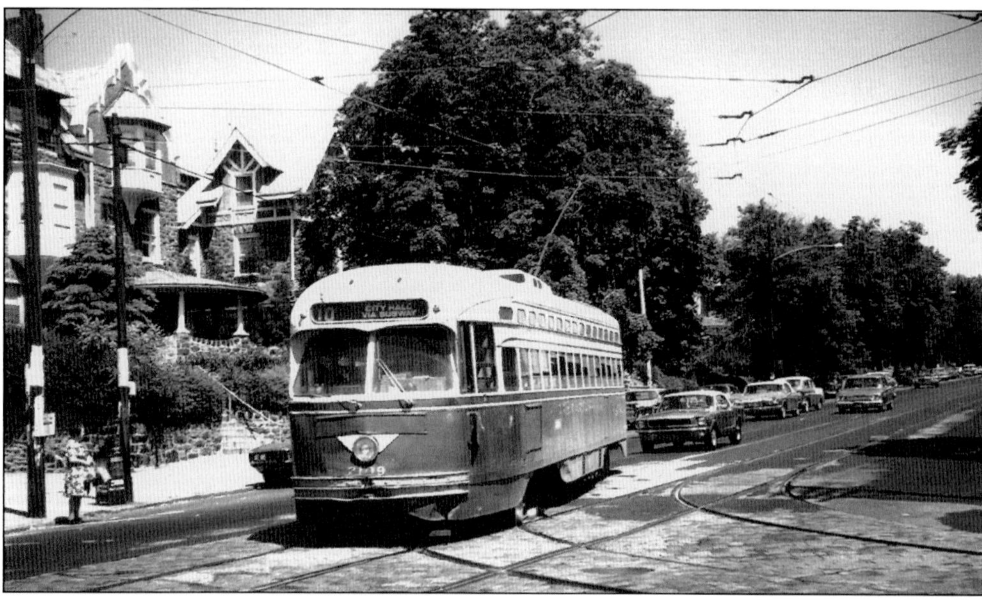

Route 10 Presidents' Conference Committee car No. 2109 is turning from Sixty-third Street to Lansdowne Avenue on May 31, 1969. Built by the St. Louis Car Company in 1948, this car was overhauled in 1982. It was sold to Colorado Springs in September 1995. The trackage that continues straight on Sixty-third Street was once used by route 41 trolleys and was retained to reach Callowhill Depot. (Photograph by Kenneth C. Springirth.)

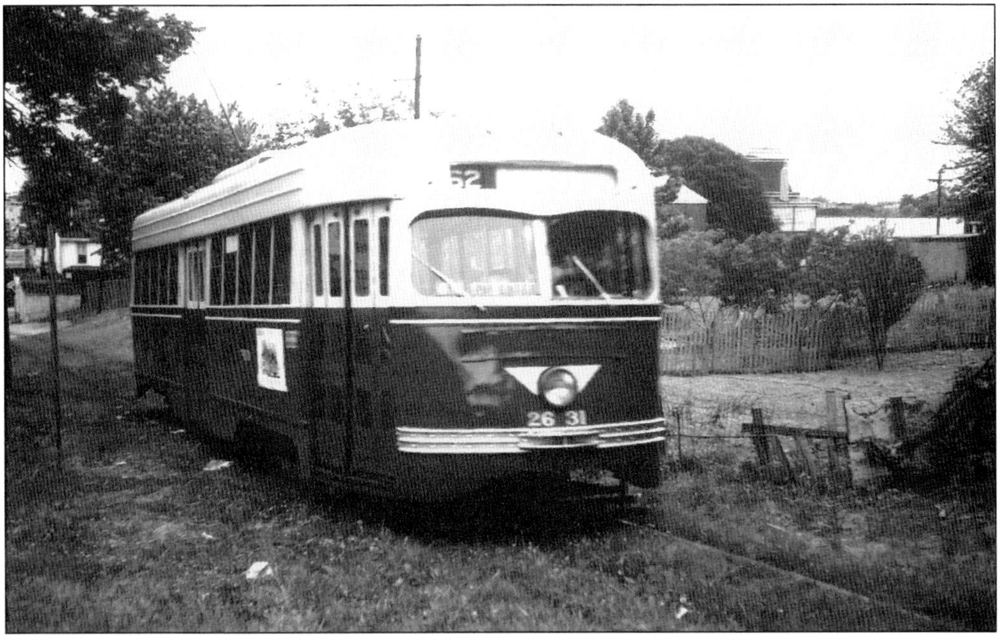

Philadelphia Transportation Company route 62 Presidents' Conference Committee car No. 2631 is on the private right-of-way near Darby Terminal on June 2, 1963. This car, built by the St. Louis Car Company in 1942, was scrapped during 1977. Route 62, operating from Darby to Yeadon, was discontinued with certain route 13 trips operating via Yeadon to Darby beginning on January 23, 1971. (Photograph by Kenneth C. Springirth.)

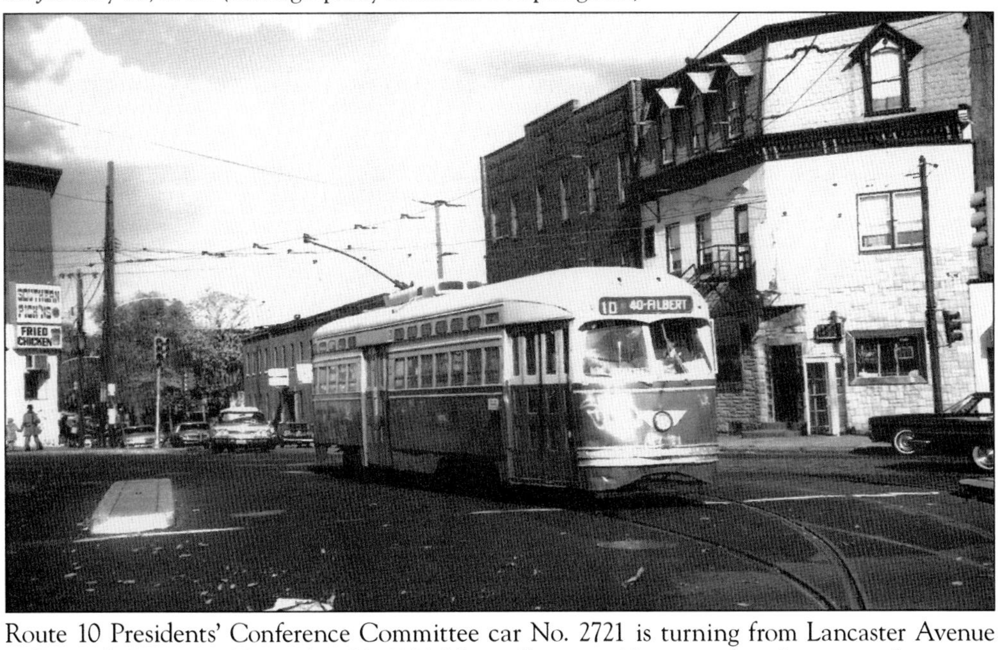

Route 10 Presidents' Conference Committee car No. 2721 is turning from Lancaster Avenue to Fortieth Street on November 21, 1971. Normally route 10 operated on Lancaster Avenue to Thirty-sixth Street where it entered the subway south of Market Street. This car, built by the St. Louis Car Company in 1947, was sold to San Francisco Municipal Railway in February 1993 and became car No. 1053. (Photograph by Kenneth C. Springirth.)

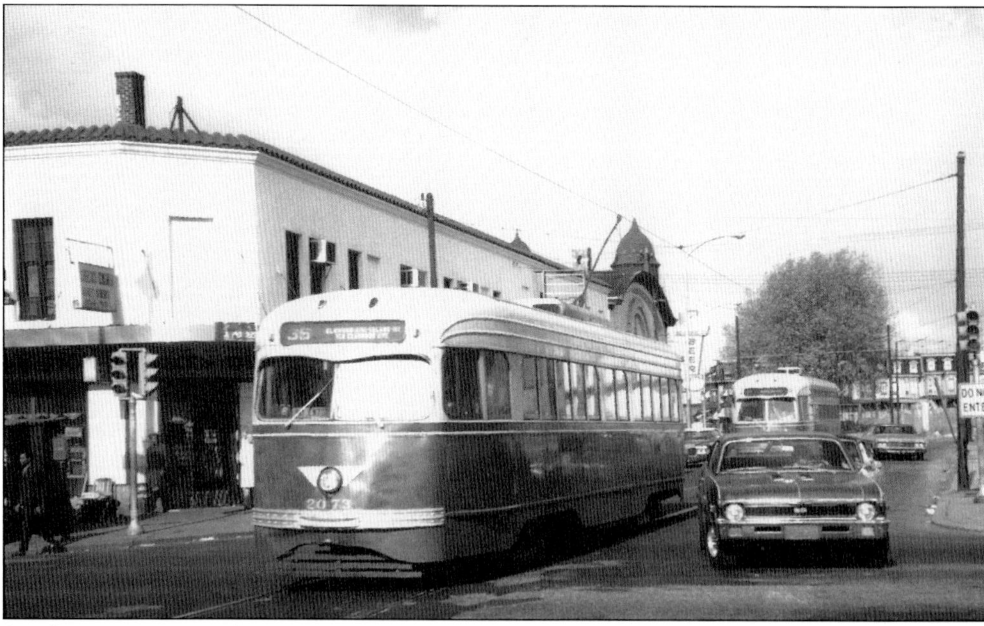

Southeastern Pennsylvania Transportation Authority route 36 Presidents' Conference Committee car No. 2073 is on Fortieth Street crossing Market Street on November 21, 1971. This car, built by the St. Louis Car Company in 1941, was scrapped during 1977. When the subway is closed, routes 10, 11, 13, 34, and 36 are diverted to Fortieth Street and passengers transfer to the Market-Frankford Subway-Elevated Line for downtown Philadelphia. (Photograph by Kenneth C. Springirth.)

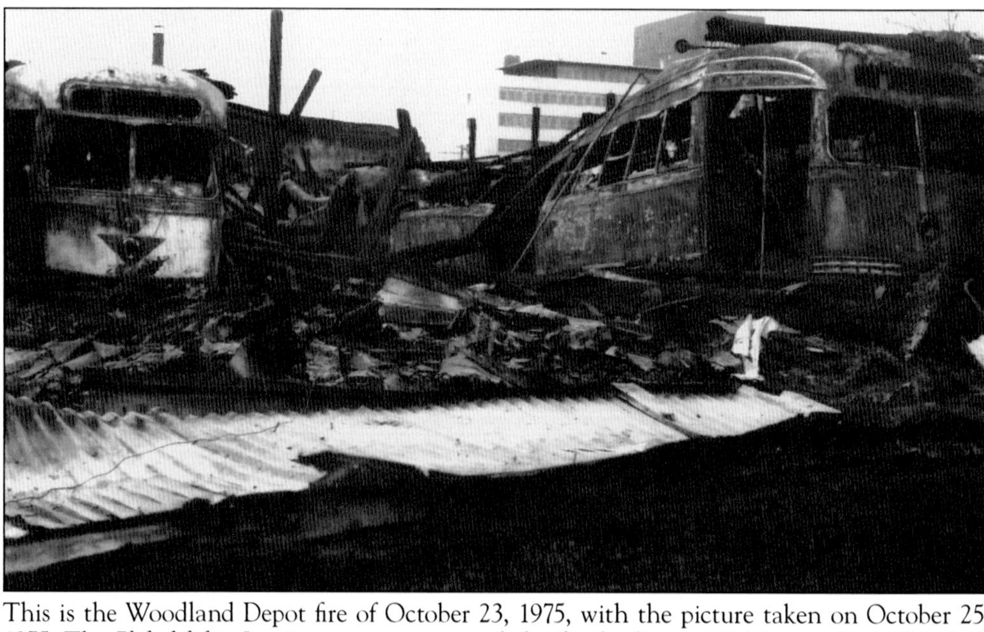

This is the Woodland Depot fire of October 23, 1975, with the picture taken on October 25, 1975. The *Philadelphia Inquirer* newspaper noted the fire broke out 12:40 a.m., destroying half the building. With 60 trolley cars lost, buses were substituted on route 11, using Fortieth and Market Streets as a transfer point for the Market-Frankford Subway-Elevated Line. Trolleys were transferred from Luzerne Depot to restore service. (Photograph by Kenneth C. Springirth.)

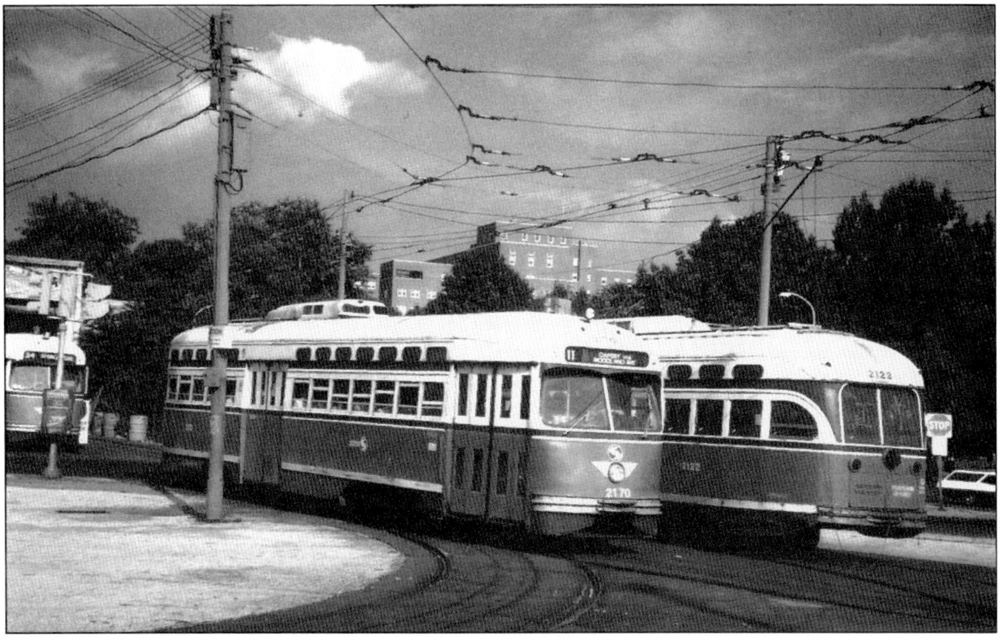

Southeastern Pennsylvania Transportation Authority cars Nos. 2170 and 2122 are at the Fortieth Street Subway portal on July 27, 1979. The St. Louis Car Company built both of these cars during 1948. Car No. 2122 was sold to San Francisco Municipal Railway in October 1992 and became car No. 1055. Car No. 2170 was sold to the Brookville Equipment Company for parts on February 27, 2003. (Photograph by Kenneth C. Springirth.)

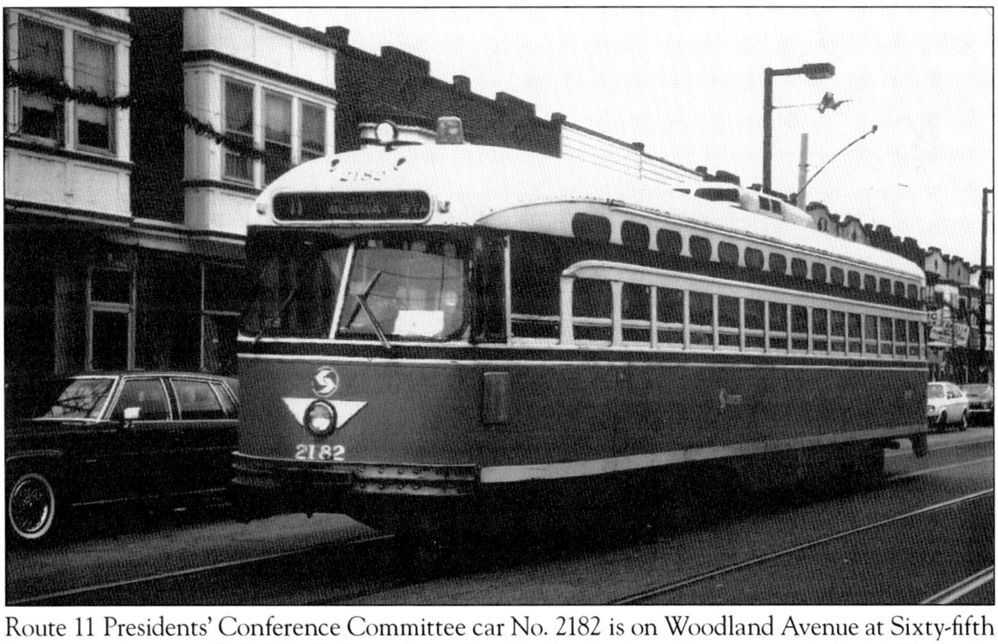

Route 11 Presidents' Conference Committee car No. 2182 is on Woodland Avenue at Sixty-fifth Street on January 6, 1982. Delivered by the St. Louis Car Company in July 1948 to the Philadelphia Transportation Company, the car was overhauled during 1986. It was rebuilt by the Brookville Equipment Company as car No. 2329 and delivered to the Southeastern Pennsylvania Transportation Authority on June 23, 2004. (Photograph by Kenneth C. Springirth.)

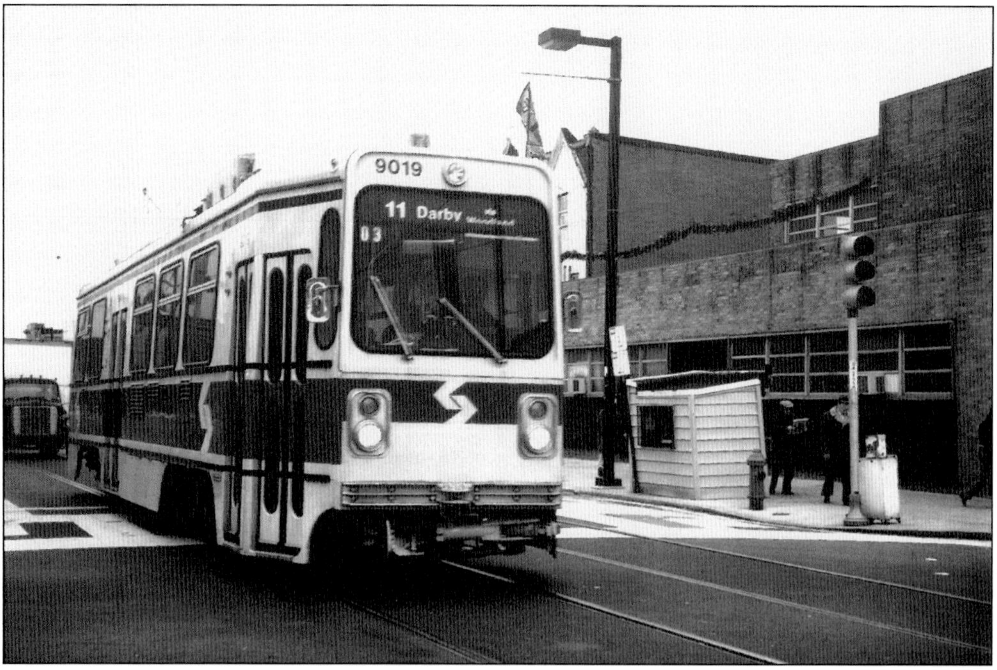

Route 11 car No. 9019 is on Woodland Avenue at Sixty-fifth Street on January 6, 1982. Built by Kawasaki Heavy Industries, this car went into Southeastern Pennsylvania Transportation Authority revenue service on November 9, 1981. The car was 50 feet long, 8.5 feet wide, weighed 57,882 pounds, and had a maximum speed of 50 miles per hour on level track. (Photograph by Kenneth C. Springirth.)

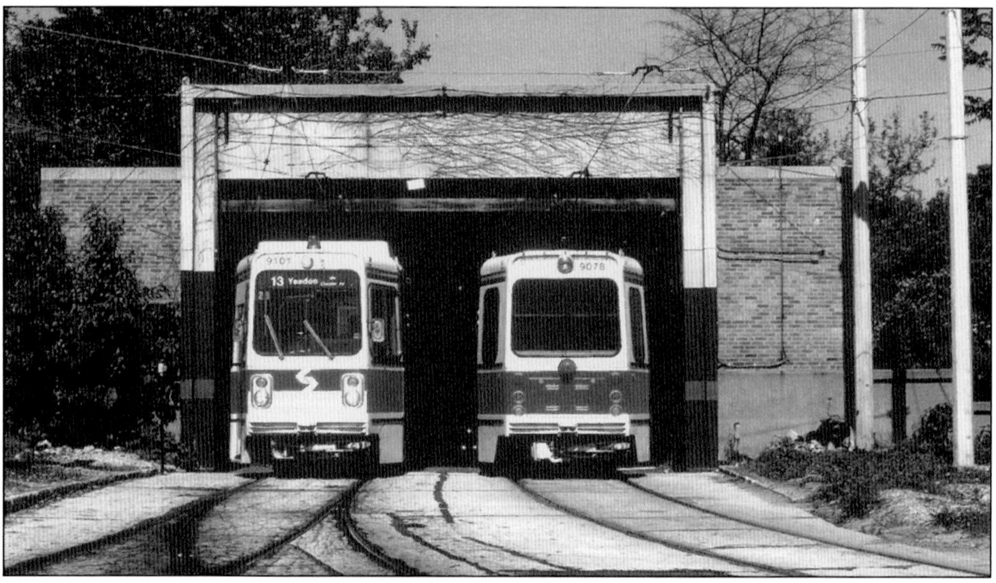

Route 11 car No. 9101 is passing car No. 9078 at the Fortieth Street subway portal on May 25, 1984. Car No. 9101 went into revenue service on March 29, 1982. Car No. 9078 went into revenue service on November 2, 1982. Kawasaki Heavy Industries built 112 cars numbered 9000 to 9111. These cars featured an automatically controlled comfort system for air-conditioning and heating. (Photograph by Kenneth C. Springirth.)

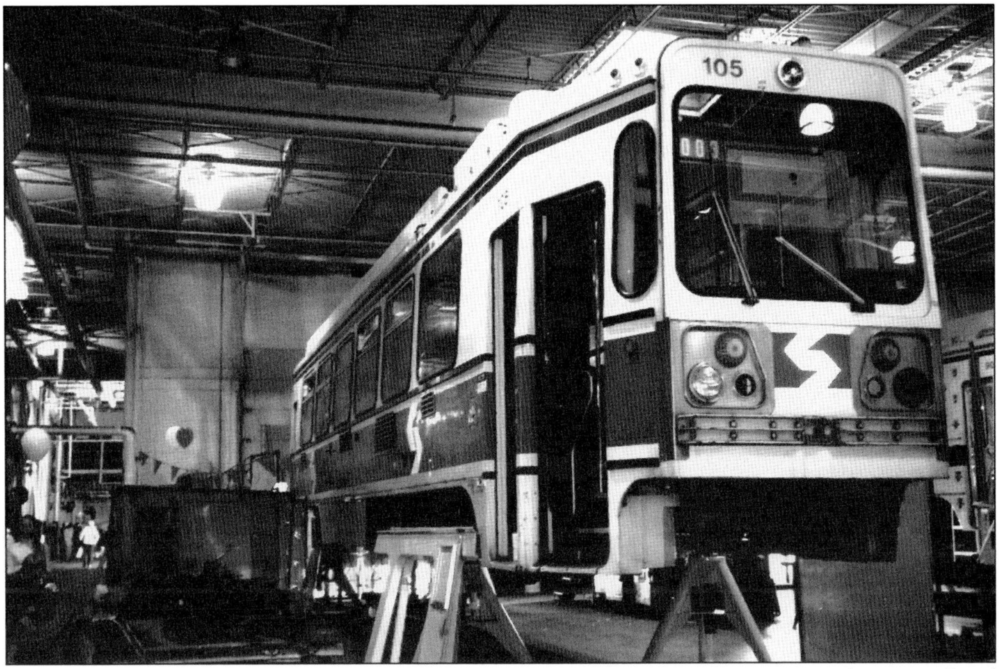

Southeastern Pennsylvania Transportation Authority car No. 105 is at the Woodland Maintenance Facility on October 2, 1993. Built by Kawasaki Heavy Industries, it began revenue service on October 7, 1982. One of 29 cars numbered 100 to 128, it was 53 feet long, 8.83 feet wide, weighed 60,043 pounds, and had a maximum speed of 62 miles per hour on level track. (Photograph by Kenneth C. Springirth.)

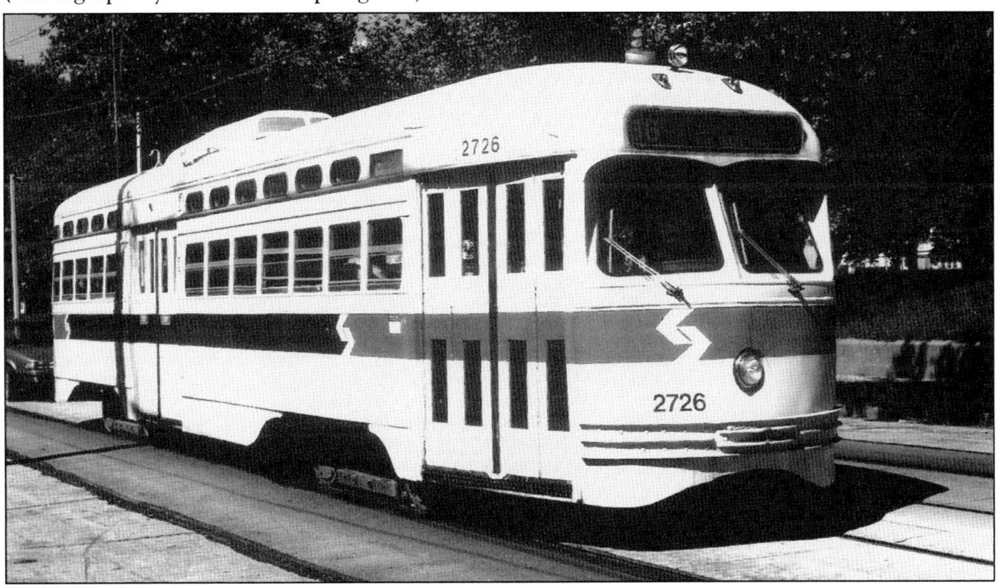

Presidents' Conference Committee car No. 2726 is on Elmwood Avenue at Sixty-fourth Street on August 7, 1994. The Philadelphia Transportation Company received this car from the St. Louis Car Company in March 1947. It was overhauled in 1987. The Brookville Equipment Company rebuilt this car as Number 2328 with delivery to the Southeastern Pennsylvania Transportation Authority on May 27, 2004. (Photograph by Kenneth C. Springirth.)

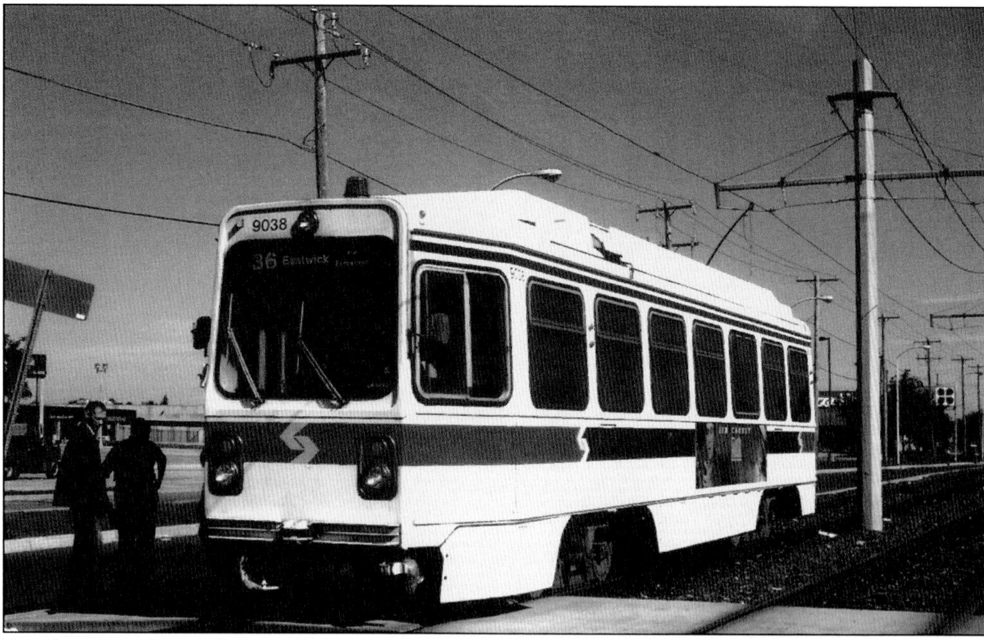

Southeastern Pennsylvania Transportation Authority route 36 car No. 9038 is on the reserved median of Island Avenue near the terminus at Eightieth Street and Eastwick Avenue on August 7, 1994. Built by Kawasaki Heavy Industries, it was placed in revenue service on May 25, 1982, and is equipped with Westinghouse Electric motors, gear boxes, and controls. (Photograph by Kenneth C. Springirth.)

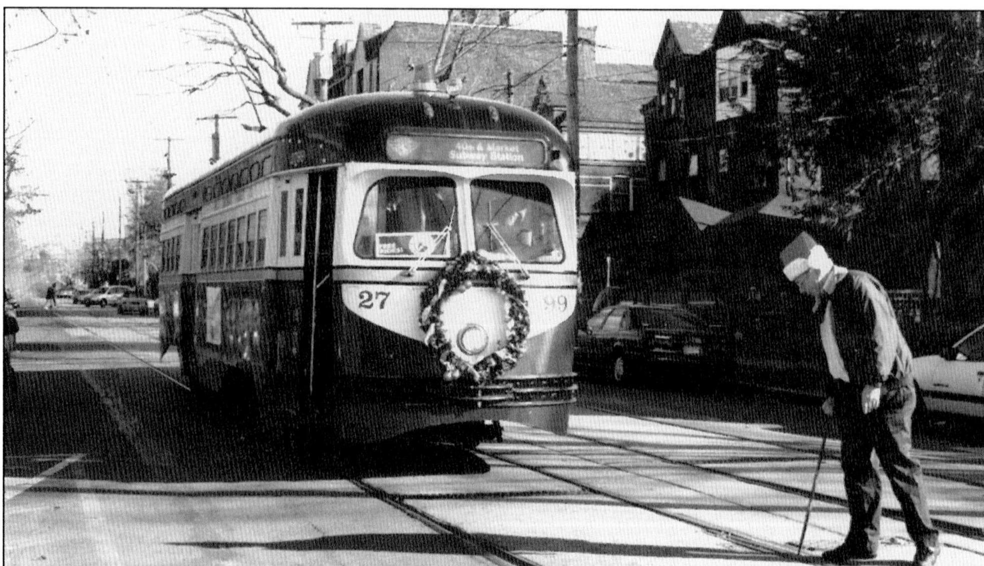

Southeastern Pennsylvania Transportation Authority car No. 2799 is on Chester Avenue at Forty-second Street on the University City Holiday loop, with the operator setting the switch on December 15, 2001. This special Christmas service operated every 20 minutes using Fortieth Street, Spruce Street, Forty-second Street, Chester Avenue, and Forty-ninth Street returning via Woodland Avenue, Forty-second Street, Spruce Street, Thirty-eighth Street, and Filbert Street to Fortieth Street. (Photograph by Kenneth C. Springirth.)

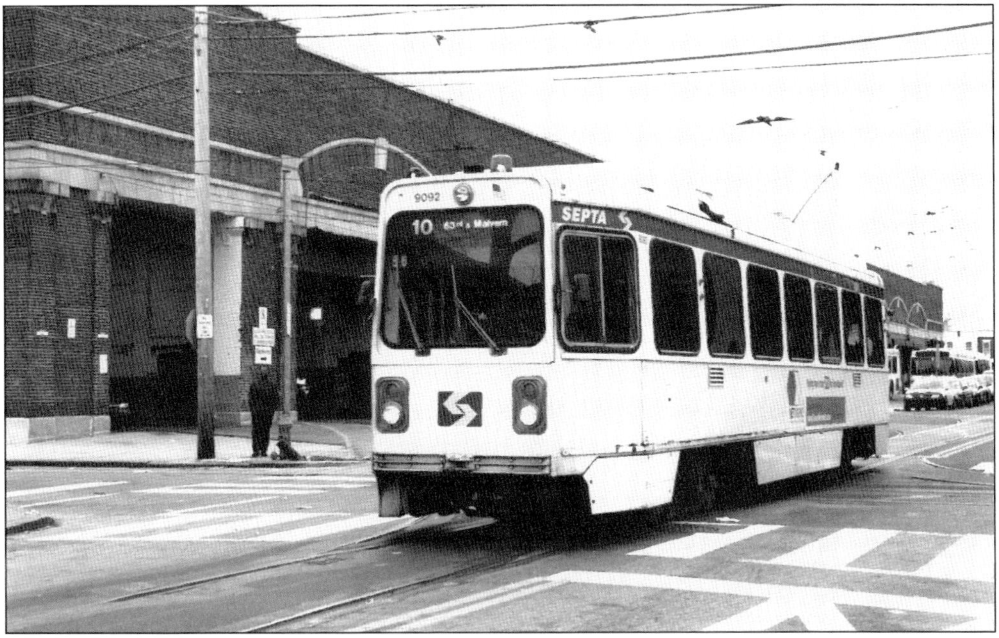

Leaving Callowhill Depot on February 4, 2006, car No. 9092 is on Fifty-ninth Street crossing Callowhill Street and will use route 15 trackage to go into service on route 10. The Southeastern Pennsylvania Transportation Authority received this car from Kawasaki Heavy Industries on November 4, 1981. (Photograph by Kenneth C. Springirth.)

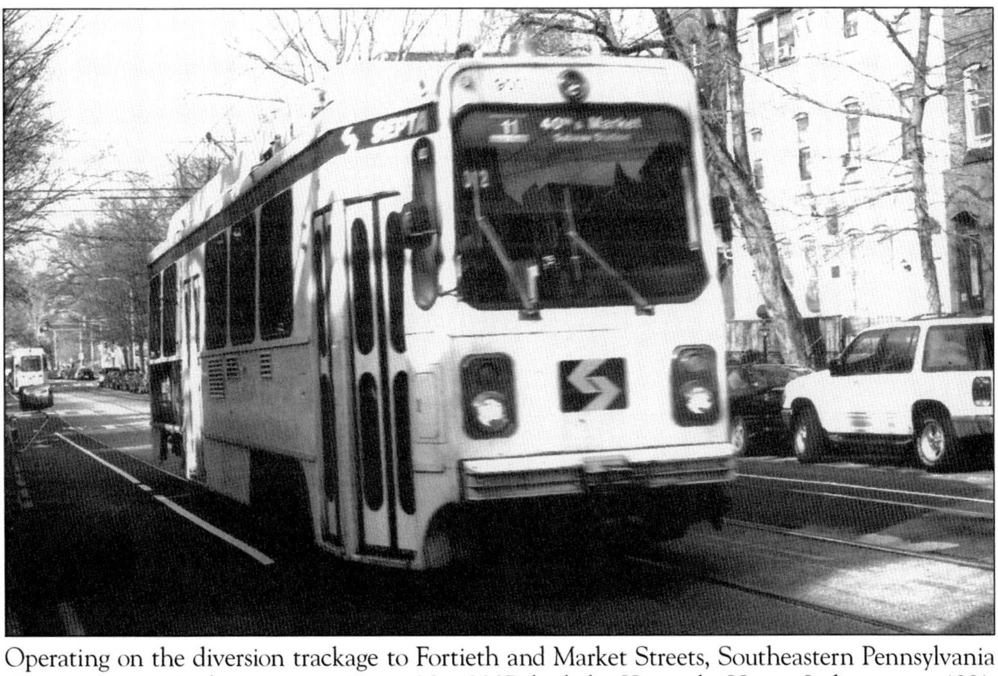

Operating on the diversion trackage to Fortieth and Market Streets, Southeastern Pennsylvania Transportation Authority route 11 car No. 9007, built by Kawasaki Heavy Industries in 1981, is on Spruce Street at Forty-first Street on February 5, 2006. When the subway is closed, the subway surface lines are routed to Fortieth Street, necessitating a transfer to the Market-Frankford Subway-Elevated Line to reach downtown Philadelphia. (Photograph by Kenneth C. Springirth.)

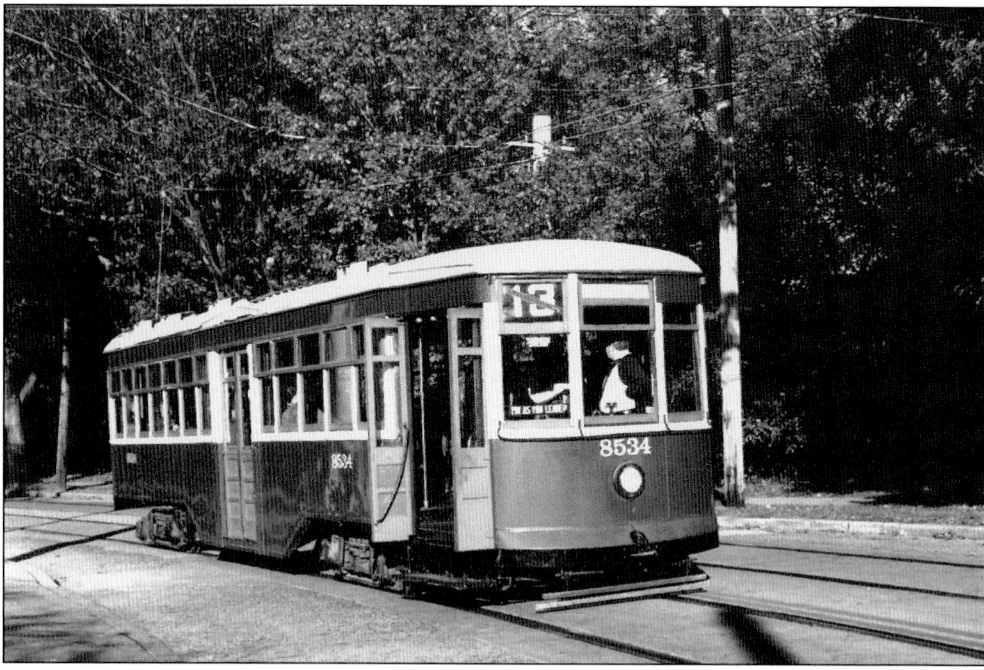

Westbound on Chester Avenue at Church Lane in Philadelphia on trolley route 13 is car No. 8534 on a rail excursion on October 28, 2001. J. G. Brill Car Company built this car in 1926 for the Philadelphia Rapid Transit Company. It has been preserved at the Electric City Trolley Museum. (Photograph by Kenneth C. Springirth.)

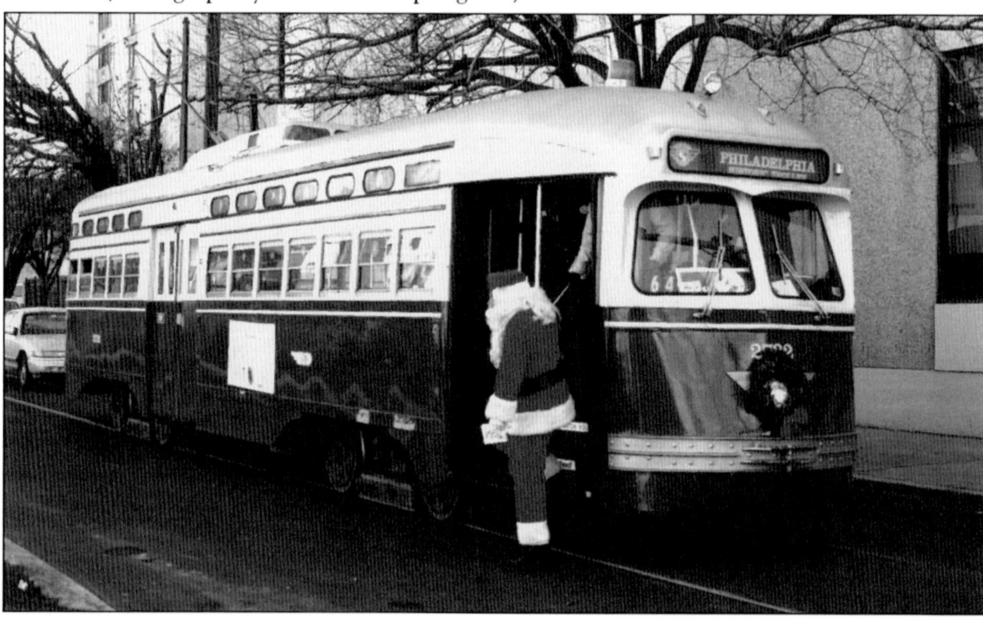

Presidents' Conference Committee car No. 2732 is on Filbert Street at Fortieth Street on December 15, 2001, for the University City Holiday loop operated by the Southeastern Pennsylvania Transportation Authority and sponsored by the University City District and the University of Pennsylvania. Santa Claus was Joel Spivak, who along with Allen Myers wrote *Philadelphia Trolleys*. (Photograph by Kenneth C. Springirth.)

Five

Girard Avenue Trolleys

The Girard Avenue Line, which later became route 15, began operation on May 30, 1895, from Girard Avenue and Fifty-fourth Street to Richmond and Norris Streets. The western end of the line was extended via Girard Avenue to Sixtieth Street on July 2, 1900, and reached Sixty-third Street via Haverford and Girard Avenues on April 1, 1902. The eastern end of the line was extended via Richmond Street to Allegheny Avenue on July 22, 1903, and was extended to the Arsenal Gate via Richmond and Bridge Streets on December 3, 1922. Presidents' Conference Committee trolley cars were placed in service on route 15 on June 20, 1955. Effective September 11, 1955, the eastern end of the line was cut back to Richmond Depot at Allegheny Avenue and Richmond Street. A new loop at Richmond and Westmoreland Streets was placed into service on February 24, 1956, and operation through Richmond Depot was discontinued. On September 12, 1992, the last trolley car runs were made in a temporary bus conversion. The Southeastern Pennsylvania Transportation Authority agreed to restore trolley car service. Eighteen Presidents' Conference Committee trolley cars, originally built by the St. Louis Car Company, were stripped down to their bare frame and completely rebuilt by the Brookville Equipment Company with new propulsion and electrical systems, new trucks, air-conditioning, cloth upholstered seats, wheelchair lift, and the original "bull's-eye" interior lighting. A new modular substation was installed at Callowhill Depot at Fifty-ninth and Callowhill Streets. Track along the 8.2-mile line was renewed and or repaired. The overhead electrical power lines were repaired. New island passenger platforms were constructed. In the center section of the line, Girard Avenue is wide, but at each end of the line, trolleys travel narrower streets. On September 4, 2005, trolley car service was restored on route 15. This is the only surviving trolley line that links West Philadelphia to North Philadelphia. Route 15 is not considered a tourist line but serves a variety of business and residential districts, Girard College, and the Philadelphia Zoo, plus it intersects both the Broad Street Subway and the Market-Frankford Subway-Elevated Line, providing accessibility to densely populated neighborhoods.

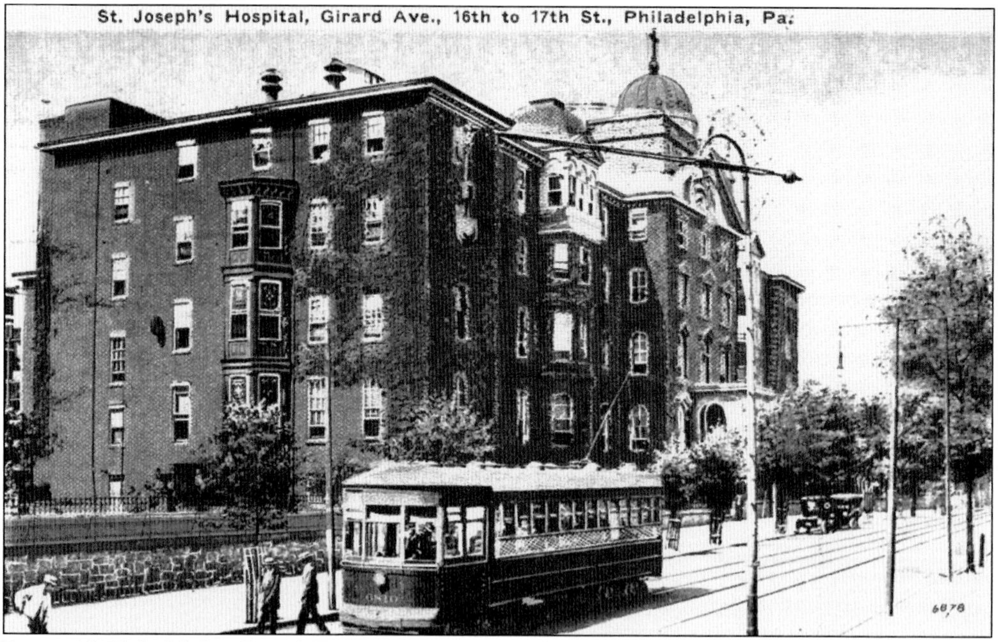

Route 15 Philadelphia Rapid Transit Company trolley car No. 6810 is at St. Joseph's Hospital on Girard Avenue between Sixteenth and Seventeenth Streets on this postcard postmarked February 27, 1920. This car series, numbered 6000 to 7499, represented the largest single group of trolley cars ever acquired by the Philadelphia Rapid Transit Company.

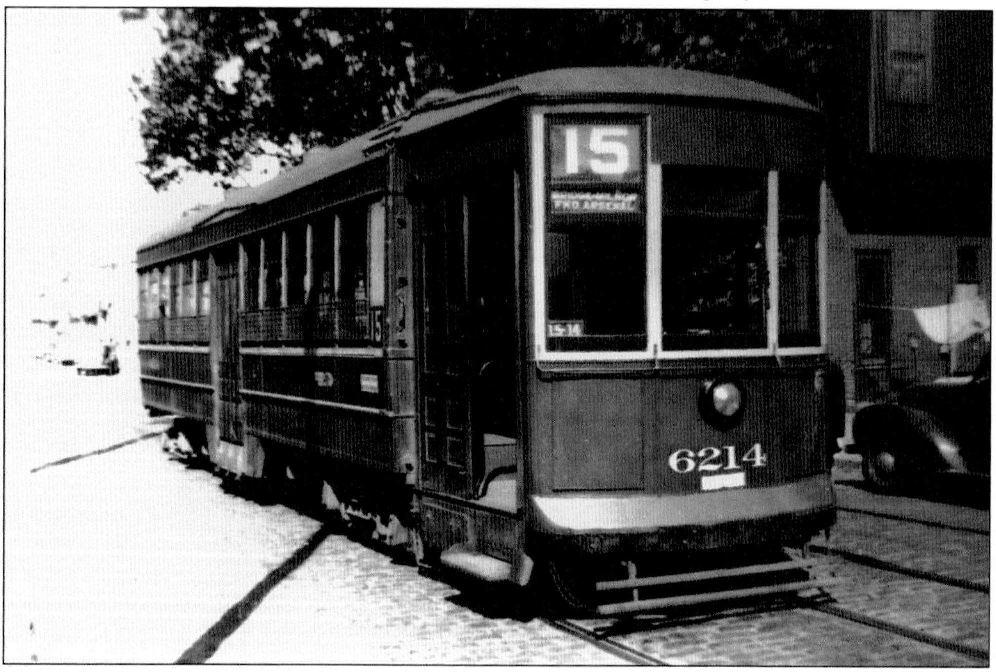

Philadelphia Transportation Company car No. 6214 is on route 15 at Sixty-third Street and Haverford Avenue around 1947. Built by J. G. Brill Car Company during 1912, as part of an order of 500 cars numbered 6050 to 6549, this car was 45.5 feet long, 8.5 feet wide, and was scrapped during January 1955. (Craig Knox collection.)

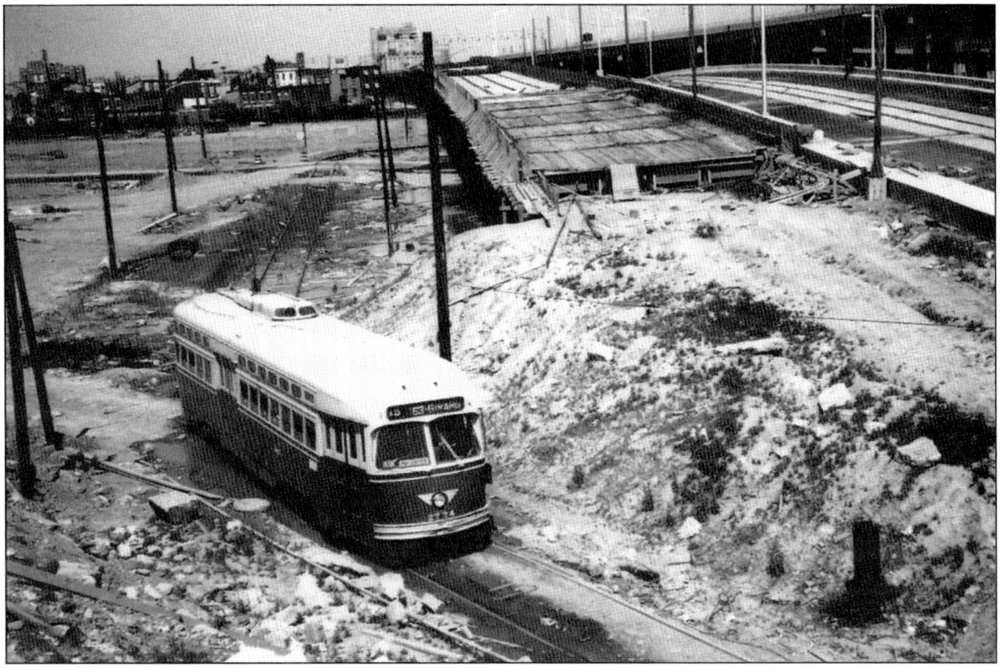

Southeastern Pennsylvania Transportation Authority route 15 Presidents' Conference Committee Car No. 2724 is westbound on temporary trackage during the construction of the Girard Avenue interchange with Interstate 95 on May 31, 1969. The St. Louis Car Company delivered this car to the Philadelphia Transportation Company in March 1947. (Photograph by Kenneth C. Springirth.)

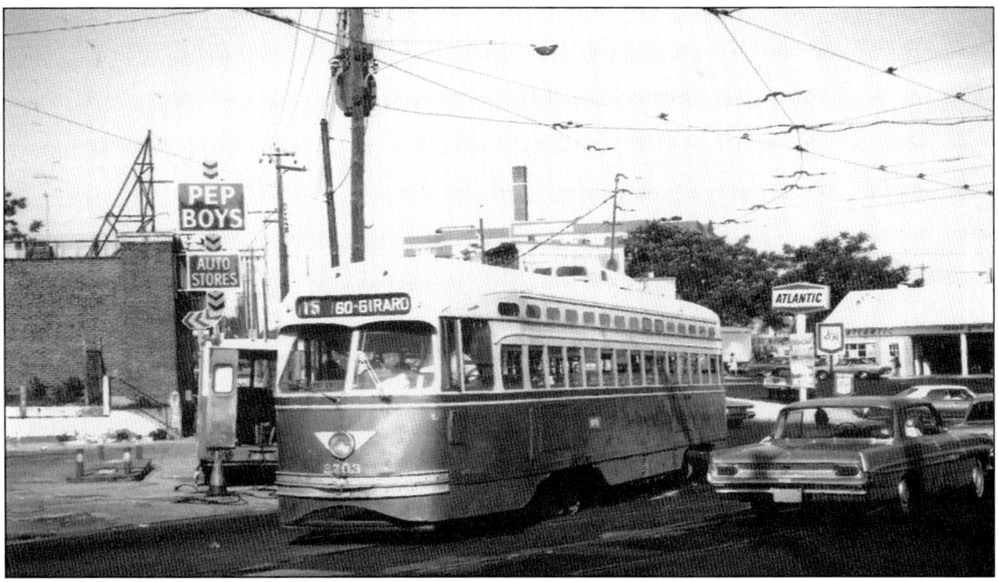

Presidents' Conference Committee car No. 2703 is turning from Girard Avenue onto Lancaster Avenue on a May 31, 1969, route 15 trip. Rebuilding of the Girard Avenue bridge resulted in the line cutback from Sixty-third Street to Twenty-sixth Street and Girard Avenue on October 26, 1969, and the entire line bus operated beginning June 21, 1970, with trolley service restored on January 30, 1972. (Photograph by Kenneth C. Springirth.)

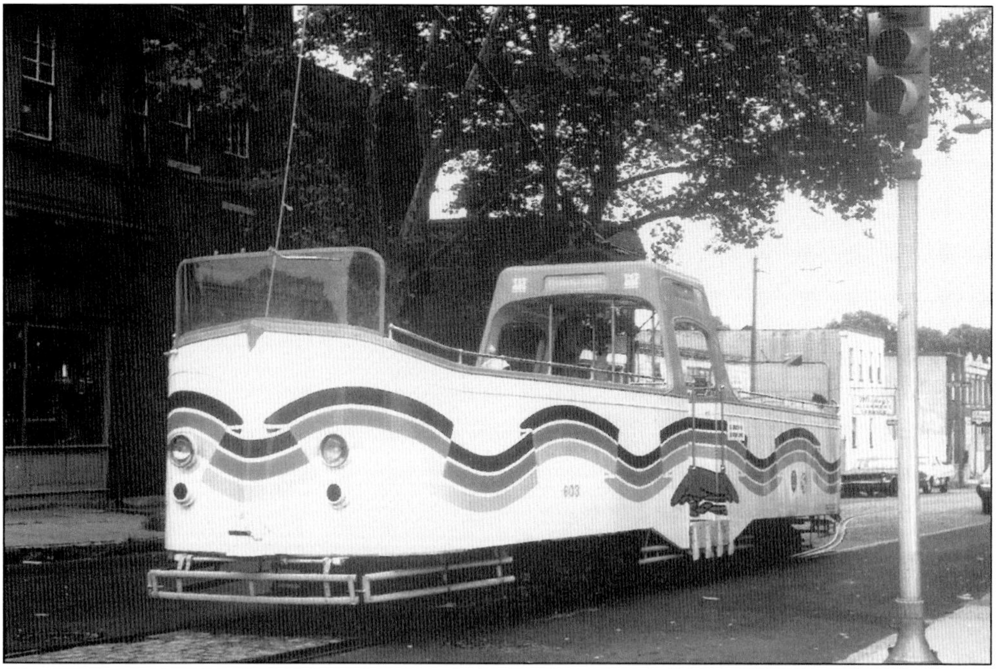

The Blackpool boat trolley is on route 15 on Girard Avenue at Sixty-third Street on August 6, 1977. This car had been regauged to meet Philadelphia's city trolley line gauge of 5 feet, 2.25 inches, repainted, and was on loan to the Southeastern Pennsylvania Transportation Authority. It operated on a special bicentennial loop on a portion of route 50 during 1976. (Photograph by Kenneth C. Springirth.)

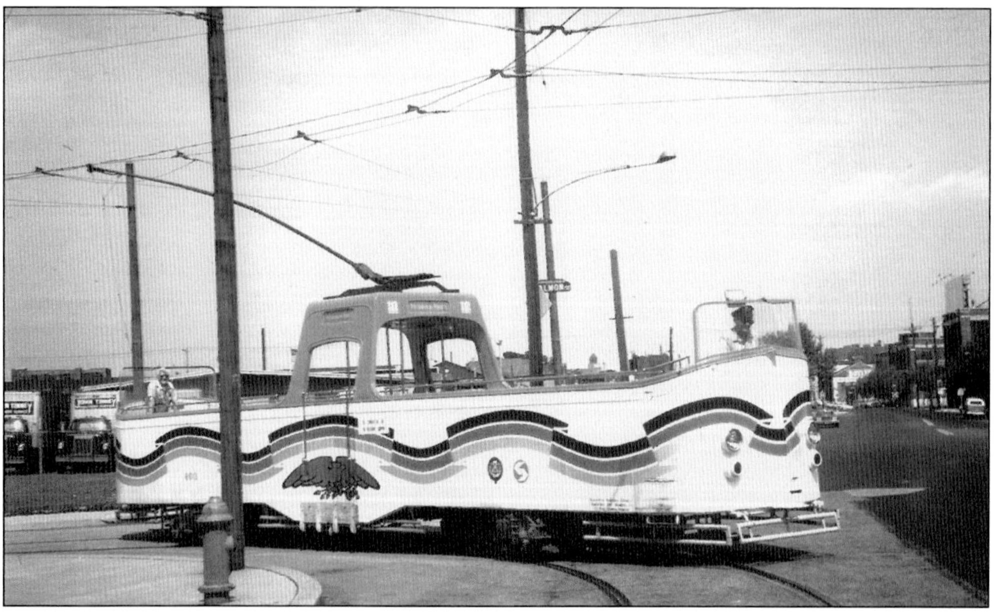

The Blackpool boat trolley is turning from Salmon Street onto Cumberland Street on route 15 on August 6, 1977. In 1984, the boat trolley was acquired as a gift to the Municipal Railway of San Francisco. It was restored to the standard gauge of 4 feet, 8.5 inches. In 1995, it began operating on San Francisco's F-Market Street line. (Photograph by Kenneth C. Springirth.)

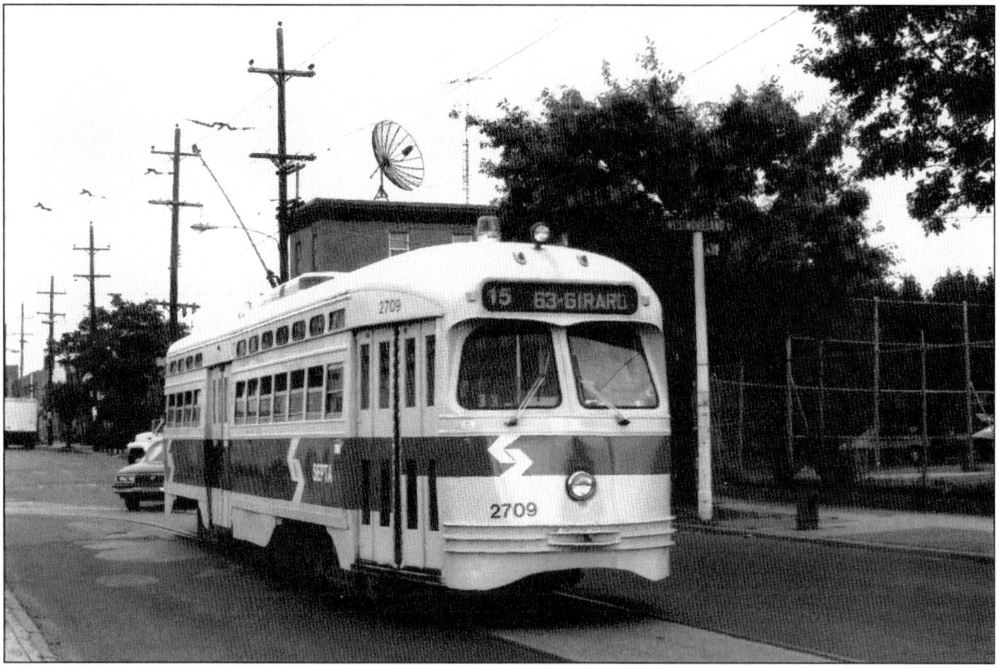

Southeastern Pennsylvania Transportation Authority route 15 Presidents' Conference Committee car No. 2709 has just turned from Westmoreland Street onto Richmond Street on August 31, 1990. This 1947 product of the St. Louis Car Company was acquired by the Seashore Trolley Museum of Kennebunkport, Maine, in February 1995. (Photograph by Kenneth C. Springirth.)

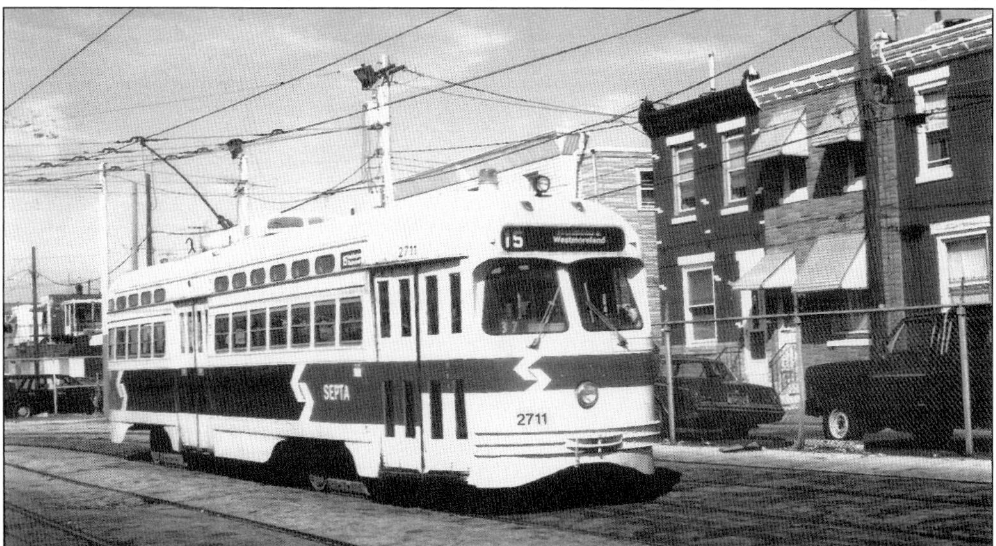

Richmond and Westmoreland Streets loop finds Southeastern Pennsylvania Transportation Authority route 15 Presidents' Conference Committee car No. 2711 on a layover on May 18, 1992. The Philadelphia Transportation Company received this car from the St. Louis Car Company during 1947. It was purchased by the Pennsylvania Trolley Museum at Washington, Pennsylvania, during 2000 and was rebuilt by Bombardier Transportation. (Photograph by Kenneth C. Springirth.)

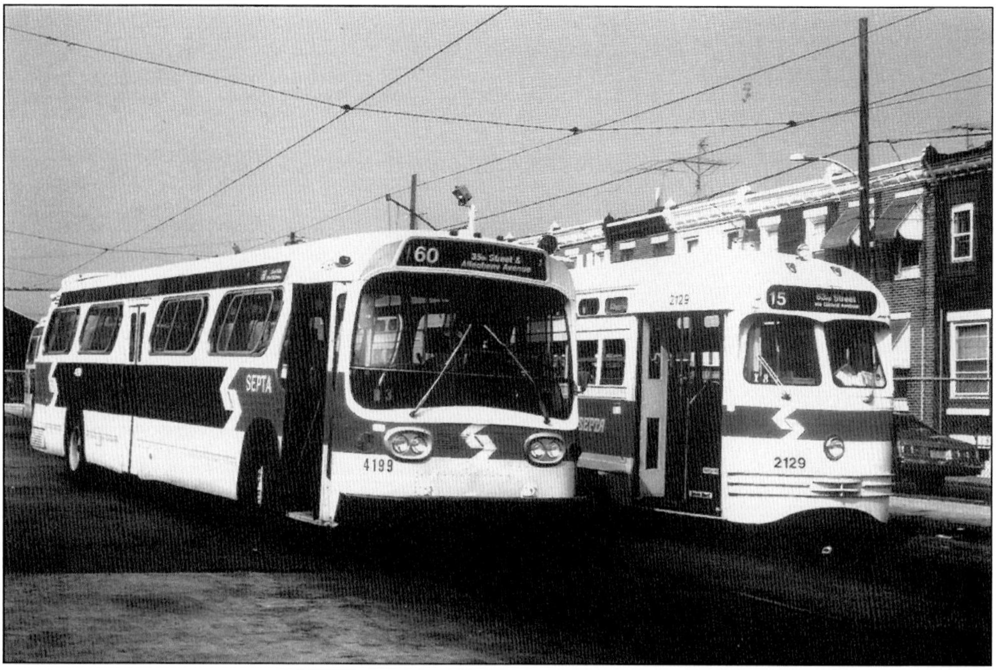

Southeastern Pennsylvania Transportation Authority route 60 bus No. 4199 model TDH5304, built by General Motors in 1967, and route 15 trolley car No. 2129, built by the St. Louis Car Company in August 1948, are at the Richmond and Westmoreland Streets loop on August 6, 1984. Car No. 2129 was overhauled in 1982 and sold to Colorado Springs in May 1995. (Photograph by Kenneth C. Springirth.)

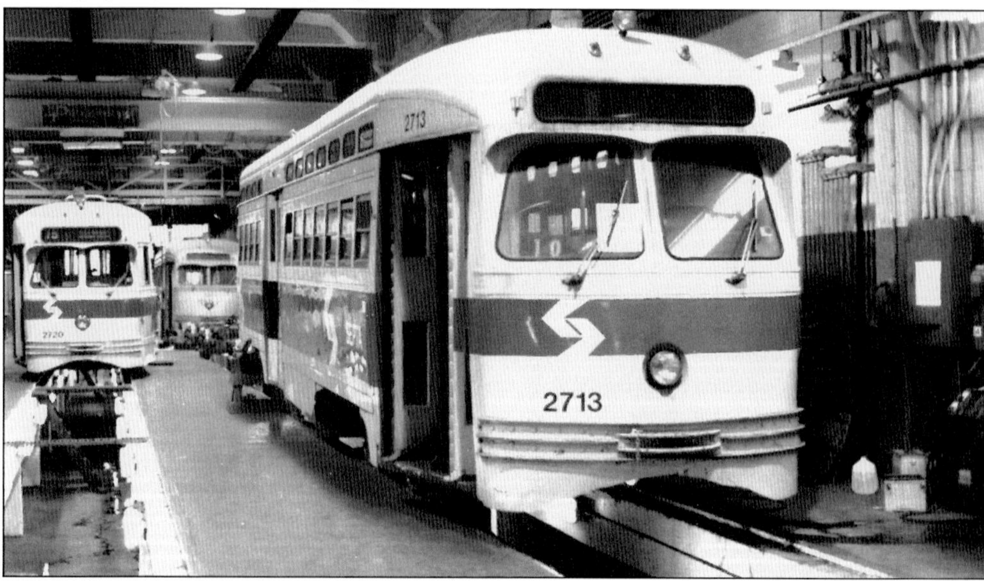

An inside view of Callowhill Depot on August 9, 1991, finds Presidents' Conference Committee cars No. 2713 with No. 2054 in the rear and No. 2720 in the left section of the picture. Car No. 2713 was sold to the Brookville Equipment Company in 2004. Car No. 2054 was sold to the Electric City Trolley Museum in 2005. Car No. 2720 was sold to the Gomaco Company in 1994. (Photograph by Kenneth C. Springirth.)

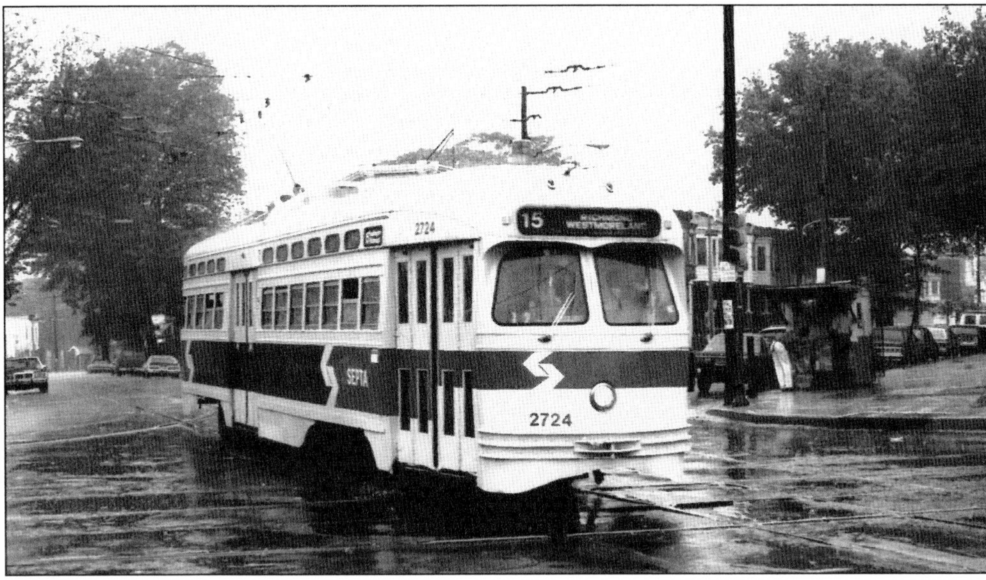

On August 9, 1991, route 15 Presidents' Conference Committee car No. 2724 is on Girard Avenue crossing Sixtieth Street. The Southeastern Pennsylvania Transportation Authority overhauled this car in June 1983. It was sold to the Vintage Electric Streetcar Company on December 28, 1993. Route 46 trolleys operated on Sixtieth Street until conversion to bus operation on August 11, 1957. (Photograph by Kenneth C. Springirth.)

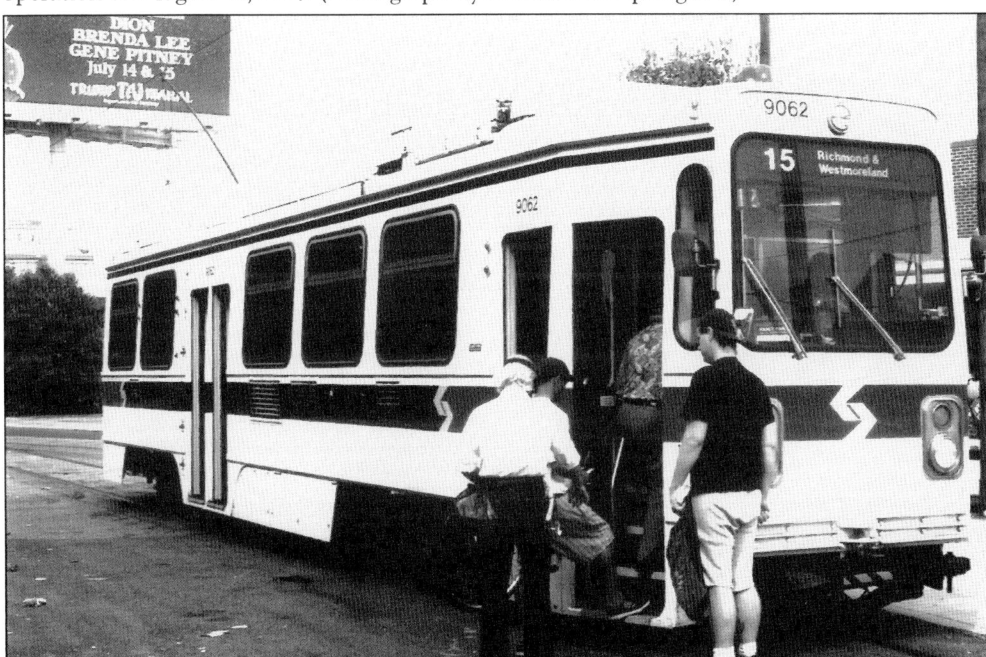

Southeastern Pennsylvania Transportation Authority route 15 car No. 9062, delivered by Kawasaki Heavy Industries on October 7, 1981, is at Richmond and Cumberland Streets loop on July 14, 1995. Kawasaki Heavy Industries trolleys operated route 15 from June 18, 1995, to September 9, 1995, because route 10 operated as a bus route due to a Philadelphia Water Department project at Forty-eighth Street and Lancaster Avenue. (Photograph by Kenneth C. Springirth.)

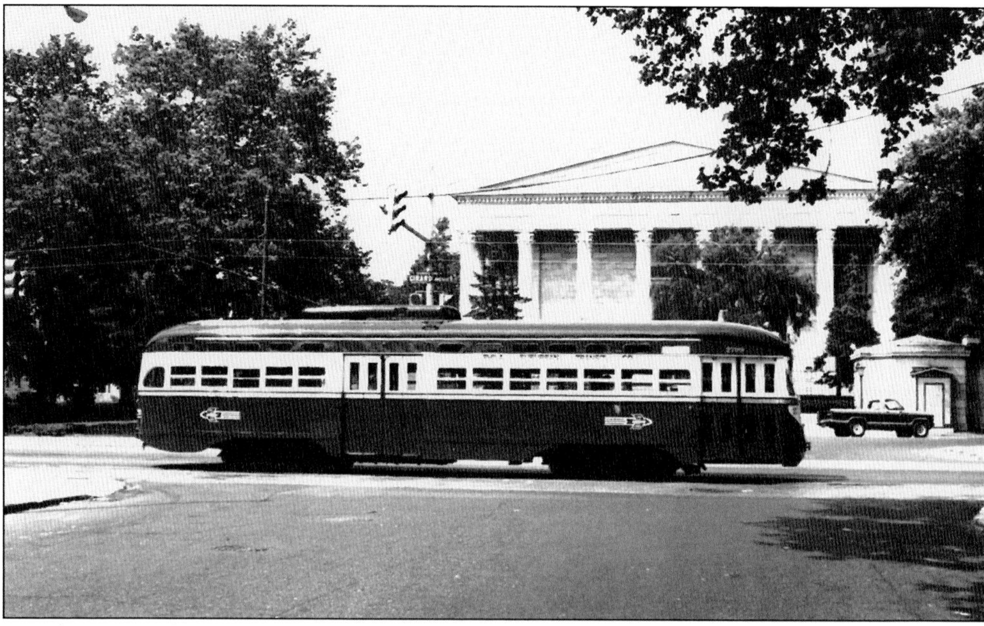

Presidents' Conference Committee car No. 2799 is passing by Girard College on South College Avenue at Corinthian Avenue on July 15, 1995 on the route 51 Welcome Line that used routes 15 and 23 trackage. The *Philadelphia Inquirer* of May 19, 1995, headlined, "City welcomes trolley back to Center City," noting that it had been three years since trolleys were in Center City. (Photograph by Kenneth C. Springirth.)

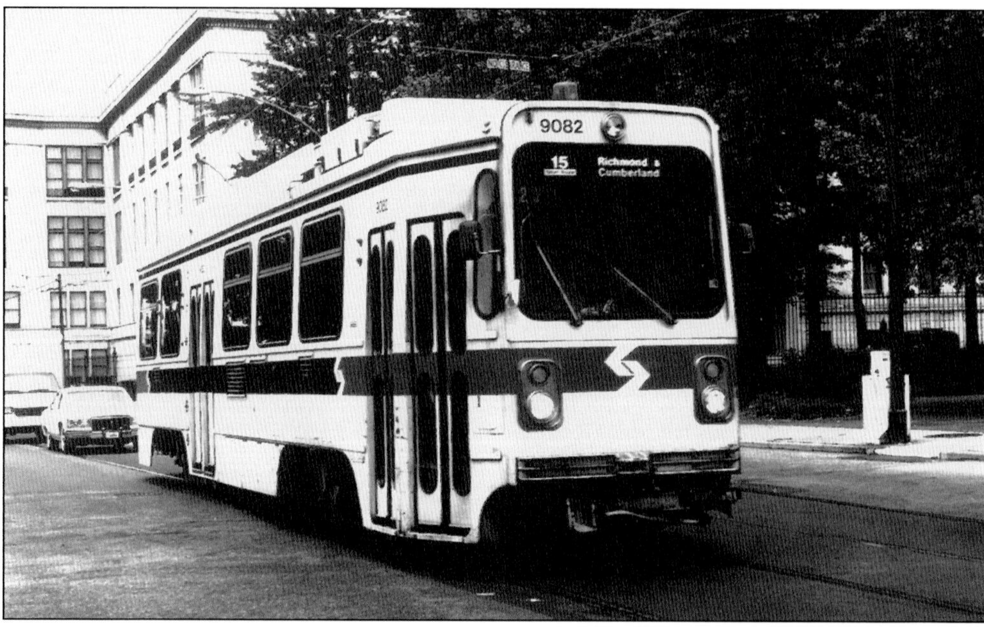

Southeastern Pennsylvania Transportation Authority route 15 car No. 9082, a 1981 product of Kawasaki Heavy Industries, is on South College Avenue at Corinthian Avenue on July 6, 1995. Buses replaced route 15 trolleys on September 13, 1992. Kawasaki Heavy Industries trolley cars served route 15 from June 18, 1995, to September 9, 1995, operating from Sixty-third Street and Malvern Avenue to Richmond and Cumberland Streets. (Photograph by Kenneth C. Springirth.)

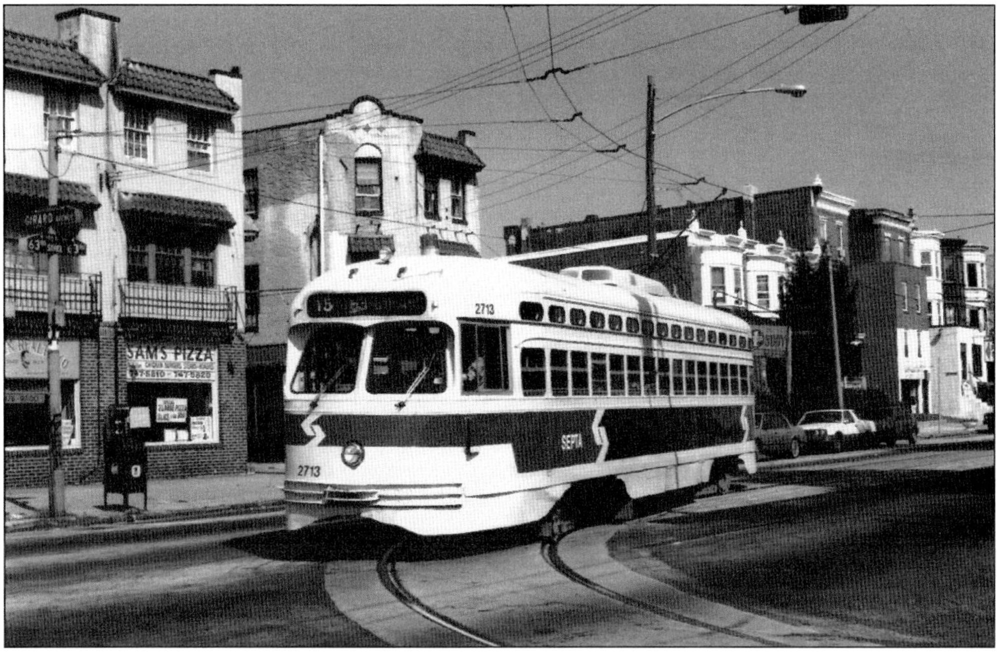

Presidents' Conference Committee car No. 2713 is on route 15 turning from Sixty-third Street onto Girard Avenue on September 2, 1990. The St. Louis Car Company delivered this car to the Philadelphia Transportation Company in February 1947. It was overhauled by the Southeastern Pennsylvania Transportation Authority in 1982 and was sold to the Brookville Equipment Company in 2004. (Photograph by Kenneth C. Springirth.)

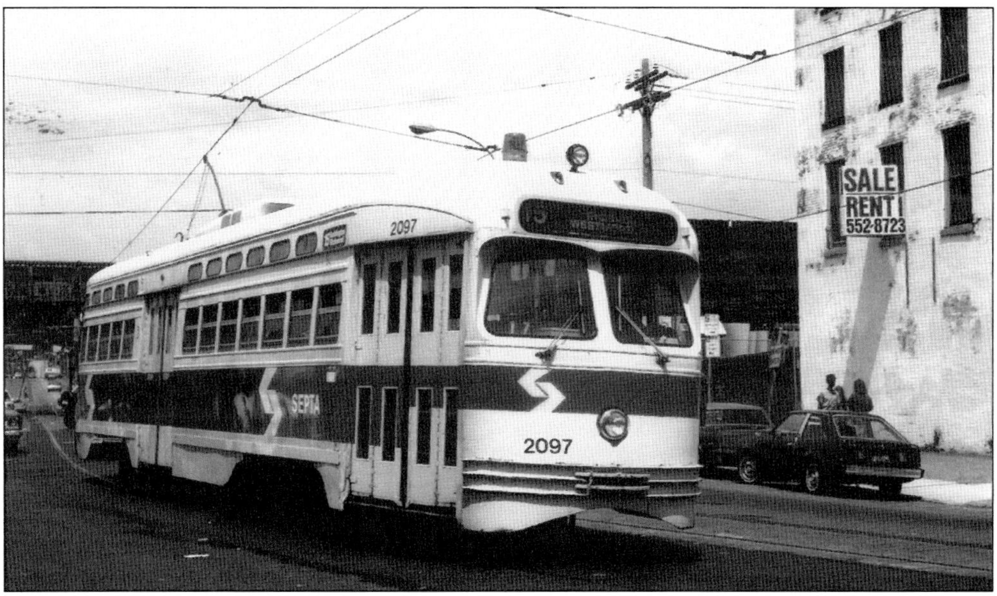

Southeastern Pennsylvania Transportation Authority route 15 Presidents' Conference Committee car No. 2097 is on Girard Avenue at Frankford Avenue on July 13, 1992. Built by the St. Louis Car Company for the Philadelphia Transportation Company in 1948, it was overhauled by the Southeastern Pennsylvania Transportation Authority in July 1981 and was sold to Colorado Springs in June 1995. (Photograph by Kenneth C. Springirth.)

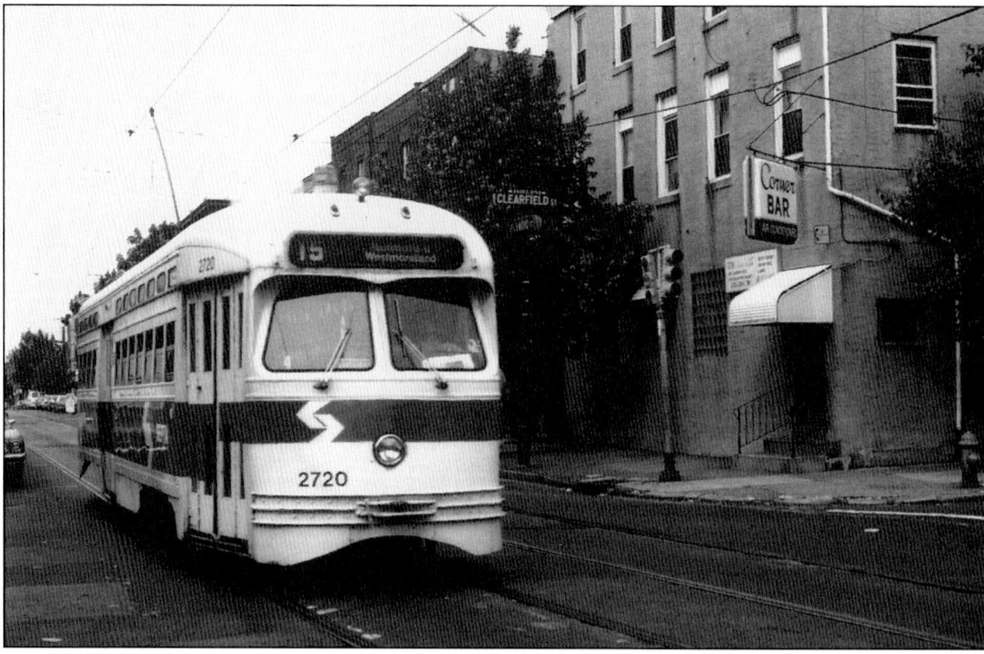

Route 15 Presidents' Conference Committee car No. 2720 is on Richmond Street crossing Clearfield Street on July 13, 1992. The St. Louis Car Company built this car in 1947 for the Philadelphia Transportation Company. Cars 2701 to 2725 had four Westinghouse model 1432D motors. Cars 2726 to 2800 had four General Electric model 1220A motors. (Photograph by Kenneth C. Springirth.)

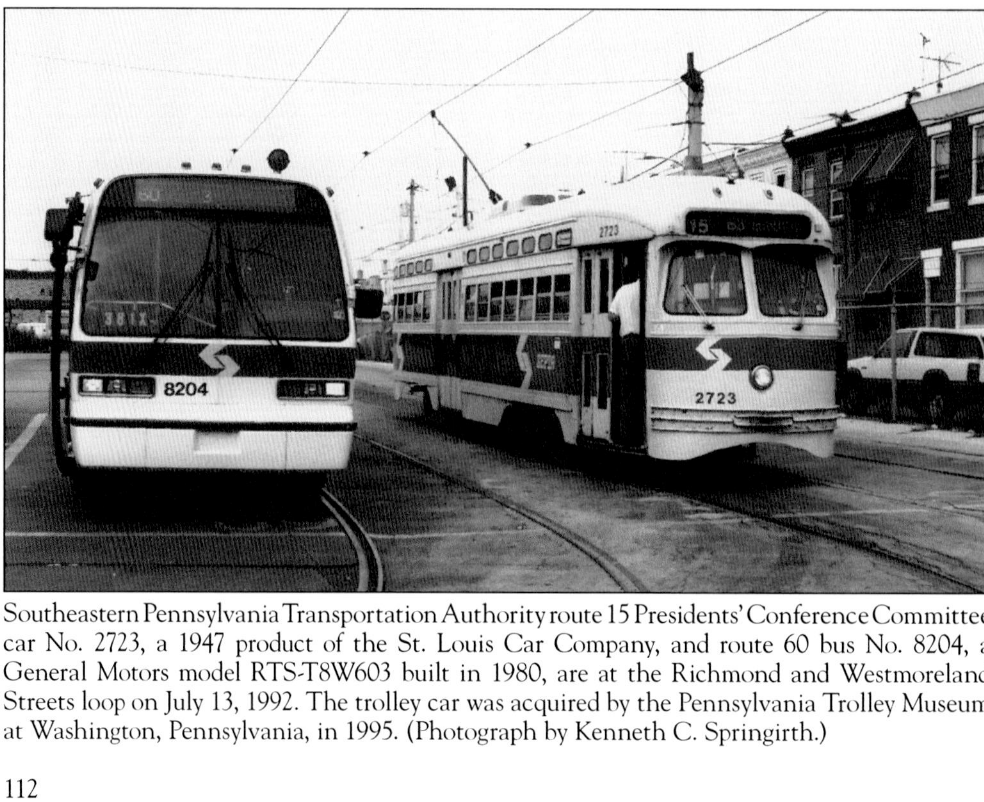

Southeastern Pennsylvania Transportation Authority route 15 Presidents' Conference Committee car No. 2723, a 1947 product of the St. Louis Car Company, and route 60 bus No. 8204, a General Motors model RTS-T8W603 built in 1980, are at the Richmond and Westmoreland Streets loop on July 13, 1992. The trolley car was acquired by the Pennsylvania Trolley Museum at Washington, Pennsylvania, in 1995. (Photograph by Kenneth C. Springirth.)

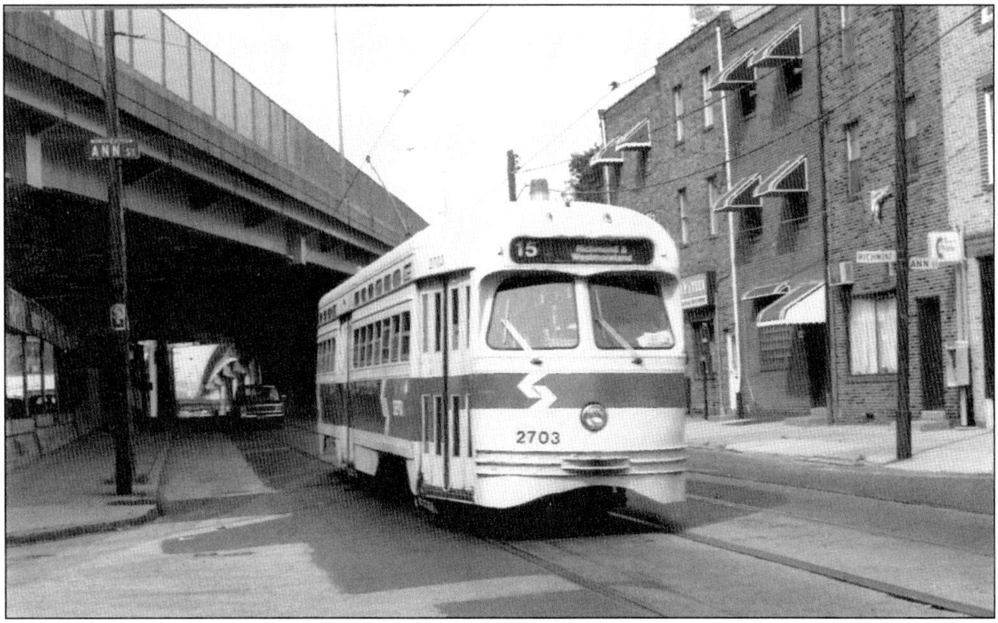

Route 15 Presidents' Conference Committee car No. 2703 has passed under Interstate 95 and is on Richmond Street at Ann Street on July 13, 1992, less than a half mile from the terminus at Richmond and Westmoreland Streets. The Southeastern Pennsylvania Transportation Authority overhauled this car in November 1982. It was sold to the Gomaco Company in October 1994. (Photograph by Kenneth C. Springirth.)

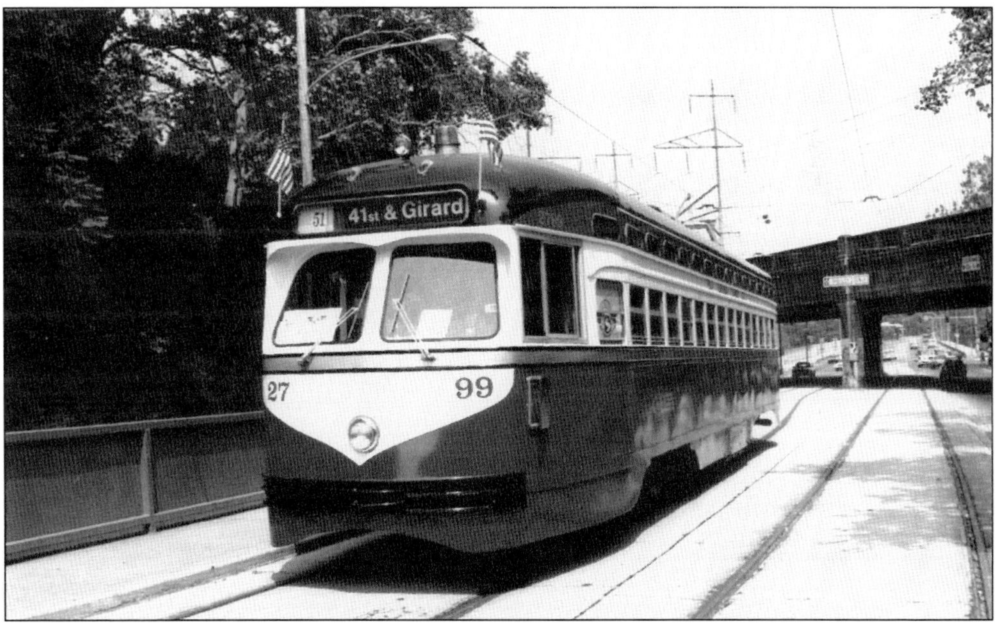

Presidents' Conference Committee car No. 2799 is on Girard Avenue at the Philadelphia Zoo on July 15, 1995. Beginning on May 19, 1995, the route 51 Welcome Line operated weekends between downtown Philadelphia and the Philadelphia Zoo using cars Nos. 2728, 2732, and 2799 that were refurbished at the Woodland Maintenance Facility and painted in historic color schemes. (Photograph by Kenneth C. Springirth.)

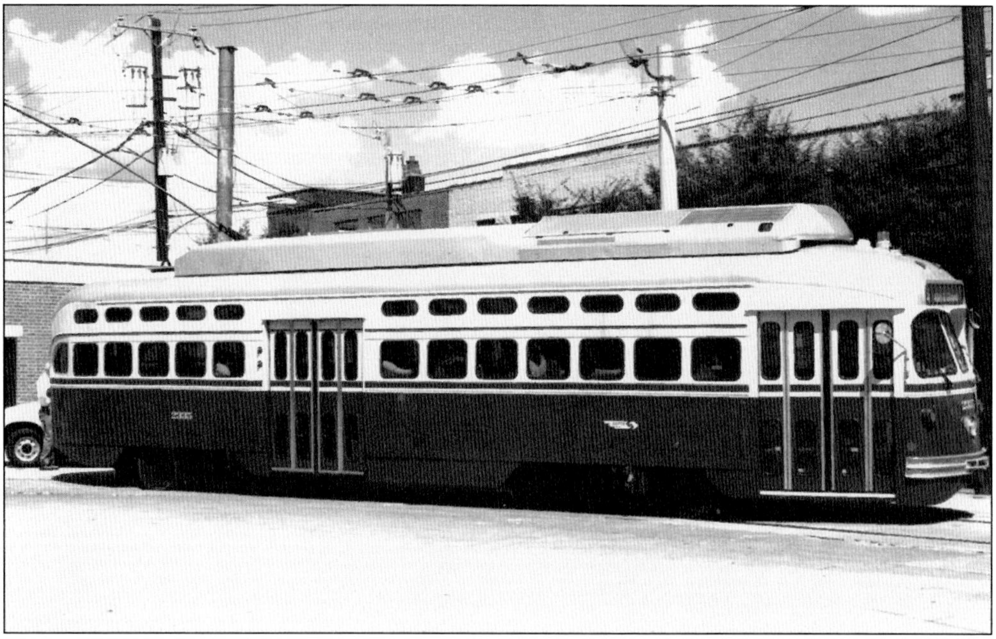

Southeastern Pennsylvania Transportation Authority route 15 trolley No. 2335 in Philadelphia Transportation Company colors is leaving Richmond and Westmoreland Streets on September 4, 2005, the first day of operation on the restored trolley line. This was originally car No. 2158 built by the St. Louis Car Company and delivered in June 1948. It was rebuilt by the Brookville Equipment Company and delivered on October 19, 2004. (Photograph by Kenneth C. Springirth.)

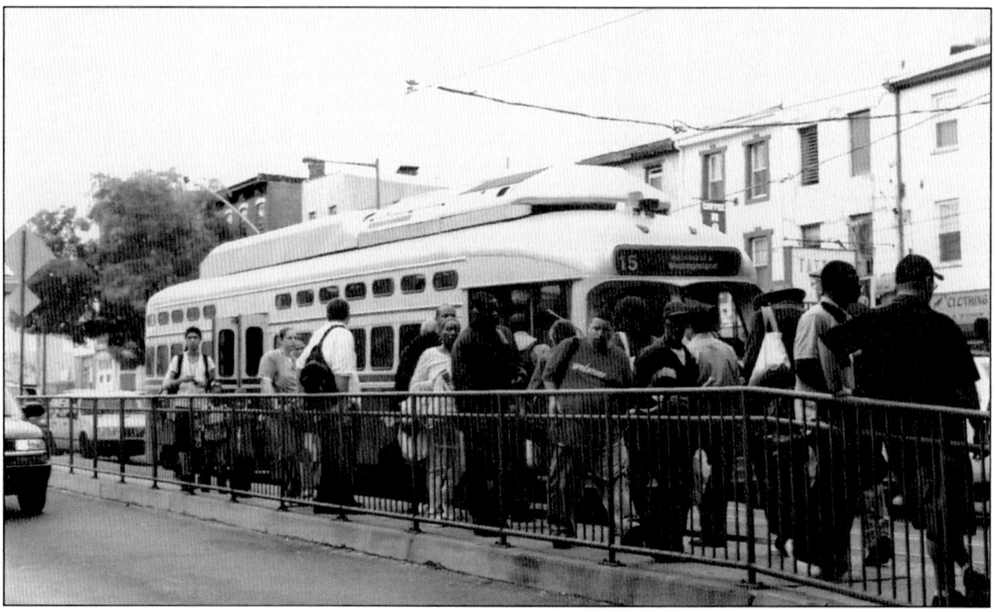

People are boarding Southeastern Pennsylvania Transportation Authority route 15 trolley No. 2329 at 4:00 p.m. on Girard Avenue at Front Street on October 19, 2007. This was originally car No. 2182 built by the St. Louis Car Company and delivered in July 1948 with rebuilding by the Brookville Equipment Company and delivery on June 23, 2004. (Photograph by Kenneth C. Springirth.)

Six

Philadelphia's Trackless Trolleys

Trackless trolleys are electric-powered rubber tire transit vehicles similar to a bus. Two poles draw power from the overhead trolley wires. The Philadelphia Rapid Transit Company began trackless trolley operation on October 14, 1923, on route 80 (Oregon Avenue). Route 61 (Ridge Avenue) began trackless trolley operation on October 5, 1941. Route 80 was converted to bus operation on May 15, 1960, followed by route 61 on March 31, 1961. Trolley car route 29 (Tasker Morris) was temporarily converted to bus operation on August 10, 1947, for the installation of trackless trolley overhead wires and became a trackless trolley route on December 14, 1947. On January 11, 1948, it was extended westward to Thirty-third and Dickinson Streets. Trolley car route 75 (Wyoming Avenue) began operation on November 15, 1931. On April 18, 1948, buses replaced trolleys with conversion to trackless trolleys the next day. Trolley car route 59 began operation on November 5, 1922, and became a trackless trolley line on June 25, 1950, operating via Castor Avenue from Margaret-Orthodox elevated station to an off-street loop at Castor Avenue near Bustleton Avenue. On January 2, 1926, trolley car route 66 began operation from Bridge Street via Frankford Avenue to City Line loop replacing the Frankford, Tacony and Holmesburg Street Railway Company. On July 31, 1955, route 66 was temporarily converted to bus operation for the installation of trackless trolley overhead wires. On September 11, 1955, trackless trolley operation began from Bridge Street Terminal via Frankford Avenue to Gregg Street loop reaching City Line loop on October 2, 1955. Trolley car route 79 (Snyder Avenue) began operation on January 1, 1912, and became a bus line on October 28, 1956, with conversion to trackless trolleys on June 18, 1961. Trackless trolley routes 59, 66, and 75 were temporarily converted to buses on June 16, 2002, because of the reconstruction of the Bridge-Pratt Elevated structure and station. Route 29 was converted to bus operation on February 23, 2003, because of construction at the western end of the line. Route 79 was converted to bus operation on July 1, 2003, as a cost-saving measure. New Flyer Industries Incorporated will supply 38 new trackless trolleys for routes 59, 66, and 75 during 2008.

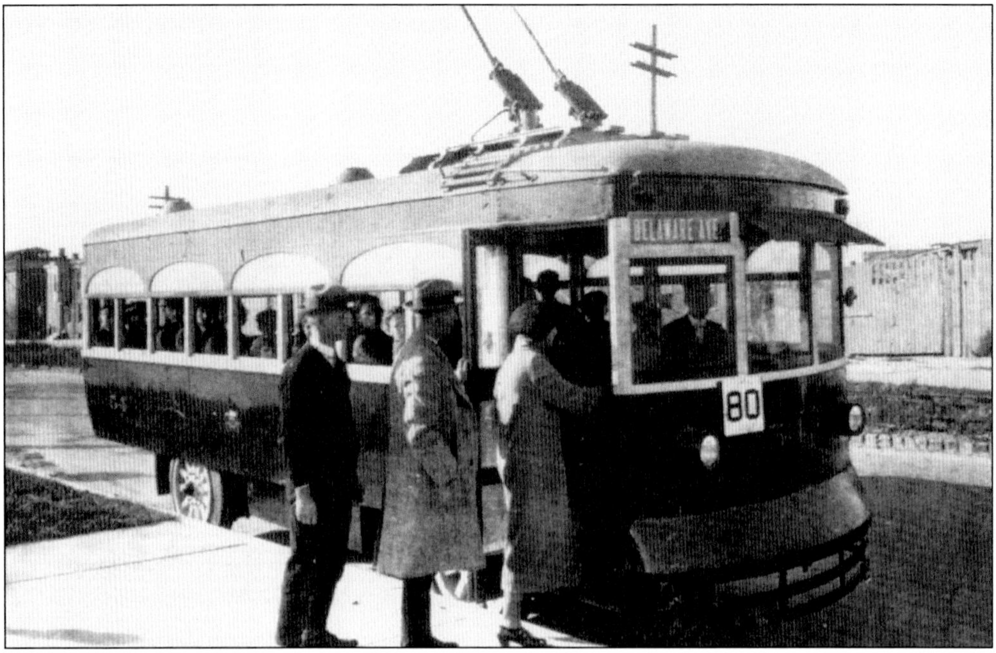

Philadelphia Rapid Transit Company trackless trolley No. 54, built by J. G. Brill Car Company during 1923, is on route 80, Oregon Avenue, on the first permanent trackless trolley line in the United States that began operation on October 14, 1923. This vehicle was 23.208 feet long, 7.5 feet wide, seated 28 passengers, and was retired in 1935. (Oliver J. Ogden, Museum of Bus Transportation photograph.)

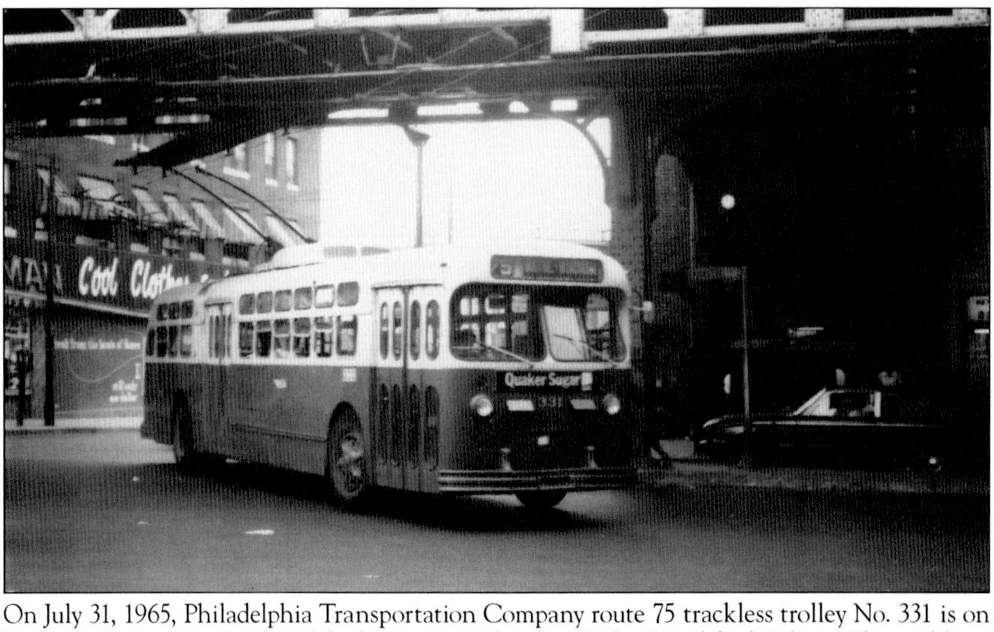

On July 31, 1965, Philadelphia Transportation Company route 75 trackless trolley No. 331 is on Margaret Street crossing Frankford Avenue under the Market-Frankford Subway-Elevated line. The City of Philadelphia owned this model TC-49 trackless trolley, built by Marmon Herrington in 1955 seating 49 passengers. On April 3, 1966, the line was cut back from Richmond Street to the Arrott Street Terminal. (Oliver J. Ogden, Museum of Bus Transportation photograph.)

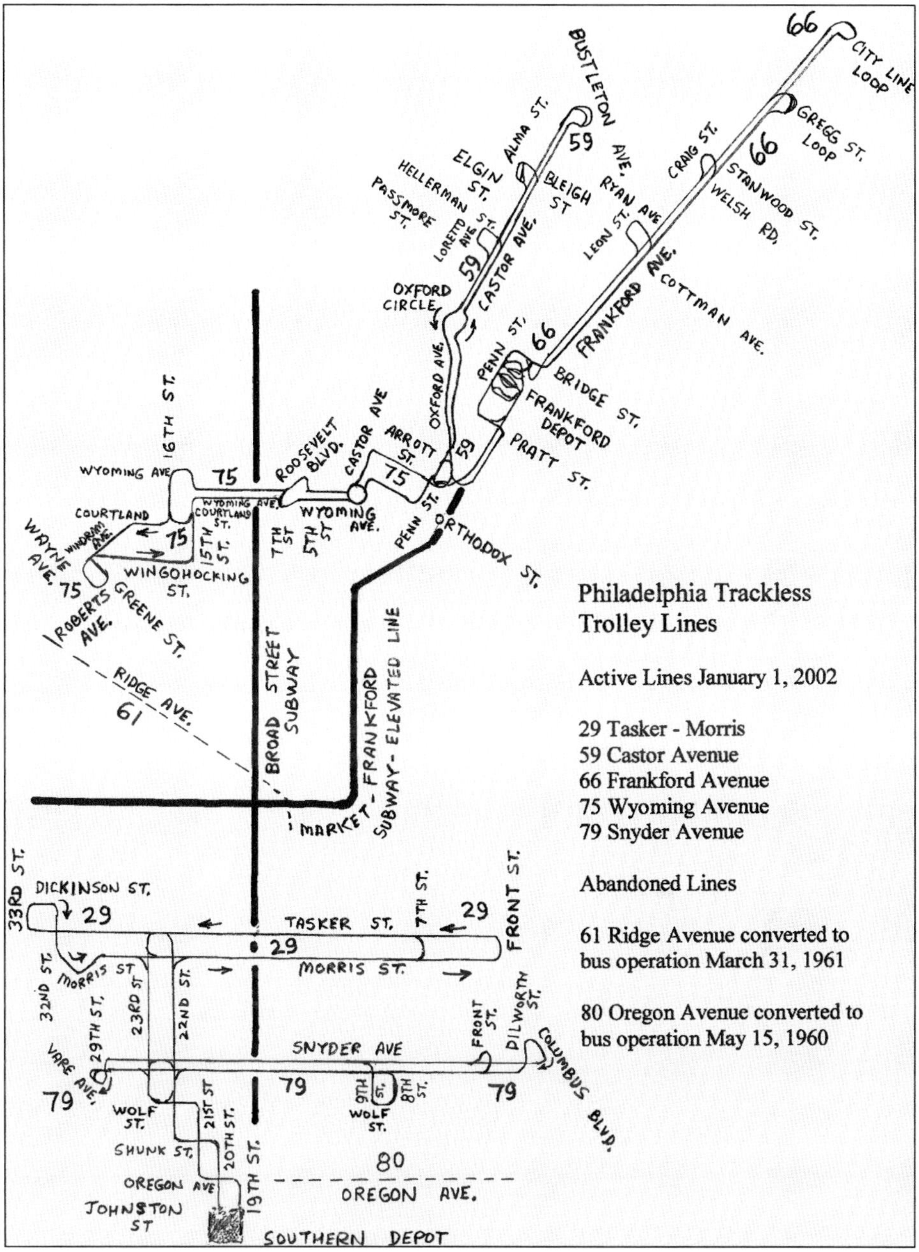

This map shows the Philadelphia trackless trolley routes. Route 80 (Oregon Avenue) was the city's first trackless trolley line beginning service on October 14, 1923. On November 30, 1896, the Manayunk trolley line, which became route 61, operated via Ridge Avenue to Front and Arch Streets and was temporarily converted to bus operation on August 10, 1941, and became the second trackless trolley line on October 5, 1941. The route 29 (Morris-Tasker) trolley line was established on November 16, 1913, and became a trackless trolley route on December 14, 1947. Route 59 (Castor Avenue) became a trackless trolley line on June 25, 1950. Route 75 (Wyoming Avenue) became a trackless trolley line on April 19, 1948. Route 66 (Frankford Avenue) became a trackless trolley line over its full length on October 2, 1955. Route 79 (Snyder Avenue) became a trackless trolley line on June 18, 1961.

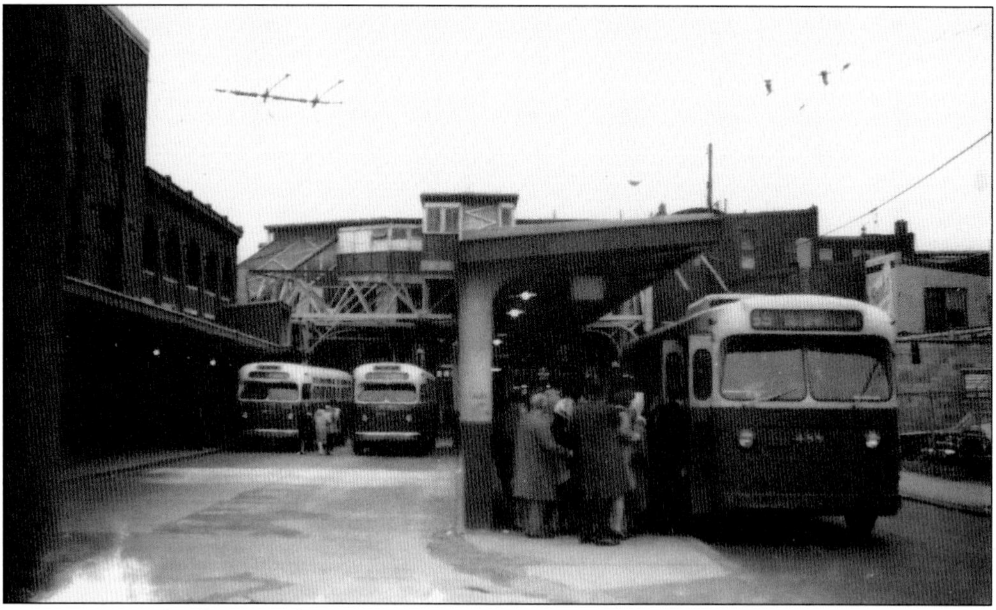

Arrott Terminal is the scene for route 59 trackless trolley No. 488 loading passengers on March 26, 1966. Marmon Herrington built trackless trolleys numbered 471 to 498 in 1949. These vehicles model TC-46 were 37.229 feet long, 8.5 feet wide, seated 46, and were retired during 1981. This was an important terminal point for trackless trolley routes 59 and 75. (Oliver J. Ogden, Museum of Bus Transportation photograph.)

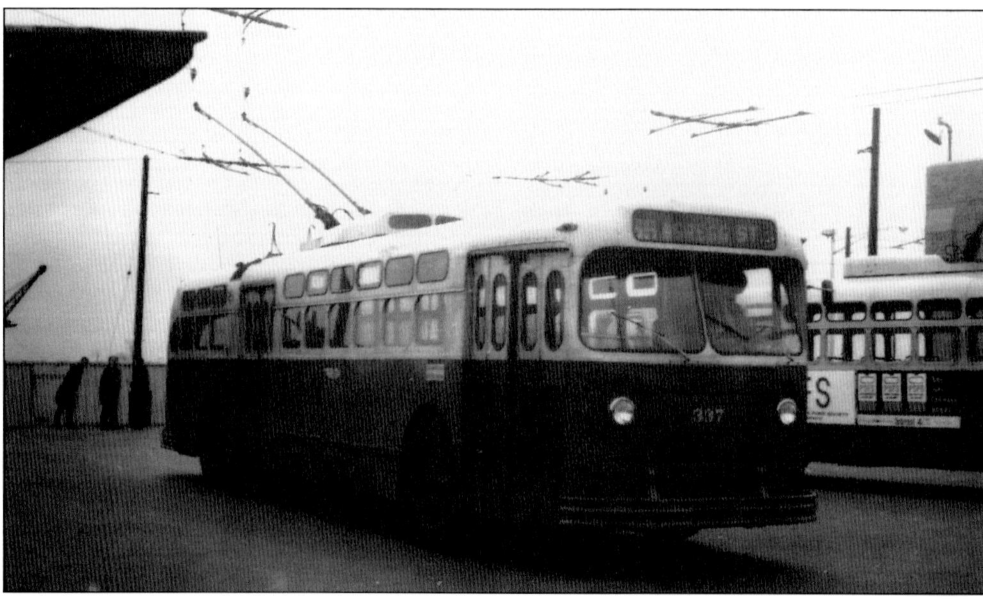

Trackless trolley No. 337 is on Philadelphia Transportation Company route 66 at Gregg Street loop on April 2, 1966. Marmon Herrington built trackless trolleys Nos. 301 to 343 in 1955 for route 66, which was converted to trackless trolley. These model TC-49 vehicles were 39.885 feet long, 8.5 feet wide, seated 49 passengers, and were retired during 1981. (Oliver J. Ogden, Museum of Bus Transportation photograph.)

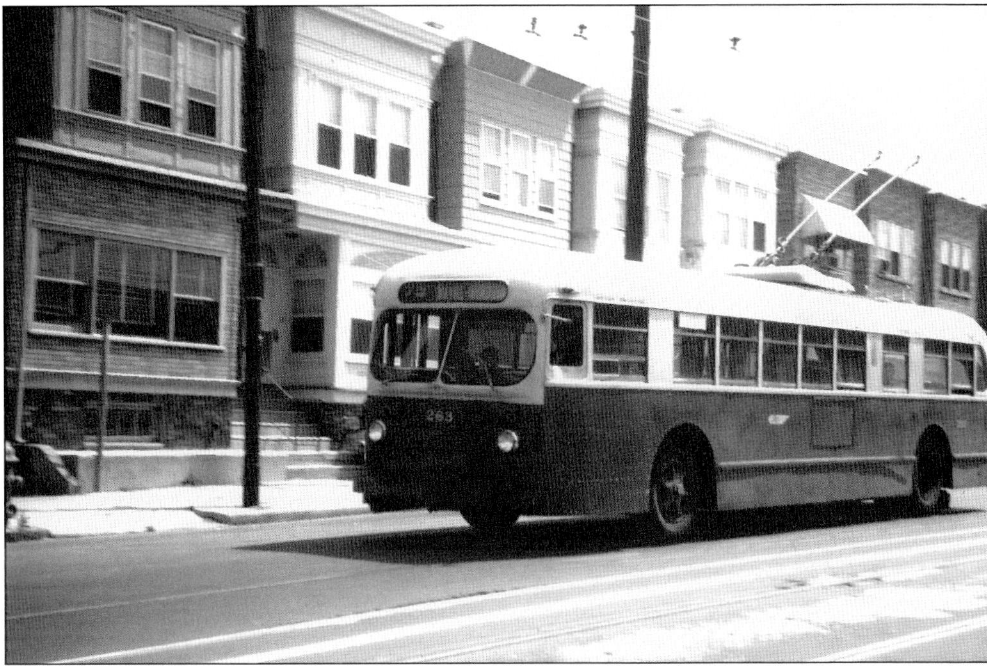

Philadelphia Transportation Company route 75 trackless trolley No. 263 is on Wyoming Avenue at Third Street on May 31, 1968. These 65 model TC-44 trackless trolleys Nos. 201 to 265, built by A. C. F. Brill during 1947, were 36.813 feet long, 8.5 feet wide, and seated 44 passengers. They served routes 59 and 75 and later routes 29 and 79, with retirement during 1981. (Photograph by Kenneth C. Springirth.)

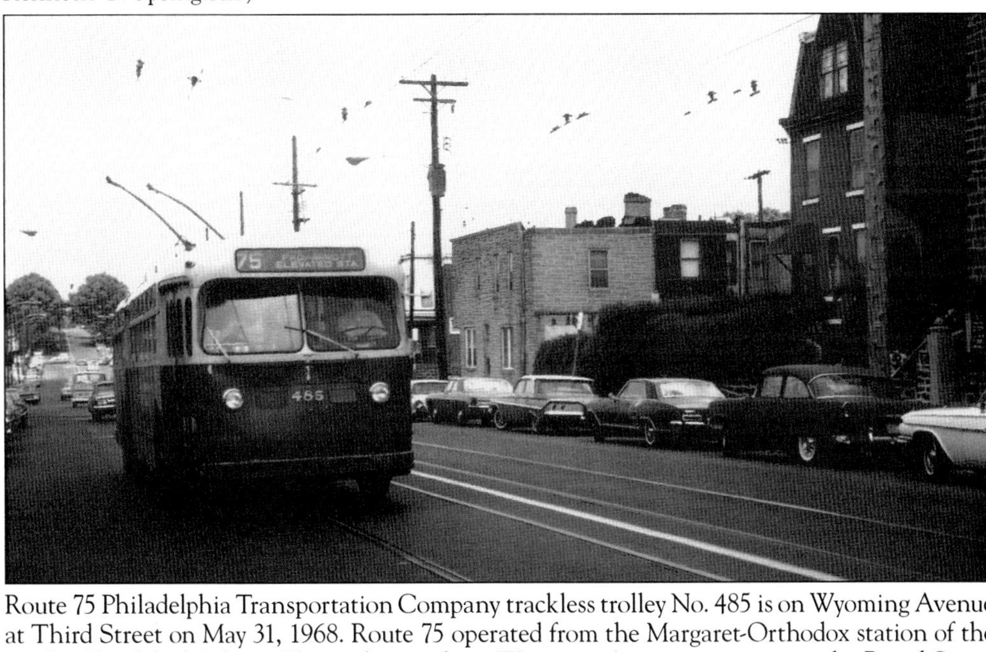

Route 75 Philadelphia Transportation Company trackless trolley No. 485 is on Wyoming Avenue at Third Street on May 31, 1968. Route 75 operated from the Margaret-Orthodox station of the Market-Frankford Subway-Elevated west along Wyoming Avenue intersecting the Broad Street Subway and connected with trolley car routes 23 and 53 at its western end. (Photograph by Kenneth C. Springirth.)

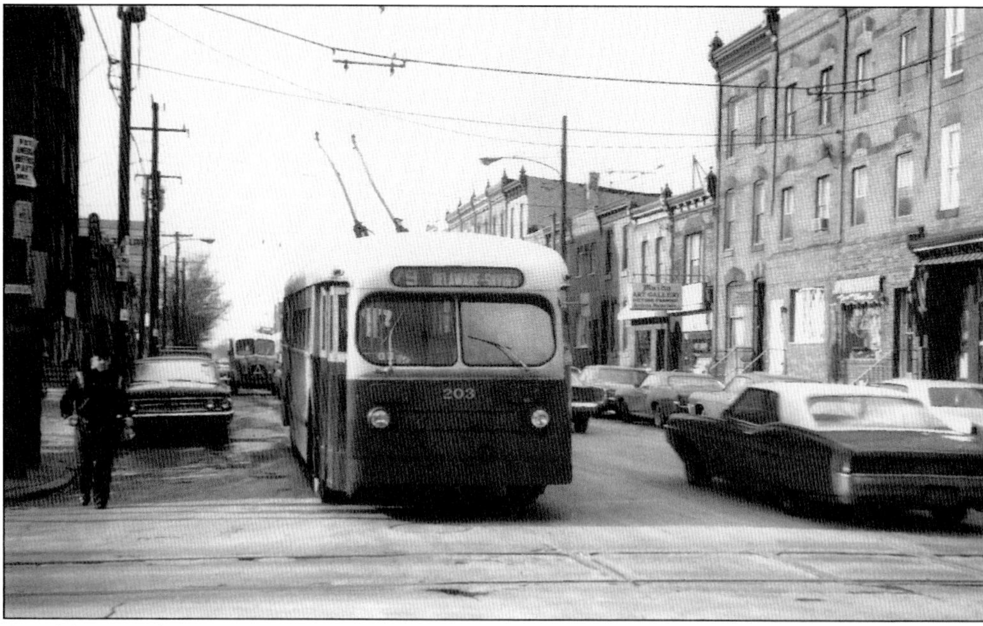

A cold December 26, 1970, finds Southeastern Pennsylvania Transportation Authority route 79 trackless trolley No. 203 on Snyder Avenue at Twelfth Street ready to cross the southbound track of trolley route 23. Route 79 was established as the Snyder Avenue trolley line on January 1, 1912. It became a bus line on October 28, 1956, and on June 18, 1961, became a trackless trolley line. (Photograph by Kenneth C. Springirth.)

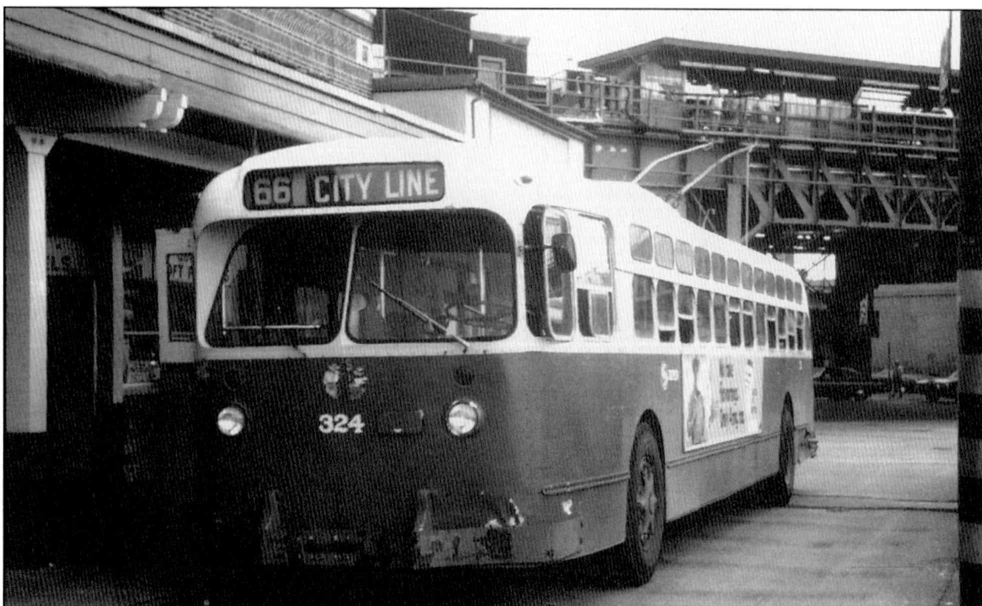

Southeastern Pennsylvania Transportation Authority route 66 trackless trolley No. 324 is at Frankford Terminal on July 29, 1977, with the Bridge Street Station of the Market-Frankford Subway-Elevated in the background. During peak periods route 66 had express service over a portion of the line plus trips that used the Gregg Street and Cottman Avenue cutback loops. (Photograph by Kenneth C. Springirth.)

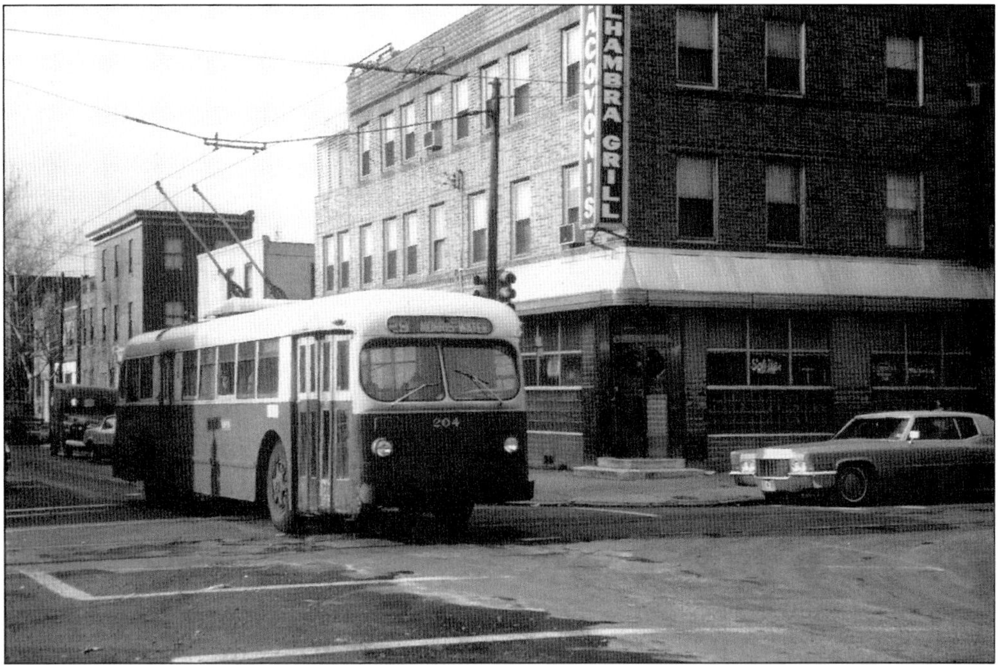

On December 26, 1970, Southeastern Pennsylvania Transportation Authority trackless trolley No. 204 on route 29 is eastbound on Morris Street at Twelfth Street. This was a transfer point for southbound trolley car route 23. In the 1950s, most of Philadelphia's trolley lines became bus lines. (Photograph by Kenneth C. Springirth.)

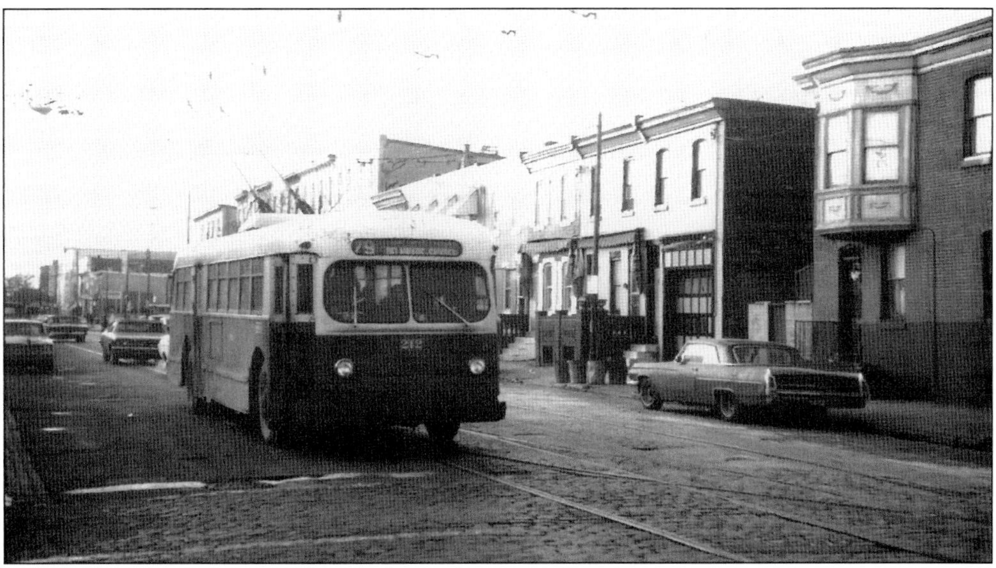

Southeastern Pennsylvania Transportation Authority trackless trolley No. 212 is eastbound on route 79 on Snyder Avenue at Fourth Street on December 26, 1970. Routes 29 and 79 serving South Philadelphia were not physically connected to trackless trolley routes 59, 66, and 75 in Northeast Philadelphia. (Photograph by Kenneth C. Springirth.)

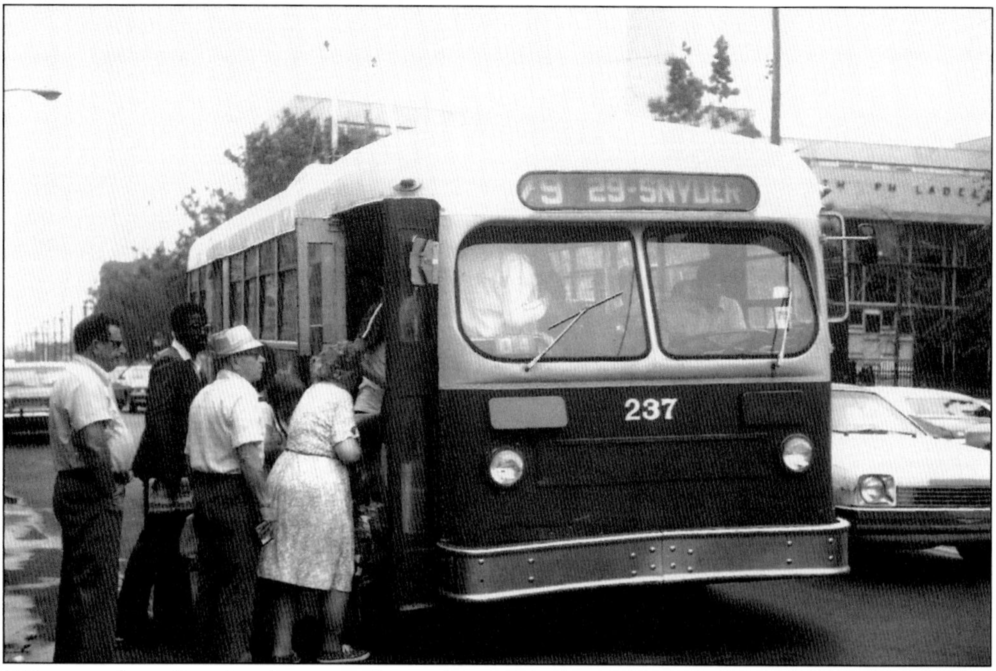

Riders are boarding Southeastern Pennsylvania Transportation Authority route 79 trackless trolley No. 237 on Snyder Avenue at Broad Street on July 24, 1978. Trackless trolleys used on route 80, which became a bus line on May 15, 1960, and route 61, which became a bus line on March 31, 1961, were reassigned to route 79, which became a trackless trolley line on June 18, 1961. (Photograph by Kenneth C. Springirth.)

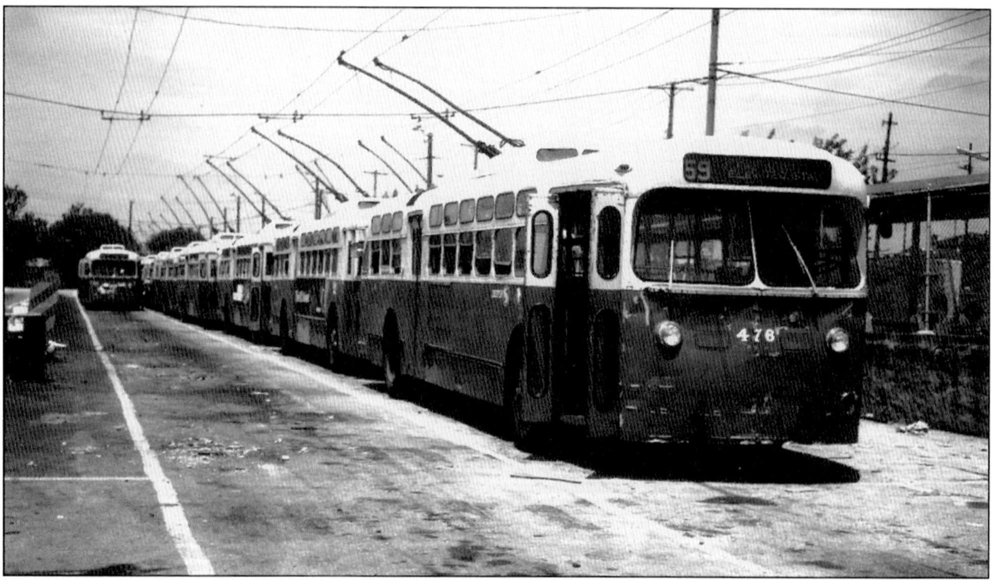

Southeastern Pennsylvania Transportation Authority trackless trolley No. 476 heads the lineup at Frankford Depot on July 28, 1979. Trackless trolley routes 59 and 75 were connected to that depot by wire on Frankford Avenue under the elevated tracks of the Market-Frankford Subway-Elevated Line while trackless trolley route 66 started directly from that depot. (Photograph by Kenneth C. Springirth.)

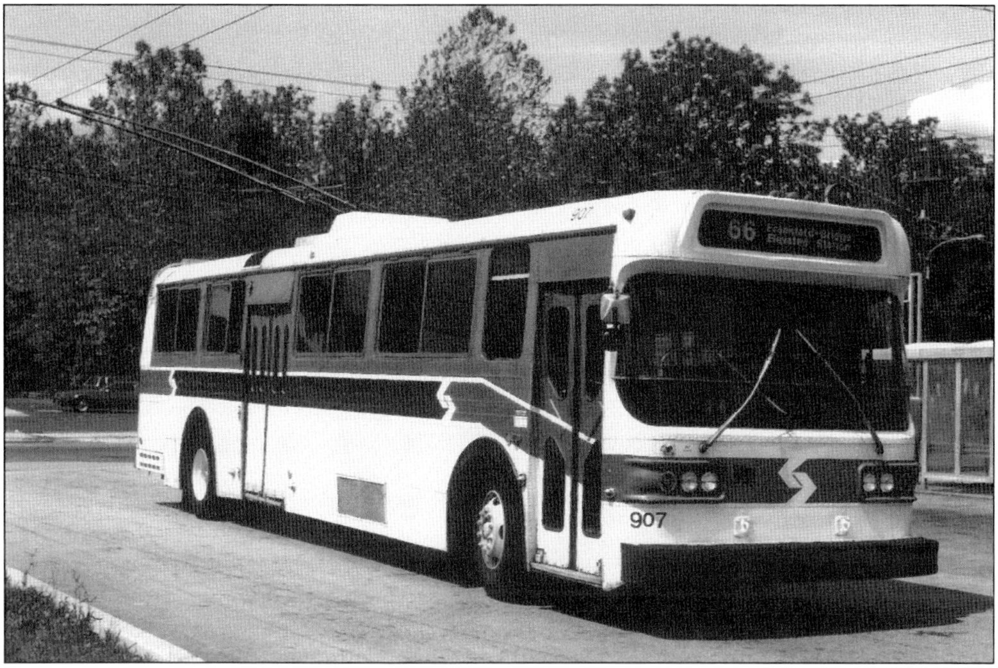

City Line loop is the scene for route 66 trackless trolley No. 907, waiting the departure time on May 29, 1992. This was one of 110 vehicles numbered 800 to 909, model 10240-E trackless trolleys built by AM General during 1979 for the Southeastern Pennsylvania Transportation Authority. (Photograph by Kenneth C. Springirth.)

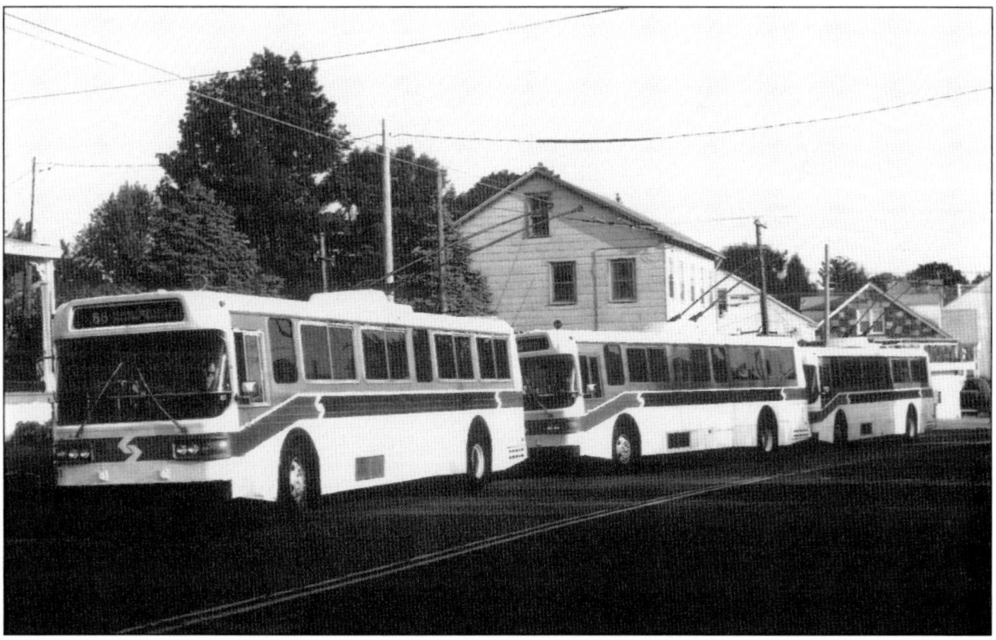

Three Southeastern Pennsylvania Transportation Authority trackless trolleys are at the route 66 Welsh Road cutback in the morning rush hour of May 29, 1992. At that time, there were morning trips scheduled from that loop. In later years, no official trips were shown on the public schedule from that loop. (Photograph by Kenneth C. Springirth.)

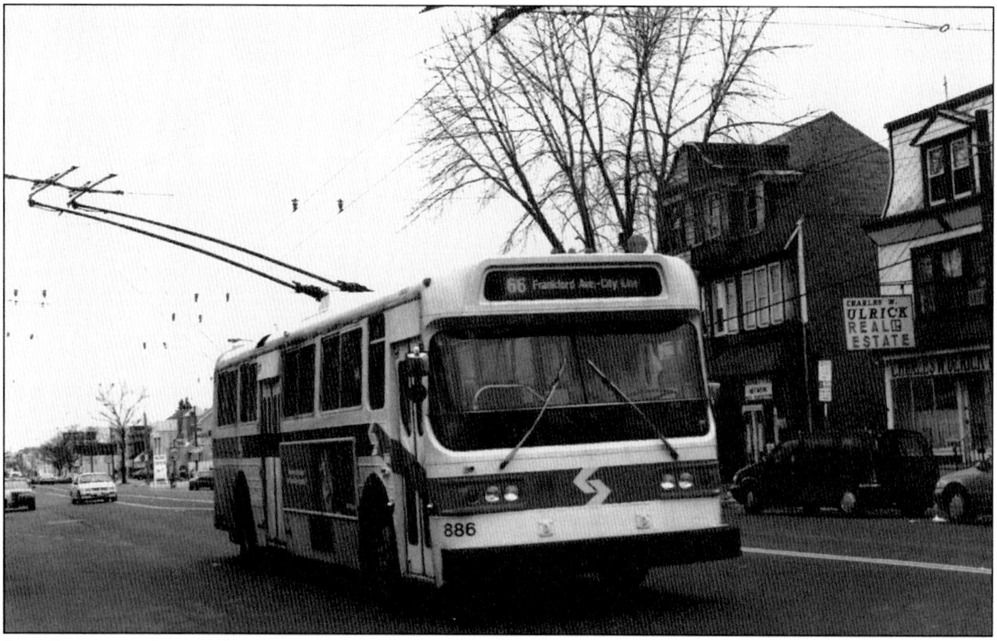

Southeastern Pennsylvania Transportation Authority route 66 trackless trolley No. 886 is on Frankford Avenue at Rhawn Street on December 30, 1996. On June 19, 1961, limited express service northbound began during the afternoon rush hour from Bridge Street to Cottman Avenue. On September 24, 1962, limited express service began southbound in the morning rush hour. (Photograph by Kenneth C. Springirth.)

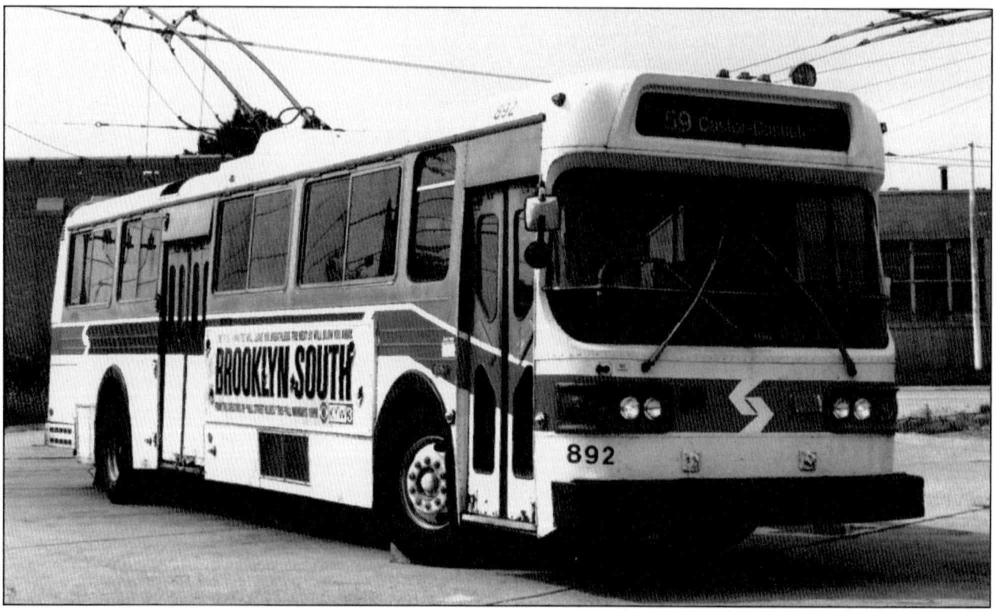

The route 59 off-street loop on Castor Avenue just south of Bustleton Avenue is the location for Southeastern Pennsylvania Transportation Authority trackless trolley No. 892 on September 1, 1997. Marmon Herrington model TC-46 trackless trolleys, numbered 471 to 498 and built during 1949, were assigned to this line until they were retired during 1981, with replacement by AM General trackless trolleys numbered 800 to 909. (Photograph by Kenneth C. Springirth.)

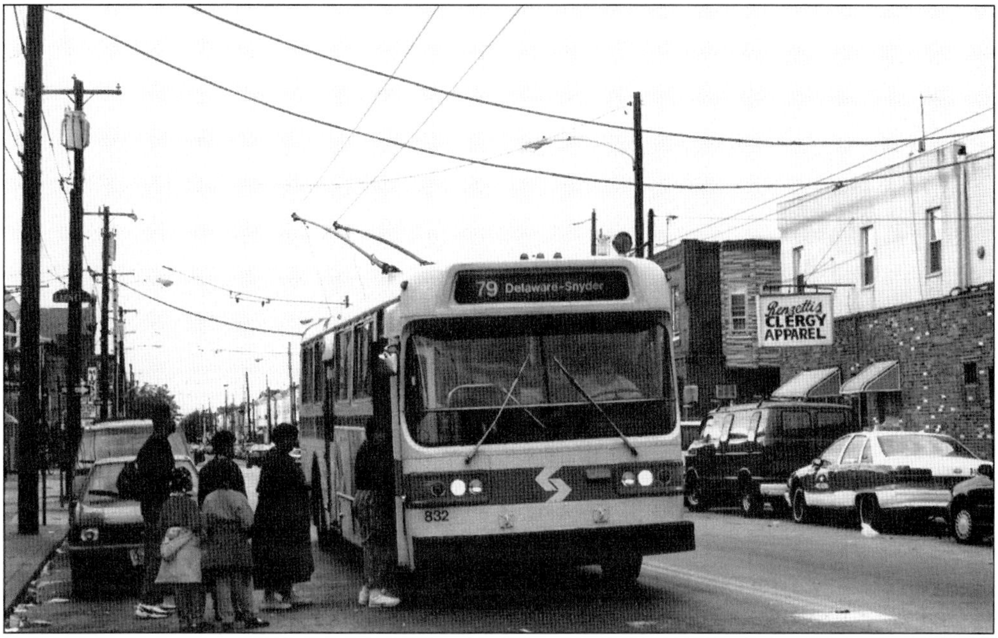

Snyder Avenue at Nineteenth Street finds route 79 trackless trolley No. 832 loading passengers for its eastbound trip on October 3, 1997. Route 79 was converted to bus operation on July 1, 2003. During 2008, trackless trolley service will be restored for routes 59, 66, and 75. The option to purchase trackless trolleys for routes 29 and 79 was not exercised. (Photograph by Kenneth C. Springirth.)

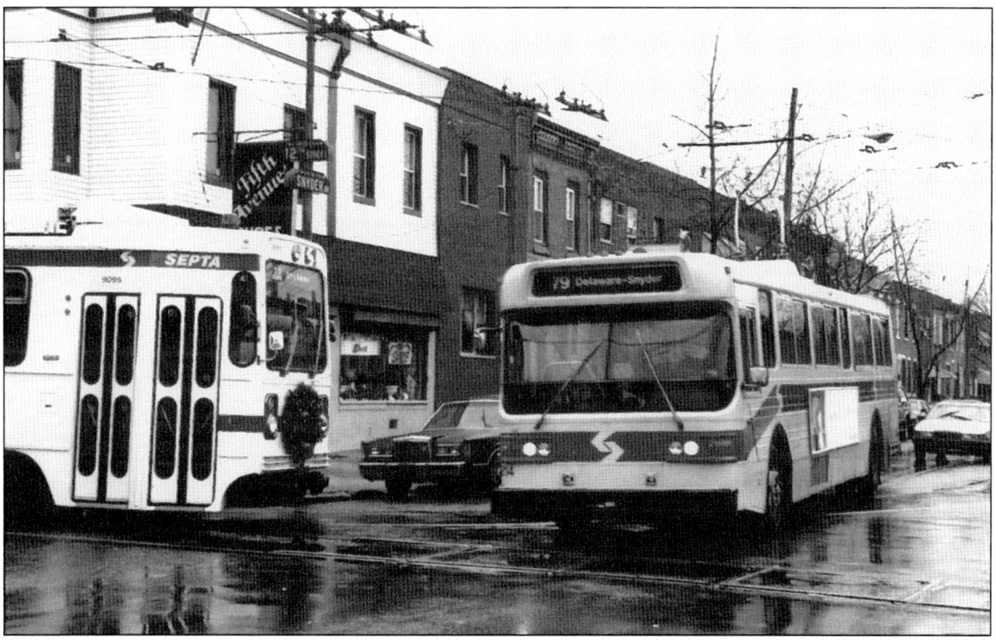

Holiday trolley car No. 9095 is on Twelfth Street ready to turn onto Snyder Avenue as route 79 trackless trolley No. 814 is westbound on December 12, 1997. Snyder Avenue was once a cutback point for route 23 trolley cars. This was a transfer point between route 23 trolley cars and route 79 trackless trolleys. (Photograph by Kenneth C. Springirth.)

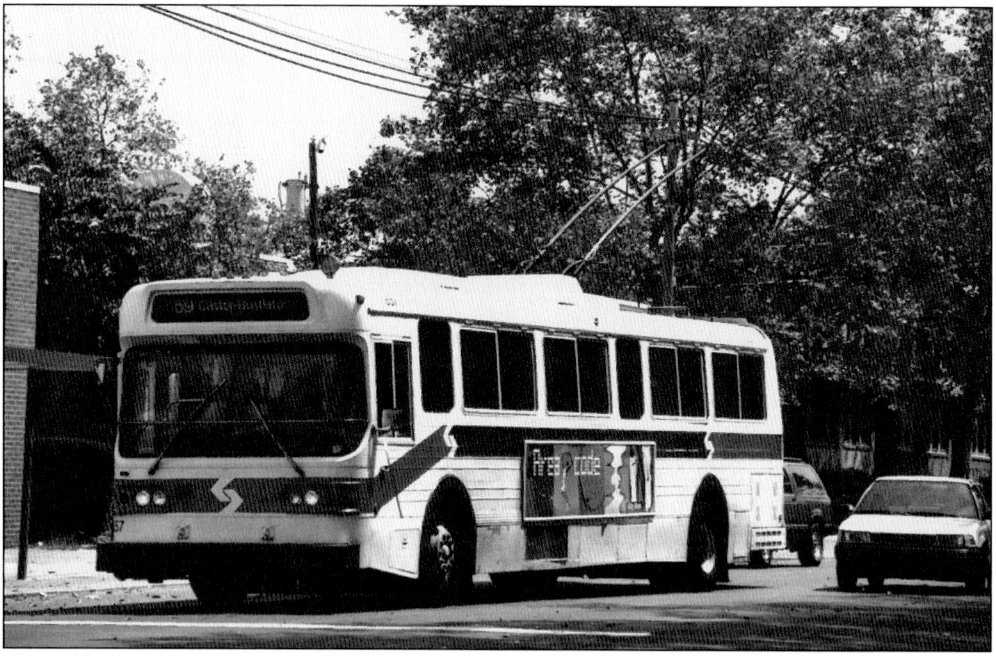

Route 59 Southeastern Pennsylvania Transportation Authority trackless trolley No. 857 is on Oxford Avenue at Pratt Street on July 29, 1998. The March 1, 1987, schedule showed additional service Monday through Friday from Arrott Street Terminal to Alma Loop (Cottman and Bleigh Avenues) from 6:38 a.m. to 7:31 a.m. and from 1:37 p.m. to 6:05 p.m. (Photograph by Kenneth C. Springirth.)

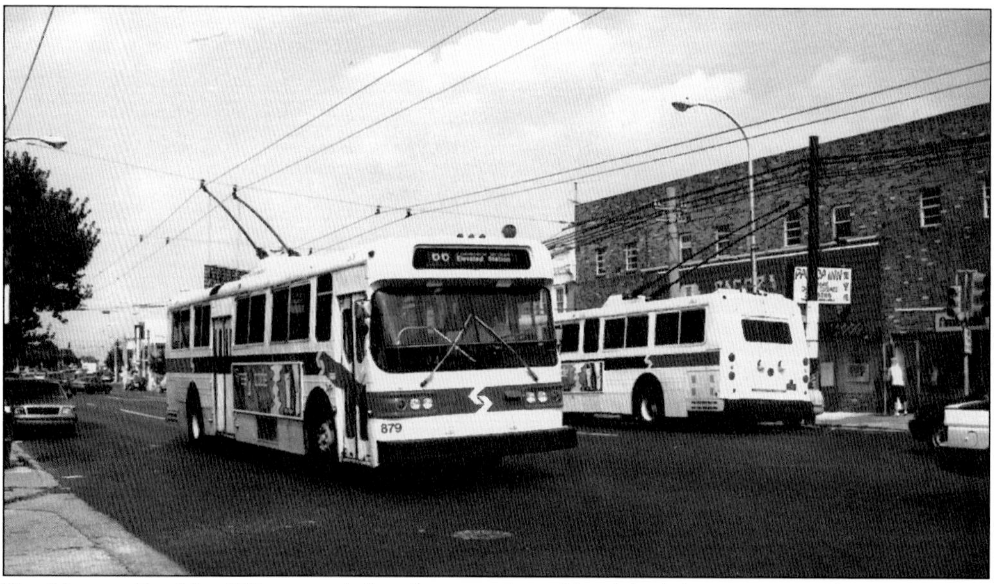

Trackless trolley No. 879 is quietly heading south on Frankford Avenue at Wellington Street, passing northbound No. 863 on route 66 on July 29, 1998. There was an extra set of wires on this section of Frankford Avenue with the local trackless trolleys using the two outer wires and the rush hour express trackless trolleys using the inner set of wires. (Photograph by Kenneth C. Springirth.)

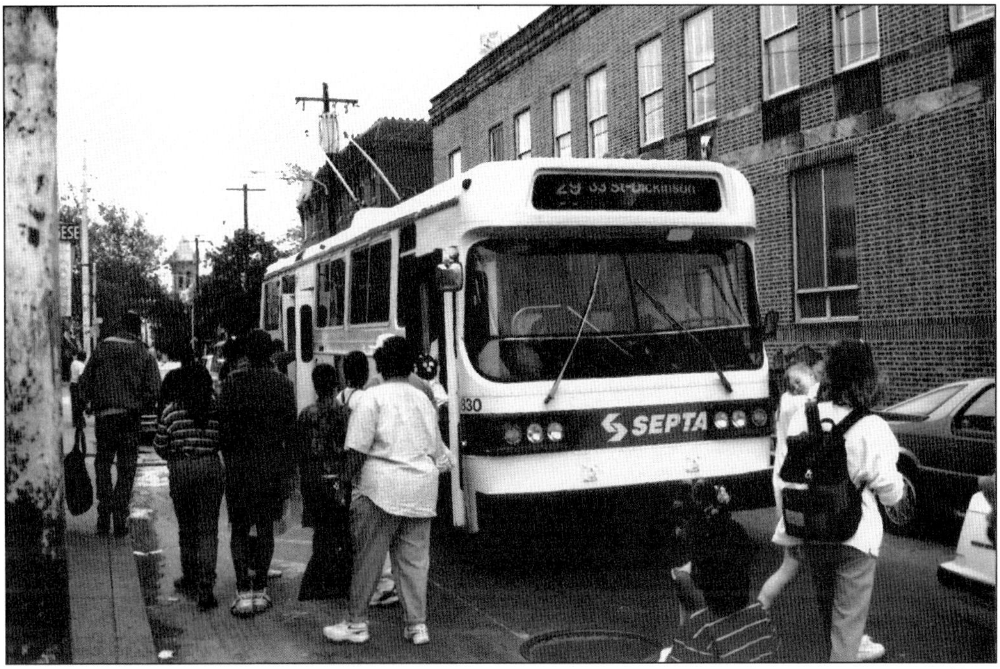

Passengers are boarding Southeastern Pennsylvania Transportation Authority route 29 trackless trolley No. 830 on Tasker Street at Broad Street in the early afternoon of July 31, 1998. Route 29 was converted to bus operation on February 23, 2003, due to construction at the western end of the line. (Photograph by Kenneth C. Springirth.)

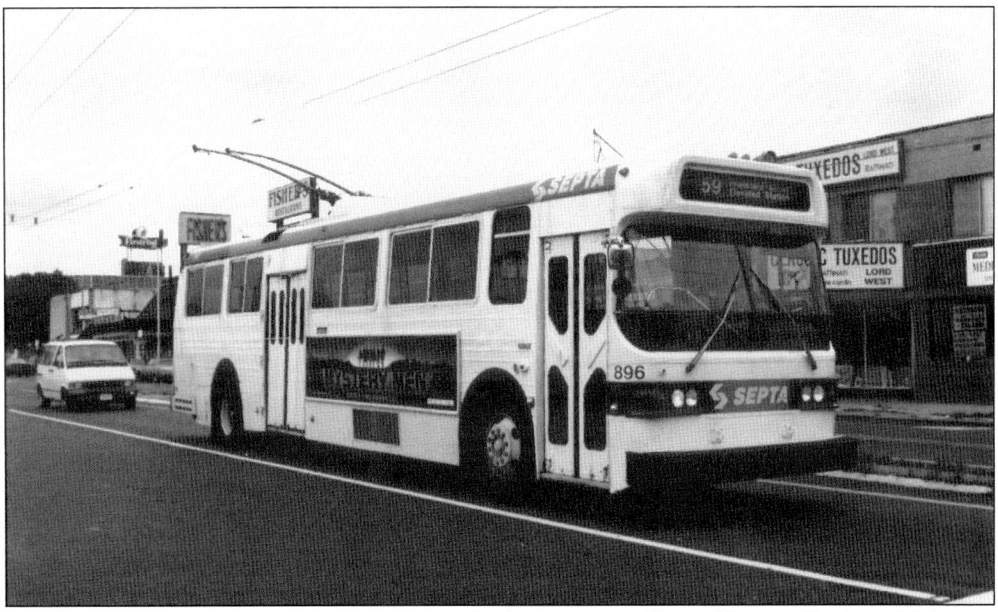

Southeastern Pennsylvania Transportation Authority route 59 trackless trolley No. 896 is on Castor Avenue at Bleigh Avenue on July 2, 1999. In February and March 2002, 44 of the 110 AM General trackless trolleys were scrapped, with the remainder scrapped by June 2006. New Flyer Industries Incorporated will be supplying 38 new trackless trolleys during 2008 to the Southeastern Pennsylvania Transportation Authority. (Photograph by Kenneth C. Springirth.)

Consistent with our mission to preserve history on a local level, this book was printed in South Carolina on American-made paper and manufactured entirely in the United States. Products carrying the accredited Forest Stewardship Council (FSC) label are printed on 100 percent FSC-certified paper.

MADE IN THE USA